LIVING
RICHLY
IN AN AGE OF
LIMITS

LIVING RICHLY IN AN AGE OF LIMITS

BILL DEVALL

GIBBS·SMITH
P
PUBLISHER

SALT LAKE CITY

First edition
98 97 96 95 94 93   10 9 8 7 6 5 4 3 2 1

This is a Peregrine Smith Book, published by
Gibbs Smith, Publisher
P.O. Box 667
Layton, UT 84041

Design by J. Scott Knudsen, Park City, UT
Jacket photograph by Burton Pritzker, Venice, CA
Manufactured in the U.S.A.

Library of Congress Cataloging-in-Publication Data
Living richly in an age of limits
p.   cm.
ISBN 0-87905-559-6
1. Environmental protection—Citizen participation.
2. Human ecology. 3. Deep ecology. 4. Quality of life.
TD171.7.L57 1993
362.70525—dc20   92-40241
                                      CIP

CONTENTS

PREFACE

This is the third in a series of books I have written on the deep, long-range ecology movement. The first, *Deep Ecology* (written with George Sessions) introduced the basic frame of reference of the deep ecology movement. Deep ecology is based on ecocentric philosophy and on practices that seek harmony between humans and all other parts of nature. Ecocentric philosophy is a philosophical approach based on our broad identification in nature. In *Deep Ecology*, ecocentric philosophy was explored through the writings of a diverse group of thinkers ranging from Christians such as Francis of Assisi and Thomas Berry, to philosophers such as Spinoza, and to naturalists such as Rachel Carson, Henry David Thoreau, and John Muir.

In *Simple in Means, Rich in Ends* I discussed some of the social policy implications of the deep, long-range ecology movement.

In this third book, I focus on lifestyle. I have always considered myself a social ecologist. I was educated as a social scientist and I tend to look at social and cultural reasons for behavior. While lifestyle is a concept derived from the literature on psychological theory, I see lifestyles based on the intuition of deep ecology emerging in a changing natural, social, and cultural landscape.

Many of the guidelines and suggestions in this book are not new. They have been made by numerous other authors over the past twenty years. It is my opinion that we would be better off in the 1990s if we had changed our ways in the 1970s and 1980s. It is even more urgent in the 1990s that we change our lifestyles.

I was particularly motivated to focus on the themes developed in this book by three series of events—by participating in events surrounding Earth Day 1990, by observing the rapid change in life conditions experienced by many people in the United States brought about by the persistent recession of the early 1990s, and by reading the accumulation of scientific data indicating that ecological life support systems may have passed thresholds beyond which deterioration of whole natural systems may be occurring.

The general theme promoted by organizers of Earth Day 1990 was "greening our lifestyles." I strongly agree with those who say that residents of the United Stated and Canada, two extremely wealthy nations in comparison to most other regions of the earth, have a responsibility to decrease the load they are putting on life systems of the earth—air and water pollution, total amount of consumption, and unsustainable patterns and practices concerning use of forest products, water, and soil.

I was dissatisfied, however, with the tone of much of the literature published around Earth Day 1990. In particular I saw an attempt to co-opt themes of "green lifestyles" by many corporations. Other writers have explored "greenwashing" by corporations. I will mention only an example from my home bioregion. Logging corporations that have been overcutting their own lands for many years, and that are in the process of clearcutting the remaining stands of ancient redwood forests, used the occasion of Earth Day to proclaim in numerous ads, press releases, and massive public relations efforts that "every day is earth day for X corporation." This is obscene. Unless ordinary citizens make every day earth day in their own lifestyles and denounce corporate behavior and government agencies who "greenwash" their irresponsible behavior with doublespeak, then the term "green" will mean little more than rhetorical advertising.

I was also dissatisfied with the tone of some of the literature appealing to consumers. *Fifty Simple Ways to Save the Earth* was certainly a catchy title, and I strongly agree with most of the suggestions in such books. However, books such as that lack philosophical, psychological, and cultural context. Simple ways are not always easy. Changing to simpler lifestyles frequently involves making difficult choices and requires addressing philosophical or religious questions. I wanted to address some of the deeper questions such as how does a higher standard of living dilute or degrade the quality of life of human and nonhuman beings? Is it possible that drastic changes in our lifestyles, including reduction in our rate of consumption, can enrich our lives?

In the Age of Ecology, many of the assumptions about our relationship with nature held dear by many members of the middle classes in the United States and Canada have been called into question. It seems less and less likely that future generations will experience ever increasing economic growth and higher and higher standards of living. Furthermore, the values held most dear by the middle classes—neatness, tidiness, control over the environment, and domination of whole landscapes with the goal of transforming those landscapes into "factories in the fields" to produce more and more commodities—now seem less desirable values.

Philosophers, social activists, people in all kinds of occupations and life situations are in the process of articulating a new philosophy of nature. These philosophers and many ordinary people use phrases such as "living in harmony with nature" or "living in balance with nature" and "sustainable culture." They are trying to discover fuller understanding of these phrases. These phrases are rich with meanings that need to be more fully explored.

In my opinion, increasing numbers of people are reexamining the meaning of the phrase the "good life." Some people, and I include myself among them, realize that no matter how well-educated, how committed they are to the ecological movement, it is not always clear how to change the habits of a lifetime.

Thus this book was written from personal concerns as well as professional concerns. When speaking about needed changes in forest policy, for example, I am frequently asked, "You live in a wood house, don't you?" "You drive to your place of work, don't you?" "You watch TV, don't you?" Yes, yes, yes.

From my own experiences with attempting to be more faithful with my own practice, for example, with my recycling habits, with attempting to increase the insulation of my house, with trying to find the financial resources to purchase a more fuel efficient vehicle, I have developed great compassion for anyone trying to balance a family budget, fulfill work obligations in a demanding job, and, at the same time, develop habits of good citizenship on this earth.

I am a nonparent, but I have supported children, and I have supported a household while at the same time helping to support my parents during their retirement years. Now I live in an aging, energy-inefficient ranch-style house which I inherited from my parents. It is expensive to upgrade this house to current energy efficiency standards. I have many choices, but I also must consider the costs.

I am not an expert gardener, but I like to have a garden. I have struggled with my desire to raise certain domesticated plants in my garden such as my mother grew, and the desires of a multitude of slugs and snails to eat those delicate flowering plants. After a difficult personal struggle with my conscience, I gave up the use of pesticides. I now plant only species that the snails and slugs show no taste for. My next challenge is to convert my yard into a semi-natural garden.

The point of this story is not just that I am an inept gardener, which I readily confess. The point is that I think we all carry in our minds images from the past that we use to judge our current actions. I carry images in my mind of gardens filled with blooming flowers in Kansas during my childhood. I carry in my mind images of neatly trimmed suburban lawns, tidy gardens, neat and clean storage areas. Many of these images are outdated, even dangerous, in terms of our current situation. Changing how we live means changing our images of how we should be living.

I am also committed to the conclusion that drastic changes are desirable in our consumption habits. I am not, however, a champion of sacrifice. Unless forced by necessity, I cannot see myself living as a hermit in a small room. I am a champion of rich experiences in life, diversity of experiences, and richness in our relationships with each other. I am a champion of what the Buddhists call the "middle way." In Buddhist terms, "right livelihood" means mindful consideration of the precepts and attention to the consequences of our actions in search of appropriate actions in specific circumstances.

I am not a champion of a dogmatic approach to changing our lifestyles. I am not a fundamentalist who preaches the True Way. I am promoting the proposition that there are diverse lifestyles that are compatible with the principle of greening our lifestyles. I do not know what the result would be if millions of people in the United States and Canada chose a "middle way." I am convinced that the process of making changes toward a green lifestyle is valuable in itself.

I am convinced that literate, relatively well-educated, relatively affluent residents of the United States and Canada have more options and possibilities to enrich their own lives than any other people on the earth. Furthermore, we need not be motivated only by altruism or by guilt. The basic proposition presented in this book is that if we see ourselves more clearly, if we broaden our identification with nature, we naturally will seek "right livelihood" for ourselves-in-nature, and we will see that this is a more rewarding lifestyle than our current lifestyle.

ACKNOWLEDGMENTS

The author is grateful for permission to include the following previously copyrighted material:

Excerpt from *The Invisible Pyramid* by Loren Eiseley, © 1970 Loren Eiseley and published by Macmillan Publishing Company.

Excerpt from *Beyond Environmental Crisis* by Alan Drengson, © 1989 Peter Lang Publishing Company.

Excerpt by Peter Berg from *Raise the Stakes* #11, Summer 1986, © Planet Drum Foundation, P.O. Box 31251, San Francisco, CA, Shasta Bioregion.

Excerpts from *A Place in the Wild: The Dynamics of Structures Integrated Into Fragile Natural Sites*, © 1991 by Noel Bennett, Jim Wakeman and Michael McGuire.

Excerpts from *"The Standard Remembering of our Ancestors in the Times of Nuclear Peril"* and *"The Guardianship Ethic,"* © 1992 Nuclear Guardianship Project, 1400 Shattuck Ave. #41, Berkeley, CA 94709.

INTRODUCTION

The Cold War officially ended in 1991. For four decades the leaders of the United States justified building a massive arsenal of nuclear and conventional weapons by arguing that they were protecting the Free World from the "evil empire"—the U.S.S.R. With the collapse of communism in Eastern Europe and the breakup of the U.S.S.R., national attention in the United States and Canada could focus on the hard reality that high levels of consumption, rapid population growth, pollution, and inappropriate land use practices in industrialized nations have led to an environmental crisis more serious than any in the history of civilization.

In 1991 national governments and non-governmental organizations (NGOs) around the world began preparing for an Earth Summit, held in Rio de Janeiro, Brazil, in June 1992, to address these urgent environmental and social issues, including rapid deforestation of tropical and temperate forests, loss of biodiversity due to destruction of habitat, global warming, and depletion of the protective ozone layer. Neither the issue of rapid human population growth nor basic philosophical issues concerning human responsibility for nature were on the official agenda of the Rio Summit nor were these topics discussed by the official delegates at the conference. The United States government delegation, headed by President George Bush, played an obstructionist role at the Rio Summit by refusing to sign a biodiversity treaty approved by a majority of governments, by demanding that a proposed forest treaty be taken off the agenda, by refusing to discuss the issue of rapid population growth, and by refusing to help third world nations in developing strategies for a sustainable society. As a result, the Rio Summit received mixed reviews. Some saw the results as hopeful first steps to massive transformations needed during the 1990s. Other commentators concluded the Rio Summit was a failure which will discourage necessary international cooperation.

There was broad agreement among politicians, scientists, environmentalists and informed citizens in the United States and Canada, however, that the decade of the nineties, for better or worse, will be decisive for human and nonhuman inhabitants of the earth. The Union of Concerned Scientists, in November, 1992, issued a "World Scientists Warning to Humanity," signed by over fifteen-hundred scientists in sixty-nine nations, stating that "human beings and the natural world are on a collision course." The "Warning" was signed by ninety-nine of the one-hundred ninety-six living scientists who have won the Nobel Prize. Monumental changes never experienced during the history of civilization are occurring virtually overnight. The 1992 edition of *State of the World,* an authoritative compilation of environmental trends on the earth, summarizes some of the findings of scientists and projections of current human interventions on life processes of the planet:

The protective ozone shield in heavily populated latitudes of the northern hemisphere is thinning twice as fast as scientists thought just a few years ago.

Atmospheric levels of heat-trapping carbon dioxide are now 26 percent higher than the preindustrial concentration, and they continue to climb. The earth's surface was warmer in 1990 than in any year since record keeping began in the mid-nineteenth century; six of the seven warmest years on record have occurred since 1980.

Forests are vanishing at a rate of some 17 million hectares per year, an area about half the size of Finland.

A minimum of 140 plant and animal species are condemned to extinction each day.

World population is growing by 92 million people annually, roughly equal to adding another Mexico each year; of this total, 88 million are being added in the developing world.

Cholera is pandemic in Latin America and is endemic along the Mexico-U.S.A. border.

The AIDS pandemic is worse than predicted and is expected, by epidemiologists, to lead to a net decrease in the population of some African nations during the 1990s.

In 1992 a United Nations report on the state of the world's environment documented marked deterioration over the past twenty years in most of the environmental and social indicators included in the report. Mustafa Tolba, head of the United Nations Environment Program, which produces the annual report, said, "Time is running out. Critical thresholds may already have been breached."

In the United States a persistent economic recession during the early 1990s, with characteristics unlike any recession of the past two decades, led many people to question some of the conventional assumptions that guided political decisions, career choices, and self-conceptions over the past several generations. From the end of World War II, to the beginning of the 1990s, surveys indicated that most Americans believed that continuing economic growth would bring prosperity, and prosperity would make it possible for Americans (and Canadians) not only to achieve ever higher standards of living but greater happiness and a greater sense of well-being.

Americans believed that nature would always be a constant provider of fresh air, trees, food, and fiber for our use. They believed that bigger was better. They became addicted to bigness—bigger human population, bigger spending, bigger government, bigger corporations, bigger military, bigger public works projects. During the 1980s, the United States government went on a huge binge of appropriations for bigger and bigger military expenditures in the name of fighting the Cold War against the Soviet empire.

Personal lifestyles of many Americans became focused on consumption of material things and on the idea that technology could solve all problems. Many believed that medical technology could solve our health problems, that nuclear technology could solve our need for new energy sources, that military technology could solve our problems of national defense. Americans bought more and more of everything—houses, automobiles, appliances. Americans used more and more electricity and fossil fuels per capita in the belief that in consuming more energy they were increasing their standard of living.

Many believed that ever-increasing prosperity would provide the means to solve intractable social problems including poverty, crime, dysfunctional families, and relations between the sexes.

Many people lost their sense of community and pursued their own careers without thought of their obligations and responsibilities to the larger community—to the ecological community we call nature.

Collectively, the most wealthy nations—the United States and Canada—went on a forty-year spending binge, ignoring the lessons of ecology, and oblivious to most of the great wisdom of religions of the world. I call this forty-year spending spree the Age of Exuberance.

In the early 1990s the Age of Exuberance ended. But to maintain a high-roller lifestyle for some people, some corporations and government agencies continue in an all-out war on nature, on every continent, in every ocean, and in the atmosphere of the planet. Many if not most people are still in denial, refusing to acknowledge that the Age of Exuberance is over, but the bills of the Age of Exuberance have come due. The costs of excess are very high.

Overriding all other concerns in the 1990s is our relationship—as individuals, as members of communities, as nations, as a species—with nature. Vast parts of the web of life are dying due to human interventions in natural processes. If we focus too narrowly on the economy and especially the recession of the early 1990s, we might not see the larger context of structural changes in society and the changing context of our relationship with non-human nature.

As residents of the United States and Canada, we are faced with harsh realities that will require major changes in our social policies, our daily habits, and our lifestyles.

We have begun to understand that we must address questions that were considered heretical a decade ago. Can economic growth, measured by the outdated standards of Gross National Product, provide the means to "solve" our collective environmental and social problems? In other words, is it possible to grow our way out of environmental dilemmas such as deforestation, species extinction, atmospheric imbalances, and toxic pollution on a massive scale, when economic growth in itself contributed to these problems?

On a personal level, more and more people are asking if there is something more to life than fighting to maintain a job or earn a slightly bigger paycheck.

Long-established habits of consumption are already rapidly changing. For example, "no smoking" ordinances, higher taxes on tobacco products, educational programs, and growing concern for our health are reasons for rapid decline in smoking, a previously widely accepted habit. Waste reduction laws, bottle and can deposit laws, and general public acceptance of the fact that we are wasting scarce resources are turning many Americans and Canadians into recyclers. Rising prices and decreasing supplies of water in many regions are encouraging residents to be more frugal with water. For similar reasons we are becoming more conscious of the amount of fossil fuel we use. Other changes in our patterns of consumption will come about due to conscious choices by consumers and by economic and ecological necessity.

Adults have the ability to make rapid and drastic conscious changes in lifestyle based on clear understanding and acceptance of certain philosophical principles. In particular, the global environmental crisis is motivating many people to understand the connection between certain patterns of consumption and the deterioration of life support systems on the planet. Surveys indicate that many people want to begin "greening" their lifestyles.

In this book, "greening our lifestyles" means developing a deeper love for ourselves as part of nature, changing our attitudes toward materialism and overconsumption, and becoming mindful of our connections to nature. It means making specific changes in our daily behavior and drastic changes in our long-range goals. There are many ways to green lifestyles. Suggestions made in this book concerning homes, gardens, participation in voluntary organizations, and perception of the land point to some of the ways anyone in a moderate or higher income household can lead a more fulfilling and life-supporting life. Readers are encouraged to be creative and adapt recommendations to their specific situations.

If we begin greening our lifestyles, we can enhance our sense of well-being, add meaning to our lives, and revitalize our sense of purpose and self-esteem, as well as contribute to the community of all beings, not only the community of human beings. I argue that by practicing the three Rs of reduction, recovery, and responsibility, we can enhance possibilities for richness of life, realization, and revitalization. Paying our debts to nature will not be simple or easy. It will be difficult to change some of our wasteful and destructive habits. But if we find congenial social support for our efforts, we can help each other on the road to recovering our balance.

The question is, will we only be reactive to large-scale changes in society, in philosophy, that are occurring around us, or will we also be proactive? Will we be full, voluntary participants in the challenge of change during this decade, or will we reluctantly, and perhaps fearfully, conform to the demands for change imposed on us by forces beyond our control?

The answer to this question is based on our attitude. If we welcome, accept, and embrace the opportunities for change—vast changes in our approach to the rest of nature, to society, and to economic changes—then we can feel empowered. Through changing our lifestyles, we can live richly—in experience of life, not in yearly income.

The major philosophical issue is one of anthropocentric versus ecocentric perspectives. Stated briefly, an *anthropocentric* perspective means that one views humans as the "highest" or most advanced or important species on the planet. All other species are "lower" in some ordained hierarchy, less intelligent, and less important than humans. Humans, in various versions of anthropocentric doctrine, have a right or even a duty to "develop," control, dominate, and manage all of natural creation. Whether as "stewards" or gardeners or resource developers, those who use anthropocentric arguments see their first responsibility and duty to be "serving the needs of people." Indeed, the slogan "Putting People First" is frequently used as a shorthand statement of anthropocentrism. *Ecocentrism,* or deep ecology, as it is often labeled, presents the idea that humans are part of nature, not apart from nature, that the human place in nature is more modest, even humble, than under anthropocentrism. Humans will be helping some of the tendencies in natural processes, but humans no longer are Lord Man and Lord Woman. We are, in the phrase coined by famed ecologist Aldo Leopold, "plain citizens" of the biosphere, of the cosmos.

For the past two decades, philosophers have been arguing some of the major philosophical issues in the ecocentric versus anthropocentric controversy. A short bibliography of some of the best and most relevant and accessible literature on the ecocentric movement is included as an appendix of this book.

For the most part, the focus in this book is on changes we can make—as individuals, as members of families, as partners, or as small household groups—in our attitudes toward work, recreation, leisure, and daily consumption. This book focuses on changes in our lifestyles based on principles developed over the past several decades in the deep, long-range ecology movement and articulated by Norwegian philosopher Arne Naess.

Although less well known in North America than in Europe, Naess has been writing for the past four decades on the interconnections between issues of social justice and ecological social movements. His work provides an intellectual framework for the suggestions contained in the following chapters of this book.

Many of the principles stated in the following chapters are expressed in somewhat broad, some would even say vague, terms. This is done purposefully to encourage dialogue, and to encourage creative approaches to the complex and frequently ambiguous situations in which we find ourselves.

The collection of essays that constitute this book should be considered as a progress report on thinking on the issues introduced within these pages.

As westerners, relatively affluent residents of North America, we are asked to address the fundamental question, what does it mean to live in harmony within nature? What changes in our philosophy, attitudes, lifestyles, and habits are necessary to begin the process of reconstructing a meaningful, joyful, harmonious way of dwelling with nature, with the biosphere, with earth?

Philosopher Neil Evernden has called our species a "natural alien" species. Similar to exotic species that invade an ecological niche, disrupting the pattern of relationships, our species tends to disrupt, to encourage entropy wherever we go on this planet. We are, in Evernden's words "perennially youthful creatures, ambivalent, agitated, and uncommitted to an environment." We seem to lack commitment to any place, lack a sense of direction or grounding. By organic standards, Evernden concludes, this is a "monumental deformity."

Our task is to become more mature—as individuals, and as a species—in order to live well and so as not to endanger whole systems and natural processes that have developed intricate relationships over time. Our job, our "real work" to use a phrase from Gary Snyder, is to live well, with integrity, in the midst of vast social and biological changes that we cannot fully understand, much less control. We cannot know the outcome of our efforts. We can only set ourselves on a pathway toward maturity. The Chinese say, "A journey of a thousand miles begins with a single step." The journey we have embarked upon is a journey home. It will be long and difficult, never easy. This book is about taking the first steps on that journey, to a reconstruction of our lives, of the meaning we find in life, and a reaffirmation of the process of life in the broadest sense of that term.

In the first chapter, some of the myths of the Age of Exuberance are reviewed.

In the second chapter, some philosophical principles for greening our lifestyles are discussed.

In succeeding chapters, the needs for change in various aspects of our lifestyles are discussed. These topics include the need for changing some of our language, revitalizing our connection with our home place—our bioregion—deepening our experience in nature, changing our food-consumption habits, examining our attitudes toward travel and recreation, and redefining our relationships with major institutions such as schools, churches, and communities.

CHAPTER 1

SISTER/BROTHER, CAN YOU SPARE A HUNDRED BUCKS?

LIVING IN THE HEARTLAND— KANSAS IN THE FIFTIES

My parents came of age in Kansas during the Great Depression of the 1930s. They witnessed unemployment lines, and they learned, from their parents, who were small farmers and manual laborers, the value of frugality, regular work habits, and cooperation in the family household. My grandparents always raised some of their household food supply in a summer garden and canned the surplus for the winter.

My first memories are of the war years of the 1940s. We had ration cards for milk, sugar, coffee, and paper products. My mother planted a Victory Garden (not much different from the usual garden my grandparents planted during the 1930s but renamed by government edict as a Victory Garden to encourage support for the war effort). During the war years my father worked an average of sixty hours a week helping to build a fleet of small boats for the military. The military considered him too old to enlist in the military, but his strong sense of patriotic duty and his commitment to helping his community drove him to work long hours with no overtime pay.

After the war my father continued to work overtime coordinating production of a steel manufacturing firm that was expanding with the great postwar economic boom. He had steady employment throughout his forty-plus-year career, but he never earned more than $11,000 a year in his life.

My mother, the first person in her family ever to receive a college education, was employed as a school teacher until she married. Following the custom of her generation, she then became a housewife and did not work at a salaried job ever again. Housewife was an honorable title for married women during the 1940s and 1950s. As homemaker and housewife, she kept the household budget, managed the house and a family of four, gardened, and worked in her church groups.

On my father's salary my parents managed to own their own home and a recent-model automobile, take a two-week vacation trip each year, and put two sons through college at a state university. When my parents retired, they managed to live comfortably on their Social Security, and supplemental income provided by my brother and me, for nearly two decades. When they died, they left no estate, but neither did they leave any debts. Medicare paid most of their medical bills during bouts of severe illness during their older years.

While my parents were still living, many of their friends moved up to more expensive houses. Some were promoted to vice presidents of the corporations for which they worked. Some sent their children to private colleges and seemed to be able to afford a new vehicle every year and maintain membership in a country club. My parents sometimes expressed the desire for more material possessions—a bigger house in a new, "all-electric" subdivision, more expensive vacations, more expensive automobiles, but in comparison to their parents' generation, they felt that they were successful. They were getting ahead in life—in a material sense—and enjoying the comforts of an increasingly affluent society. In the comfortable pews of the Protestant church of which they were lifetime members, they heard only rumblings of the emerging civil rights movement, of battles over integration of churches, equal opportunities for blacks, and only vague comments about the nuclear arms race.

In retrospect, I see that in comparison to many of our neighbors and friends in the affluent suburbs of Kansas City, our family had very modest material possessions—no art collection, no convertibles or fancy furniture, no country club membership, no expensive private school education for the children. But to me it seemed we always had plenty—plenty of food and a spacious suburban lot on which to play, but more important, we had plenty of family love and active participation in church, Boy Scouts, and garden club. We also lived in a state that provided us with an excellent education at a state-supported, public university, which charged no tuition at the time my brother and I attended college.

I remember the 1950s as a decade of increasing prosperity. We always seemed to have more—more meat on the table, more technology. Our leaders told us we would always have more advancement and progress. A vaccine for polio eliminated a health fear and seemed to confirm our expectations of ever better health and longer lives. New shopping centers seemed to be springing up at every intersection. Little did I know that during the next four decades the population of the United States would grow from 150 million in 1950 to over 253 million in 1990. Nothing in my high school or college education prepared me for the fact that basic philosophical underpinnings of our attitudes toward society and toward nature would be severely challenged from 1960 onward.

The first television appeared in our household about 1952. That changed the daily schedule of our household unit more than anything else during my childhood. Our schedule for supper, shopping, and conversation within the family changed to conform to the schedule of our favorite programs on TV. We finished dinner before the evening national news, followed by a favorite situation comedy. It seemed we were extolled by commercials to buy a new gadget every week—electric this and that, home appliances, power lawn mowers. New homes, in the sprawling suburbs, were advertised as all-electric homes—electric heating, electric appliances, even electric-powered air conditioners, which made our lives much more pleasant during long sultry summer nights in the Midwest. We were expected, based on the premise that we should "keep up with the Joneses," to buy a new automobile every two or three years. I can remember, as a teenager, eagerly awaiting the annual auto shows, where the new models of Fords and Chryslers and GMC vehicles were lavishly displayed.

I didn't hear of the National Interstate Highway Act of 1956 until I was much older, but I remember the thrill of seeing bulldozers grading the new freeways through the suburbs, making it easier for us to drive to new shopping malls, drive across the city, and drive across the state for summer vacations in the mountains of Colorado. Gasoline was twenty-nine cents a gallon.

I remember the slogan "Atoms for Peace." Guest speakers in our classes at school told us with great pride in their voices about the new atomic power plants and predicted that energy would soon be produced so cheaply we wouldn't have meters on our houses. Our teachers told us that conservation meant building huge dams to "tame" wild rivers, making their waters useful for productive farms and factories. Nature had only two purposes: to provide raw materials in endless supply to build bigger, more advanced cities, and, in limited areas, to provide scenic backdrops for our vacations. The scenic backdrops were provided in national parks. All other areas were farms, mining areas, tree lots, pastureland, or military reserves. Poverty, we were told in school, would be eliminated because continued economic prosperity would provide jobs for everyone who wanted a job. Medical advances would continue to conquer dreaded diseases.

Of course we had other fears. We had air-raid-alert training in school and were told that in the event of a nuclear attack we should get under our desks and put our heads down on the floor to protect ourselves from flying glass. We were told not to go outside until the all-clear signal was sounded. Some of our neighbors built shelters from atomic blasts in their backyards and stocked them with two weeks' supply of food and water in case there was lingering radioactivity outdoors after a nuclear attack. After two weeks, we were assured, we could resume our "normal" lives. We believed that new military technology—missiles and jet planes, for example—would allow us to win any war with the Russians. We were taught to hate the "Commies" who were attacking the "American way of life." The "American way of life" was defined as a model for the rest of the world, a cornucopian vision of new automobiles, new shopping malls, new factories, and new technological innovations to make our lives more and more comfortable.

Overall, each year was better than the last. My parents bought a new home about every five years. We had three-week family vacations, and many forecasters proclaimed a declining work week—maybe to a standard thirty-hour work week for forty hours of pay—longer vacations, and more leisure time. My parents stopped growing a summer vegetable garden and stopped canning for the winter. Food was more abundant and cheaper, it seemed, each year. We had fresh vegetables all year round. During the winter months vegetables were shipped fresh from California and Florida on the new interstate freeways. We ate fresh meat daily—slabs of bacon, pork chops, roasts, steaks, and deep-fried chicken with fat-rich gravy.

We were told that we were protected from any potential aggressor by a national security system built on nuclear armaments and the power of the Strategic Air Command. We had a sense of personal security in our belief that the American economy would continue to grow and American exports would be in demand in all the nations of the Free World. We had a sense of security in our household and our suburban communities. I don't remember ever hearing of a rape or mugging in my community during my childhood. None of my family or friends ever experienced violence directed against them. We rarely heard of the plight of the poor that Michael Harrington was to write about so eloquently in *The Other Americans* in 1962. We heard only vague rumblings of the psychological costs of racial segregation and the plight of African-Americans. And we never heard about the terrible wounds that industrial civilization was inflicting on the web of life, on the watersheds, forests, prairies, and other types of landscapes of North America.

The negative effects of chlorofluorocarbons (CFCs) on the atmosphere were understood by scientists, but these chemicals were widely accepted for refrigerators, air conditioning, and many other devices that made, we thought, our lives more comfortable. Many other chemicals, later to be shown to have detrimental effects on the environment, were widely accepted for the same reason. I can remember walking almost in awe down the long aisles of a new supermarket, looking at the vast array of personal-care items on the shelves and wondering how I could ever make a choice from so many products designed to make me more attractive to the opposite sex, more handsome, better groomed.

During the period from 1945 to 1965, a few perceptive writers warned us of the perils of rapid industrial growth. For example, William Vogt's *Road to Survival,* published in 1950, perceptively warned about depletion of soils and water supplies. But most Americans wanted to believe in economic expansion, progress, and technological advancement. Indeed, the phrase "baby boom generation" was to enter our language as a phrase summarizing rapid increase in consumption, hedonism, and me-first, get-it-now individualism and self-indulgence. Technology would always provide more of the good life, we were told—"Better Living through Electricity," "Progress Is Our Middle Name," and "Nuclear Energy for the Future" were only some of the slogans thrown at us by schools, corporations, and government.

The ecological costs of inappropriate technology were calculated by a few courageous scientists. Rachel Carson's *Silent Spring,* published in 1962, warned about the ecological consequences of widespread use of DDT, and by implication other pesticides, introduced during the post-World War II era, which helped increase crop production. Previous to the 1940s all food crops were grown organically, without synthetic chemical pesticides and herbicides. Carson's prophetic statement at the conclusion of her book could serve as an introduction to the dawning of the Age of Ecology. She urged an end to unnatural manipulations of nature.

> Through all these new, imaginative, and creative approaches to the problem of sharing our earth with other creatures there runs a constant theme, the awareness that we are dealing with life—with living populations and all their pressures and counter-pressures, their surges and recessions. Only by taking account of such life forces and by cautiously seeking to guide them into channels favorable to ourselves can we hope to achieve a reasonable accommodation between the insect hordes and ourselves.

Carson warned that the phrase "control of nature" was conceived in arrogance, that the science of insect control "has armed itself with the most modern and terrible of weapons," such as DDT, and "in turning them against the insects it has also turned them against the earth" (*Silent Spring,* pp. 296, 297).

FREE SPEECH AND FREE LOVE—
FREEWHEELING THROUGH THE SIXTIES

Stewart Udall, Secretary of the Interior under presidents Kennedy and Johnson in the early 1960s, warned of the "quiet crisis" in our relationship with nature. He called us to consider our actions within an ethical framework. Ecologist Aldo Leopold's book, *A Sand County Almanac* was first published in 1949, but only when it was reprinted in 1964 did it gain wide recognition. In that book, Leopold articulated what he called a "land ethic." He wrote, "A thing is right when it tends to maintain the integrity, beauty, and stability of the natural system. It is wrong when it tends otherwise." Udall called Americans to consider Leopold's "land ethic," and look again at Native American philosophy and spirituality, and seek inspiration from traditional Native American wisdom on how we might live more gently on this continent.

The integrity of natural systems was being threatened by actions of industrial societies—air and water pollution; depletion of forests, which were being cut at ever-increasing rates to serve the housing boom of the 1950s and 1960s; invasion of synthetic chemicals into ecological cycles; and many other threats to nonhuman beings.

The Sierra Club, in the early to mid 1960s, fought well-publicized battles to stop the Bureau of Reclamation from building dams in the Grand Canyon and lobbied successfully for passage of a national wilderness preservation system. A new national park was created in the redwoods of northern California in 1968. But campaigns for energy conservation, for public transportation systems, for preservation of vast wild areas to protect biodiversity were very few and very small. Nature, for most Americans and Canadians during the 1960s, was still seen as primarily a source of raw materials to keep our factories producing more and more consumer goods.

Our view of nature from the suburbs was increasingly truncated during the 1950s and 1960s. We literally lost touch with nature. Most Americans were now urban dwellers who did not till the soil. Wild nature was found only in remote areas of the continent. Predator-control programs supported by the federal government had helped eliminate the howl of the wolf, the yap of the coyote, the sight of eagles in the sky, and the paw prints of the mountain lion on the mountain trail. If we wanted to see wild animals, we went to the zoo. If we wanted green vegetables, we went to the supermarket. When my grandparents died in the 1960s, after living most of their lives on a small farm near Kansas City, my family ceased going to the farm to get smoked hams, fresh eggs, and fresh milk. All our foodstuffs were available in cellophane-wrapped packages in the supermarket. We didn't even have to recycle our glass milk containers. Milk, and virtually every other product we bought, was available in throw-away containers. Some commentators began to call America the "throw-away society."

The Age of Exuberance was consumed with its own successes through the 1960s. Big Technology projects included the mission to put a man on the moon by the end of the 1960s. Missile launchings at Cape Canaveral in Florida became a spectator sport, and the television images of the first moon walk seemed, to many, the triumph of American technological superiority. "One giant leap for mankind," Neil Armstrong said when he first stepped out on the moon's surface. Americans were leading the world into space. The phrase "spaceship earth" entered our vocabulary, a logical extension of the metaphor introduced in the seventeenth century that the earth can be understood as a gigantic machine and that once humans understand the workings of the machine they will be in control of it. Human intelligence was now extending into space, and our ingenuity and ability to control nature, so it seemed, had no bounds, not even earthly bounds.

The baby boom generation equated the good life with ever more consumption, more economic prosperity, better health care, more drugs to cure disease, more leisure time, more services provided by government, more education, MORE of everything. When the first wave of the baby boom generation was graduating from college in the late 1960s, it seemed that these expectations for MORE would be realized. Some young men faced the possibility of being drafted to serve in an increasingly unpopular war in Vietnam, but even during the height of the buildup of U.S. military forces in Vietnam, the number of active-duty men and women was small compared to the massive military mobilization during World War II.

In reaction to the excesses of the 1950s, an active protest movement did develop during the 1960s. Endless growth, boundless belief in technology, in big government, big corporations, and big military was questioned by perceptive scholars and many people struggling against agencies bent on "developing" nature. The assassination of John F. Kennedy in 1963 and both Martin Luther King, Jr., and Robert Kennedy in 1968 left a permanent scar on the body politic and opened a deep rift in the widely accepted notion that "everything is under control." Accounts of events presented by officials now seemed hollow. Truth itself seemed more elusive. Was Kennedy shot at by one or two gunmen?—was there a conspiracy to murder the president? If Martin Luther King, Jr., a leader of nonviolent social activism could be murdered, how could nonviolence ever overcome violence? How could the idealism of the Peace Corps, the counterculture, the opposition of many students to the war in Vietnam and to nuclear war be sustained when agencies of the federal government were engaged in massive repression of dissent, collecting files on all protesters, even those who protested spraying dangerous herbicides and pesticides on the forests, much less those who protested the war in Vietnam?

A dark shadow was emerging over industrial civilization, and that shadow was soon to be defined as the "environmental crisis," which perceptive commentators recognized as a cultural crisis, a spiritual crisis, and a psychological crisis for those who were brainwashed in the conventional slogans of the Age of Exuberance.

THE ME GENERATION: DISCO DANCING THROUGH THE SEVENTIES

During the 1970s the counterculture and the environmental movement provided a dramatic contrast with the business-as-usual, growth-and-development ideology of the federal government, most of the media, and most of the middle class.

Many commentators on the 1960s have highlighted free sex, freer willingness to experiment with drugs, a sense of disengagement from conventional middle-class life, and concern with issues of social justice, equality of opportunity, and environmental quality as themes of the 1960s generation. By contrast it seemed that the national mode changed in the 1970s. Frugality, service to others, lifestyles of moderation, holding money in savings accounts, cooperation in community became old-fashioned virtues.

Even after final U.S. withdrawal from Vietnam in the mid-1970s, military expansion continued, with the support of most citizens. The aerospace industry provided hundreds of thousands of high-paying jobs and thus the opportunity to participate in ever-increasing consumption and mass recreation and to satisfy—at least temporarily—narrow self-interest. Domestic air travel was booming. Corporate expansion serviced the demands of an increasingly affluent population. More and more women were entering the labor force, and the dual-income household became a standard means by which many couples were able to buy houses, automobiles, and all kinds of consumer items for the household even during periods of higher inflation and higher taxation.

Most Americans did not recognize it at the time, but the mid-1970s marked the high point in rapid growth of standard of living in the Age of Exuberance. Although there are many ways to interpret aggregate statistical data, most economic analysts agree that average income of Americans peaked in 1973. Factoring inflation into average incomes, Americans seem to have experienced at best stagnant and possibly declining incomes and buying power during the past two decades (*New York Times,* Jan. 12, 1992, The Week in Review, Section 4, p. 1). Adjusting for inflation, the median household income in America was between $30,000 and $35,000 in 1973 and remained in that range in the early 1990s.

Median or average incomes, of course, do not tell the whole story, and scholars are still debating what happened during the 1970s and 1980s. Some researchers at the Urban Institute, a liberal research organization in Washington, D.C., conclude that the poorest fifth of American families dramatically increased their average family income between 1976 and 1986 (by 77 percent, adjusting for inflation, according to these researchers), while the richest fifth increased their income by only 5 percent (*San Francisco Chronicle,* July 2, 1992, A13).

However, other researchers conclude that the top 20 percent of household incomes, and incomes with two income earners—especially if the income was derived from corporate executive positions, law, or medicine—improved between the early 1970s and 1990 to a point of affluence unprecedented in American history. Furthermore, the top 1 percent of Americans increased their share of the total aggregate wealth of the nation during the 1970s and 1980s.

Personal income stagnated between the late 1970s and early 1990s as fewer and fewer jobs were generated compared to total adult population growth. Declining opportunities for higher-paying jobs and thus declining opportunities to buy homes affected Americans under the age of thirty-five after the mid-1970s more than those in older age categories. According to a report in *Fortune,* by the early 1990s, 71 percent of families with a chief breadwinner under the age of thirty-five could not afford to buy a median-priced home in the area where they resided (*Fortune,* Oct. 21, 1991).

Average or aggregate incomes tell only part of the story of changes in income and consumption patterns of middle- and upper-income families. These statistics do not show the impact of increased consumption rates on the life-support systems of this continent and of the planet. Recognizing the fact that high-consumption lifestyles and heavy use of energy in industrial production were causing increased environmental damage, President Nixon signed the National Environmental Policy Act on January 1, 1970, and proclaimed the 1970s the Decade of the Environment, during which Americans would collectively clean up pollution in our air and water, repair human-caused damage to the natural environment, enlarge the national park system, and consider the impact on the environment of all significant public works projects.

In early 1970, Senator Gaylord Nelson called for an Earth Day demonstration. Volunteers in hundreds of communities across North America sponsored Earth Day celebrations. Earth Day 1970 was a "happening" in the 60s sense of that term—spontaneous, exuberant, somewhat innocent, and more than somewhat naive. However, it symbolized a growing awareness of our collective negative impact on the natural environment.

Paul Shepard, ecologist and teacher, published *The Subversive Science* in 1969. In his introductory essay he succinctly stated how ecological thinking would undermine the mechanistic, linear thinking that propelled the Age of Exuberance.

> Ecological thinking requires a kind of vision across boundaries. The epidermis of the skin is ecologically like a pond surface or a forest soil, not a shell so much as a delicate interpenetration. It reveals the self ennobled and extended rather than threatened as part of the landscape and the ecosystem, because the beauty and complexity of nature are continuous with ourselves (p. 2).

Shepard presented a challenge and a vision for the Age of Ecology that went far beyond the rhetoric of most speakers heard on Earth Day 1970.

> If nature is not a prison, and earth a shoddy way-station, we must find the faith and force to affirm its metabolism as our own— or rather, our own as part of it. To do so means nothing less than a shift in our whole frame of reference and our attitude towards life itself, a wider perception of the landscape as a creative, harmonious being where relationships of things are as real as the things. Without losing our sense of a great human destiny and without intellectual surrender, we must affirm that the world is a being, a part of our own body (p. 3).

Shepard cited the perceptive writings of Christian priest turned Buddhist, Alan Watts, who opened the doors of eastern ecological wisdom to the minds of westerners in the 1960s. In a series of books including *Nature, Man and Woman* (1958), and *The Book on the Taboo Against Knowing Who You Are* (1966), Watts presented us with the challenge that what we were to call the "environmental crisis" was a fundamental spiritual, philosophical crisis for those of us living during the last decades of the twentieth century in a nation beset with materialism, individualism, and a narrow focus on economic prosperity at the expense of natural processes. We were caught, Watts said, in a vicious circle.

> The essence of a vicious circle is that one is pursuing, or running away from, a terminus which is inseparable from its opposite, and that so long as this is unrecognized the chase gets faster and

faster. The sudden outburst of history in the last five hundred years might strike one as more of a cancer than orderly growth (*Nature, Man, and Woman,* p. 19).

In response to the cancerous growth of industrial civilization, the reform environmental movement focused on making changes in society through legislative action. Historians agree that some significant environmental legislation was enacted in America during the early years of the 1970s, including the Clean Air Act and Clean Water Act, the Endangered Species Act and reform of national forest policy. However "reform environmentalism" rarely challenged the underlying assumptions of industrial civilization. Reform environmentalism supported economic growth. As philosopher Arne Naess said in his ground-breaking article published in *Inquiry* magazine in 1973 discussing shallow (or reform) environmentalism and deep ecology, reform environmentalism deals primarily with the health of humans in rich nations.

There were some exceptions. David Brower, who established Friends of the Earth in 1971 after he resigned as executive director of the Sierra Club over the lack of progressive policies in the Sierra Club, published *Progress As If Survival Mattered* and other books that pointed the way to seeking a high quality of life without impairing all life on earth. Paul Ehrlich, whose book *The Population Bomb* increased awareness of the negative consequences of rapid population growth, published *The End of Affluence* in 1974 in which he called for self sufficient lifestyles. But Brower's and Ehrlich's appeals were not taken seriously by most Americans.

The Arab oil boycott of 1973 touched off some shock waves about our energy consumption, but the United States government responded in its customary manner of emphasizing more exploration and development of nonrenewable energy—oil, coal, oil shale, uranium, natural gas—rather than seriously examining the massive and wasteful use of nonrenewable energy in our culture. No society has used as much nonrenewable energy in so short a time. Only modest attempts were made to reduce the high rate of energy consumption during the 1970s. President Carter in the late 1970s wore a sweater in the White House and advised us to turn the thermostats down in our homes, but he also developed an expansionist national energy policy including research on oil shale, more exploration for fossil fuel, and more nuclear power plants. When challenged with the possibility of limits to expansion, we reacted by searching for technological solutions—even if for some of us it was a search for "appropriate technology," a vague phrase, but one that seemed to include an implicit acceptance that bigger was not necessarily better and that some conventional approaches to technology were not appropriate to caring for the earth.

Some social analysts began to detect a growing malaise in the collective national psyche. Higher and higher standards of living did not necessarily yield a greater sense of well-being. Tibor Scitovsky, an economist, used the phrase "the joyless economy." In his inquiry into human satisfaction and consumer dissatisfaction, he concluded that after a certain level of consumption is reached, further consumption yields fewer psychological rewards. People frequently continue to buy more things because of social pressure—advertising, comparisons with friends and acquaintances, exhortations from respected leaders who tell us to buy a new vehicle or buy a house to keep the economy growing, and from psychological inertia and a sense that somehow buying things will make up for the emptiness in our lives. Scitovsky wittily comments on the irrationality of lifestyles based on higher consumption in the Age of Exuberance:

> When a person spends his day surrounded by power-driven equipment and vehicles to help him save effort on his every move, at work, at home and at play, and he then proceeds on doctor's order to squander the energy he has so carefully saved on jogging around the block or riding his exercycle in the bedroom, he gives clear evidence that he realizes the irrationality, if not of his personal behavior, at least of the pattern of behavior society imposes, the pressure of which he is not strong enough to resist (Scitovsky, p. 255).

Paul Wachtel, in *The Poverty of Affluence*, argued that real buying power did increase during the 1970s, even during the inflationary period in the late 1970s, but buying power did not increase as fast as income in dollars (p. 15). However, the irony was that the more we produced and consumed, the less satisfied we were.

Our restless desire for more and more has been a major dynamic for economic growth, but it has made the achievement of that growth largely a hollow victory. Our sense of contentment and satisfaction is not a simple result of any absolute level of what we acquire or achieve. It depends upon our frame of reference, on how what we attain compares to what we expected. If we get farther than we expected, we tend to feel good. If we expected to go farther than we have, then even a rather high level of success can be experienced as disappointing. In America, we keep upping the ante. Our expectations keep accommodating to what we have attained. "Enough" is always just over the horizon, and like the horizon it recedes as we approach it (Watchel, p. 17).

With a low level of income, minimal food, and a sense of security about the future, even a small increase in consumption can increase our sense of well-being. In the wealthy economic situation of middle- and upper-class Americans and Canadians, however, "what really matters is not one's material possessions but one's psychological economy, one's richness of human relations and freedom from the conflicts and constrictions that prevent us from enjoying what we have. Such a state of affairs is a consequence of affluence" (p. 39).

THE DECADE OF DENIAL: CAREENING THROUGH THE EIGHTIES

Our sense of well-being was further undermined by the realization that our affluence was based on our commitment to a rapidly growing economy and on technology that was continuing to undermine the natural systems of the continent—indeed, of the earth. One psychological reaction to painful reality is denial. The decade of the 1980s can be called the Decade of Denial and a decade during which many affluent Americans expressed what Lawrence Shames called "The Hunger for More"—more affluence, more things, more sex, more success among our peers, more exuberant display of our wealth and more ridicule of environmentalists as "doomsayers," "spoilsports," and social deviants who don't play the game.

Denial played an important role in the rise of the wise-use movement (called in Canada the share movement and in logging communities the yellow-ribbon coalition). Ron Arnold, a self-proclaimed leader of this reactionary, industry-funded campaign, has explicitly denied that global warming is occurring, that ancient forests are endangered by massive clearcuts, that there are any problems with current dominant approaches to land-use management. Denial took many forms in the 1980s. Even in the face of testimony from many atomic scientists, for example, some people denied that nuclear weapons could destroy our civilization and myriad non-human species on this planet.

Joanna Macy, in her book *Despair and Personal Power in the Nuclear Age* (Macy, p. 5) says that denial is fueled by disbelief. "I can't believe this is happening. This is too abstract. It doesn't relate to my personal life. I only see nuclear explosions on film." She calls these quasi-disbeliefs because we know, in our hearts, that this is real. She writes:

> And so we tend to lead our lives as if nothing had changed, while knowing that everything had changed. On one level we maintain a more or less upbeat capacity to carry on as usual—getting up in the morning and remembering which shoe goes on which foot, getting the kids off to school, meeting our appointments, cheering up our friends and all the while, underneath, there is this inchoate knowledge that our world could go at any moment. Awesome and unprecedented in the history of humanity, it lurks there, with an anguish beyond the naming. Until we find ways of acknowledging and integrating that level of anguished awareness, we repress it; and with that repression we are drained of the energy we need for action and clear thinking (Macy, p. 6).

Our denial comes from our fear of pain, our fear of guilt, our fear of appearing unpatriotic and un-American, our fear of religious doubt, our fear of appearing too emotional in the context of conventional social discourse at the country club, over lunch with our friends, in discussions at the university. Our culture has different socialization for men and women. Men, especially, are suspect if they express sadness, strong fears about the future, fear of loss of control of the situation, but women also are subject to repression of emotions. "They often withhold their expressions of concern and anguish for the world lest these be treated condescendingly, as 'just like a woman'" (Macy, p. 11).

Denial during the 1980s was expressed in rejection of hard reality—for example, the reality that exponential population growth cannot continue for more than a short period.

Many denied that decisions by corporations, the military, and government natural resource management agencies in the United States and Canada were causing major environmental problems. The cheery, pro-corporate, anti-government-regulation message of Ronald Reagan resonated with millions of middle-class Americans.

Many denied that America was losing its economic superiority in a changing world order.

Many denied that their hunger for more had anything to do with their own dissatisfaction and lower sense of well-being.

Many denied that the Age of Exuberance was winding down, and if they, or their parents, hadn't made it—creating a portfolio of investments, real estate holdings, savings—in the 50s, 60s, or 70s, it was unlikely that they would make it into the affluent middle class in the 1980s. As Lawrence Shames summarizes the situation in the 1980s:

> The bottom line seems to be that the American middle class was becoming too expensive a club to join at this late date. It was even tougher to latch onto *more* unless you had a good bit to begin with, since the operative pattern had become trading up, not buying in. If you hadn't been around to stake a claim when things were good, when entry into the bourgeoisie seemed almost a perquisite of citizenship, there was a serious chance you'd missed out forever. (Shames, p. 63).

Most important, many denied that our overly consumptive lifestyle, our addiction to economic growth at any cost, was causing problems for other species, for whole ecosystems: "There's nothing wrong with nature that our technology can't fix, and anyway the environmentalists have exaggerated the problems because they want to get money for their own organizations." Though its expression here is simplistic and crude, that is what millions of Americans chose to believe.

Many Americans oohed and aahed the lifestyles of the rich and the famous—art collections, private yachts, huge houses, private zoos, billions of dollars invested in junk bonds and real estate. Stock in biotechnology corporations was considered a status symbol. Donald Trump became a media star and his book *The Art of the Deal* was read by millions of people who wanted to make it quickly into the affluent class. The quick deal, even the shady deal with junk bonds and loans from financially unstable savings and loans associations, fueled the orgy for *more*.

Concern for the common good was considered less important than concern for making a deal, making a career, making a statement with extravagant indulgences for personal pleasures. There were some environmental problems, but mostly problems with environmentalists. There were some problems of poverty, many people said, but mostly problems with welfare cheaters. There were some problems with the growth economy, but these could be solved through the market mechanisms, such as finding enough venture capital to start new businesses. If you were depressed, the solution was to go shopping. Indeed, a slogan of the 80s was "Shop till You Drop." There was so much to buy and so little time to buy it all.

Time became the scarcest resource. Some sociologists had predicted the arrival of the "harried leisure class" in the 1960s, but the reality of time scarcity became apparent for many full-time workers in two-income households during the 1980s. The solution: buy more time-saving devices—auto phones to communicate with friends and customers while commuting, FAX machines to speed written communication, computer networking, shorter vacations, one-day revitalizing treatments at the spa rather than week-long sessions as previously recommended (Lindner, *The Harried Leisure Class*).

In industrial production, time use has always been equated with efficiency. The goal of scientific management is to produce more goods during a given unit of time. Automation and time-management procedures were introduced in industry after industry. This industrial model of production was introduced even into natural landscapes. If it took a natural forest a hundred years to produce marketable timber, scientific management could reduce that time to twenty years through enhanced productivity. Forests were replaced by tree farms. Scientists began to breed "genetically superior" trees, planted in straight rows, sprayed with herbicides and pesticides to keep off "pests," that (if weather cooperated and no brush fires burned the plantations) could be "harvested" in twenty years.

Humans, it seemed, could not wait for the rhythm of nature. More and more Americans were in a hurry to get more production from nature and denied that massive human interventions in nature were detrimental to natural systems. Forests, and all kinds of ecosystems, evolve and change in complex ways, ways that humans barely understand.

As the 80s ended, denial seemed epidemic, almost a collective psychosis. In rational arguments, even the most ardent promoters of scientific management of nature were hard pressed to present a case that exponential growth could continue for the indefinite future. True, a few economists led by Julian Simon argued that human entrepreneurship would control, dominate, and enhance nature. Simon and his pronatalist supporters, including many high officials in the Reagan administration, argued that earth can support billions and billions more humans at higher and higher standards of living. They dismissed environmentalists as sentimental for advocating a reverence for nature (Simon, *The Ultimate Resource*).

More perceptive commentators saw the hard reality. Vastly increasing the gross national product during the 1970s and 1980s did not end poverty or solve environmental and social problems. The new reality—the economic, social, and environmental reality—could no longer be denied. Reports by the National Science Foundation, the National Academy of Sciences, Worldwatch Institute, and numerous other research organizations detailed the environmental and social consequences of policies and collective consumption patterns of the Age of Exuberance. The following conclusions are some of the most striking gleaned from these reports on income distribution and public services:

■ The gap between the wealthy and the middle class and poor segments of the population increased after 1970.

■ Two and a half million people at the top of the income scale in the United States had almost as much aggregate wealth in the early 1990s as 100 million people living in families that earn less than $27,000 a year.

■ People in the top 20 percent of income have the money to continue building new homes, buying memberships in country clubs, taking expensive vacations, and investing in a vast array of consumer goods even during periods of economic recession.

■ Through investments in corporate stocks, mutual funds and real estate, charitable contributions, contributions to political candidates and political campaigns, people in the top 20 percent of income have disproportionate influence on land-use policies, political decisions, and even the strategies of the environmental movement.

■ Although the United States had higher economic growth rates and lower unemployment rates than other industrialized nations, the poverty rate in the United States was higher than that in other comparative nations because welfare and transfer payments did not keep pace with inflation and because these transfer payments did not offset higher taxes paid by lower-income residents of the United States.

■ Millions of children dropped out of high school in the United States in the 1980s, at a higher rate than in comparable industrialized nations. Those children who drop out of high school or who have only a high school diploma and no college education are permanently stifled in finding higher-paying jobs, especially with the end to whole categories of traditional blue-collar, higher-paying jobs in manufacturing industries.

■ Single parents, especially females, have less opportunity throughout their adult lives to increase household income significantly.

■ Dual-income households, especially among the top 20 percent of household incomes, were the only type of households increasing their annual income and buying power year after year in the 1980s.

■ Despite dramatic increases in the number of two-income households, households in middle-income brackets increased their income between 1977 and 1988 by only 4 percent (*San Francisco Chronicle,* July 29, 1991).

■ A study published by the Joint Center for Political and Economic Studies, published in 1991, concluded that the United States did less to help poorer residents in the 1980s than seven other industrialized nations including Canada, Great Britain, Sweden, France, and Germany (*San Francisco Chronicle,* Sept. 19, 1991).

A permanent underclass was recognized at the end of the 1980s as a fact in the American class structure. For example, some studies indicate that at any given time, nearly 25 percent of African-American males between the ages of fifteen and twenty-five are in jail, on parole or probation, or otherwise in the criminal justice system. The underclass is further expanded by millions of immigrants to the United States and Canada, who are drawn, to a large degree, by belief in "freedom" and by images of the American Dream—a dream now ending. However, in comparison to conditions in most Third World nations and in Second World nations such as Mexico, opportunities for jobs, social services, education, and daily lives relatively free from violence still were perceived by immigrants and those seeking to immigrate as very good.

The myth of steady progressive advancement of society by finding rational solutions to problems through technology; by increasing government expenditures on education, welfare, health care, and social services; by capital investment in infrastructure; and by corporate investment is still widely believed, even though prosperity and economic growth during the Age of Exuberance did not lead to solutions to major social problems or environmental problems. The problems are the result of deeply held attitudes, the result of denial of ecological realities and social realities. Society, during the Age of Exuberance, did not effectively address fundamental religious, philosophical, perceptual issues created by our loss of a sense of organic nature, our reverence for nature.

A growing body of literature has been developed over the past two decades by historians, philosophers, psychologists, and social scientists, exploring the historical origins of our cultural problems. I don't want to imply that our current situation is the result of policies and attitudes expressed in America over only the past half century. What I am calling the

Age of Exuberance in North America is in many ways a logical fulfillment of assumptions found in government, business, science, and philosophy over at least the past several centuries.

I have focused in this chapter on the last fifty years because that is the lived experience of most people in this society. I contend that our faith in the icons of our society that embodied the philosophy underlying the Age of Exuberance—big government, big business, big public works projects, big education, big military-industrial complex—is now in disarray. An opening has been created for new/old approaches to living well—that is, living with integrity—and some data from surveys and other social research indicates that many people living in America and Canada recognize that the realities of the 1990s, and beyond, need to be addressed in much different ways than the way problems were analyzed and addressed during the Age of Exuberance.

Economist Robert J. Samuelson summarized the failures of the Age of Exuberance when he wrote in 1992, "Our faith in prosperity was an infatuation, and like all infatuations, we were seduced by its pleasures and blinded to its shortcomings" (*Newsweek,* March 2, 1992, p. 33). Economic growth was not a great social stabilizer. New insecurities and new international competitions were created, and old industries were drastically restructured, leading to the loss of hundreds of thousands of jobs—jobs replaced by automation, tighter cost controls, and new ways of production that are more efficient.

It is not that standards of living fell during the 1970s and 1980s, it is more that the astronomical expectations of the baby boom generation could not be attained. We cannot have it all—now. Agonizing choices have to be made.

Women are torn between responsibilities to young children and having a career. Single parents are torn between education, job, demands of case workers (if they are on welfare or receive other entitlements), and demands from children for quality time, for home time.

By the beginning of the 1990s, polls revealed that residents with median or above-median incomes said they felt the quality of their lives was decreasing because of the amount of time they spent commuting to work, the hazards of daily traffic jams, smog, fear of crime, and the higher cost of living. Friendships suffered because of hectic schedules. People holding professional jobs and couples in which both people were holding full-time jobs, had difficulty scheduling meetings with friends. When they did meet friends, they felt rushed. Owning or having access to more things—automobiles, yachts, motorcycles, all-terrain vehicles, snowmobiles, larger houses, home entertainment centers—was no longer as psychologically rewarding as it once was because environmental quality, intimate human contacts, family life, friendship, job security, and harmony in our relationship with nature were all declining.

Most important when considering prospects for sustainable culture, the very fabric of nature had been torn asunder by industrial civilization, and there was little evidence that short-term efforts by even the most enlightened and well-meaning humans could put it together again.

THERE'S NO PLACE LIKE HOME—
REALITIES OF THE NINETIES

Our modern society is based on a linear conception of time and on the expectation that things will get better as time goes by. This linear conception of time became not only the most dominant conception of time, but almost the only conception of time used by individuals, social planners, and politicians in making plans for the future. Except for periodic downturns in the economy, or recessions, people generally expect economic expansion, economic growth, and ever higher standards of living to continue for as long as they can see into the future. Jeremy Rifkin, in his book *Time Wars*, summarizes research indicating that the conception of linear time during the Age of Exuberance was out of synch with cyclical time—the coming and going of the seasons, the rhythms of natural change.

Furthermore, conventional assumptions about continued linear growth of the American economy were destroyed by the new realities of the world economic marketplace. Restructuring of the American economy in the early 1990s led to major downscaling in the automotive industry, timber industry, and computer manufacturing industry, as well as banking and education.

The planned decrease in military expenditures by the U.S. government by 25 percent before 1996 means the end of hundreds of thousands of military jobs and hundreds of thousands of more jobs in military procurement such as the aerospace industry and nuclear armaments.

By the fall of 1991, national news media were carrying daily stories profiling the economic problems of the middle classes. *Newsweek* profiled a middle-class family of four whose total income of $62,000 a year depended on three jobs, and the parents worried that they would not be able to afford a college education for their two children. A single mother with an eight-year-old child and an annual income of $19,000 worried that she was splurging to rent a $3 video to watch on the weekends. A middle-aged couple living in Florida with their two teen-aged children and their children's grandmother had been working at full-time jobs for twenty-four years and had a yearly income of $40,000. They could not afford to take a vacation or buy a house on the waterfront (*Newsweek,* Nov. 4, 1991, pp. 22–25).

Many members of the middle classes feel pinched financially and feel they can never achieve economic stability. The social safety net built during the New Deal—Social Security, old-age pensions (both public and private), welfare, public education, and job creation by government—no longer is able to deal with growing claims on entitlement.

Not only did incomes stagnate between the 1970s and early 1990s, fewer jobs were generated in comparison with population growth, and more people competed for those jobs—many of them service sector jobs. Jobs created in the service sector of the economy are lower-paying than jobs in traditional blue-collar industries, in the professions, and in public service. At the same time, the bottom 25 percent of income earners in America have lost out over the past two decades—due to inflation, loss of job opportunities, rising costs of medical care, and declining quality of education for their children—and they are more likely to live in an area contaminated with lead or other toxics or near a toxic dump site.

At the same time, social as well as environmental problems seem to have become more intractable. Child abuse, violence against homosexuals, violence against women, increased racial tensions, problems of the homeless, and the AIDS epidemic are creating interrelated financial and social problems.

Furthermore the natural resources of the nation can no longer be squandered for short-term profit or for creating jobs. The remaining 10 percent of ancient forests administered by the U.S. Forest Service are too ecologically valuable—for their contributions to biodiversity, clean water, science—and spiritually valuable to be squandered by clearcutting them. Fisheries in many oceans and rivers are at historic lows. Water is a precious source of system stability *in the rivers* without being diverted to irrigate pastures and fields.

The costs of toxic and radioactive waste cleanup, of waste created only within the past forty years, continue to grow by astronomical proportions. Some analysts suggest it will be centuries before we can contain radioactive wastes created during the great Cold War competition with the Soviet Union. Containment and disposal of other toxic substances will be very costly if we make a commitment to future generations of humans as well as to the future of other species.

The decade of the 1990s has been called the turnaround decade, the moment of truth, the revolutionary decade. Some historians believe that the decisions we make in this decade will be the most important in the history of civilization—not just western civilization, but all civilization, as historians have described it over the past two and a half thousand years. The environmental crisis is now recognized as affecting every continent on the planet and all the oceans of this planet, as well as the atmosphere. In his perceptive essay on the greenhouse effect, Bill McKibben suggests we are witnessing the "end of nature." By that he means we are witnessing the end of our ideas about nature and about time. Life on this planet may have begun over four billion years ago. Our ideas about nature were formed only during the last four hundred years. Our comforting thoughts that the earth is very large and will absorb the wastes of our civilization began to crumble when we discovered how long it will take for the radioactive particles scientists formed during the last forty years to decay into a less harmful state of being. Within four decades we have increased the rate of extinction of nonhuman life forms to the point that, at current rates, 30 to 50 percent of all the species on the earth will become extinct within the next fifty years. As McKibben says, "We have killed off nature—that world entirely independent of us which was here before we arrived and which encircled and supported human society" (McKibben, p. 96).

The new nature is unpredictable. *Nature* has now become a loaded term—that is, the very words we use to refer to our predicament may be part of the problem. In the next chapter I will discuss the importance of using words in new contexts, but for now it is enough to define *nature* as the processes that hold the earth together and the manifestations of those processes in ecological relationships, geological events, formation of landscapes, and changes due to forces not under human control. The old nature had extremes—storms, earthquakes, droughts—but summer followed winter, and over the millennia it was reliable. The old nature was so reliable we didn't have to think about it, and many attempted to avoid thinking about it all together during the Age of Exuberance. Since all food came packaged in supermarkets, they didn't even have to think about watering the vegetable garden in their yard. The new nature is so unpredictable that we *must* think about it—daily. The question is: Do we have the will to change our lifestyles drastically enough, quickly enough, and with enough commitment to the new nature to save ourselves as well as fragments of the biodiversity of this planet?

Mikhail Gorbachev, who has been a major participant in changes in his own nation as well as in East-West relationships, commented in 1992, "The truth of the matter is that today all of us, East and West, are moving toward a new type of civilization, whether we realize it or not. And it is that which compels me to think that our old stereotypes have now lost their meaning and should be radically reexamined" (*San Francisco Chronicle,* Feb 24, 1992, p. 2).

Lester Brown, president of Worldwatch Institute, in introducing the 1992 edition of *State of the World,* plainly says that only a revolution in the way we go about our lives, our means of production and habits of consumption, our social policies, can reduce the acceleration of negative human impact on all vital natural processes of the old nature—of the oceans, climate, speciation, forest growth, and atmosphere (*State of the World 1992,* Worldwatch Institute).

Dr. Mustafa Tolba, director general of the United Nations Environment

Program, predicted in his introduction to the World Conservation Strategy, that: "Unless nations change their course, we face, by the turn of the century, an environmental catastrophe as complete, as irreversible as any nuclear holocaust."

The "new world order" may be a type of civilization that is different from any seen on earth during the past ten thousand years. Civilization in the emerging Age of Ecology will be based, however, on radically different relationships to nature than those dominant during the Age of Exuberance.

What lessons have we learned from our experiences during the Age of Exuberance?

- We have learned that Bigness is not always better. Bigger human populations do not always produce high-quality civilization nor harmonious relationships among people or between people and the rest of nature.
- We have learned the dangers of addiction to Consumption for the sake of consumption. What we called a "higher" standard of living has threatened not only the quality of human lives, but the quality of life of the earth as a whole.
- We have learned some of the dangers of addiction to growth—economic growth, information growth, growth in the rate of technological change. Economic growth does not always solve social problems and may accentuate social inequality, insecurity, and dislocation from our community. Growth in accumulation of information without a framework to interpret this information can lead to apathy—increasingly people complain of "information overload." Rapid rates of technological change make it increasingly difficult to assess the social and environmental impacts of new technology.
- We have learned that community is more important for our well-being than society and that our community includes nonhuman nature.
- Perhaps we have learned that humans, as a species, would be better off taking a more modest position in the flow of energy in the biosphere than attempting always to dominate, control, and fix nature to fit our whims, our desires, our demands for straight lines, for efficient use of water and wood to fuel our industrialized civilization and the growth machine of our economy.

The Age of Exuberance is rapidly coming to a close. The Age of Ecology has arrived. Our new perceptions of nature will have only partial similarity to our old, sentimental perceptions of nature—our love of ancient forests, fuzzy animals, grand vistas, gardening, hiking in designated wilderness areas, taking a vacation at the beach. In industrial civilization, we have abused our relationship with nature, and nothing less than a fundamental change in perception of our place in nature will enable us to make amends.

Are we ready to face up to our addictions? Are we willing to admit that the assumptions we made about prosperity, economic growth, about our need for higher and higher standards of living led us in a vicious cycle to our current predicament? Therapists who deal with addictive behavior suggest that when we face up to our addictions, take the first step in changing our patterns of behavior, we have taken the most important step. Drastic reevaluation of our lifestyle and a conscious decision to change our habits—habits of thought and habits of behavior—may be the most courageous action we can take in this "moment of truth."

The message in the following chapters of this book is premised on the belief that many people have taken that first step. The overall theme explored in the following chapters is summarized in the phrase "greening our lifestyles." The meaning of this phrase is explored in the following chapters by examining how we perceive ourselves, our homes, and our communities in the context of building new habits for the hard ecological realities of the 1990s. The process of greening our lifestyles begins with reduction—reduction in wastes that are thrown into the environment, reduction in the stuff we surround ourselves with, reduction in the size of our impact on natural processes.

The recovery process, recovering from the habits developed during the Age of Exuberance, will take a long time. How long? Probably the rest of our lives. Recovery of natural systems will take many centuries.

Revitalization will take commitment from individuals in communities and by the society as a whole. It includes revitalizing our sense of place in nature. It includes revitalization of our institutions—churches, finance and savings institutions, schools—to make decisions based on the emerging ecocentric worldview. More than that, it means revitalizing our sense of wonder, our mindfulness of the processes of nature.

Change is occurring extremely rapidly—from the old to the new approach to nature, from the Age of Exuberance to the Age of Ecology. Our choices will diminish in the future—perhaps drastically diminish—but if humans have demonstrated anything during their brief appearance as a species on this planet, it is that they are adaptable. Millions of people have already begun to change their habits in a green direction. Recycling and waste reduction are widely accepted practices. Merchandisers are noting a trend toward downscaling—buying smaller houses, less furniture, appliances that are more energy efficient (that don't use CFCs or other gases that interact with the upper stratosphere to destroy the ozone layer), and smaller vehicles that are kept longer and are more efficient. There is less desire for throw-away products and more concern with quality and durability. Many people are showing more willingness to volunteer to become environmental guardians of natural areas rather than only give money to environmental organizations.

All these are positive indications that many people accept the need for changing their lifestyles toward greeness. This book is for those who are willing to create new lifestyles that conform to ecological principles. This book is for people who want to engage in real work within their communities for long-term bioregional health. Making our way, and making peace, in a sometimes intransigent world has many dimensions—spiritual, social, political. As we begin to realize the enormous impacts that industrial civilization has had on this earth, making peace with nature becomes a central theme. Greening our lifestyles in the Age of Ecology involves changes in the way we see ourselves and the way we understand our place on the earth—our place as individuals, as members of the community of humans within which we live, as one species among many dwelling and co-evolving on this earth.

2

PHILOSOPHICAL ROOTS FOR GREENING OUR LIFESTYLES

Twelve strangers gather at Pepperwood Ranch, in Sonoma County, California, during a weekend in April, preparing for two days of work and meditation. Pepperwood Ranch is maintained by the California Academy of Sciences as an oak woodlands reserve. Oak savanna is considered one of the most endangered types of plant communities in California. On this weekend, the conservation director of the ranch has brought Stephanie Kaza, a Buddhist teacher, ecologist, and environmental educator, to help a diverse group of people gain deeper understanding of our place—as humans—in the flow of change in nature.

Following Buddhist tradition, we mix periods of sitting meditation, called *zazen*, with *samu*, mindful, physical work. "Breathe into your experience," Kaza tells us. "Breathe clearly with each breath as you walk the road in the dark, each step following your breath." We are on a midnight silent walk on a ranch road; the air is warm for April, the sky is clear; and the north star is visible to guide us back to the ranch house should we become confused as to our direction. Returning from our silent walk, we go to bed without conversing, settling our minds from the distractions and business of the work week.

In the morning after a silent breakfast of hearty cereal, fruit, and tea, Kaza explains the ecological meaning of our work. The oak woodland savanna in which we are spending the weekend has been heavily grazed by domestic cattle over the past hundred years. Exotic grasses, brought into the region in the intestines of domesticated, imported cattle, have taken over the meadows from native bunch grass. Moreover, cattle have eaten the young oak sprouts throughout the ranch. Virtually all the oak trees on the ranch are older trees. Some are dying. Since cattle grazing was ended on parts of the ranch a decade ago, young Douglas fir trees have sprouted under the cover of the mature oaks. Young Douglas fir like the shade and protection provided by the oaks—shade from the summer dry season when the sun bakes down on the savanna in this Mediterranean-type climate. The Douglas fir are outcompeting the oaks. In several more decades, if left as they are, the Douglas fir may overshadow and kill the mature oaks, and young acorns will not have a chance to sprout.

Our job, for the weekend, is to cut the young Douglas fir trees under a certain grove of mature oaks and, in a fenced-in parcel of the ranch, to plant acorns of five native species of oaks. The acorns were collected the previous fall by the conservation director of the ranch from various parcels in the watershed where the ranch is located. If we cut the Douglas fir, we protect the mature oaks and give fallen acorns a chance to sprout.

In Buddhist tradition, we work not only to work on the work, but to work in the moment while realizing the far different future. Gary Snyder, poet and teacher who has spent several decades realizing his life within the Buddhist tradition, calls this type of work the "real work"—the work of becoming real to ourselves, realizing the consequences of our actions, taking responsibility for our actions while breathing into the moment.

The morning begins to warm us; sweat appears on some of our brows. It is not easy to cut Douglas fir saplings four to six inches in diameter with a handsaw. After cutting the saplings we drag them into a pile in the center of the meadow. It is noon, and Kaza asks us to gather around the pile of saplings we have cut. We have taken the lives of these trees. It is time to honor their lives.

"Why don't we just leave the Douglas firs alone?" a college student asks as she stands near the pile of saplings. "I think it is bad to cut any more trees when so much deforestation is occurring on our earth."

Kaza asks us to think of the oak woodlands five hundred years in the future. Could a minor intervention in the system today enhance chances for the survival of the whole system? Are we going with the tendency of the land, the tendency of change in the landscape toward cycles of change that can occur without human intervention? Our physical work today is part of a long-term management plan for the ranch. The hope, based on advice from ecologists who have studied oak regeneration in other places in California, is that once some specific types of human influences on the landscape have been removed—especially cattle ranching—that the natural process will tend toward healing the landscape. Our mindful practice is directed to becoming aware of each breath, breathing in the joy of the moment, breathing out the joy of the moment.

Kaza explains that after the pile of Douglas fir saplings we have cut has dried under the summer sun, it will be burned in a controlled burn in the fall, and the ashes will help fertilize the meadow under the winter rains. Native American informants tell us that it was common, before the arrival of Europeans, for tribal people to collect seeds from native grasses in the meadows of the California savanna areas and then burn the meadows in late summer to stimulate the growth of new grass.

The work project after lunch is more satisfying for some of us than cutting young trees. We plant acorns in a fenced enclosure that is designed to test the ability of acorns to sprout when planted by humans. The acorns have been held in moisturized plastic bags for several months, allowing them to begin sprouting from their hard shells.

In the evening, we say grace before a vegetarian meal, remembering, in the words of Gary Snyder that "eating is a sacrament. The grace we say clears our hearts and guides the children and welcomes the guest, all at the same time" (*The Practice of Wild,* p. 184). Again we eat in silence in the Buddhist tradition, contemplating each bite, remembering that we too are edible. After supper we gather in a circle to speak from our hearts about the work we did during the day and the work to be done in restoration.

A young woman graduate student studying ecology wonders why many of us found it more satisfying to plant acorns than to cut trees. Are we sentimental? Have we been conditioned by numerous Arbor Day exercises at school to the idea that we should plant trees rather than cut them down?

Why not burn the young Douglas fir and the grasslands in a controlled fire sometime in the fall, another woman asks? Some forest ecologists recommend that prescribed burns be set in many areas of northern California. Fire is part of healing the forest. Fire is also a powerful teacher. During the past eighty years, fire has been suppressed by massive efforts of the U.S. Forest Service and the California Department of Forestry in an effort to save harvestable timber and to prevent fires from burning through historically burned-over forested lands, including many areas that now have farms, suburban developments, and even large cities. Suppression of natural fire cycles in millions of acres of the American West has led to a huge buildup of dead material, which, during the summer drought, can be sparked—by numerous causes including lightning, carelessly thrown cigarette butts, ashes from a camper's fire—into catastrophic fires.

Our discussion of the role of fire in the ecology of oak savannas leads to a more general discussion of the meaning of "natural" and "restoration." How can we ever "restore" an area to naturalness after massive human interventions in the system, a philosophy student asks. Isn't a "restored" oak savanna merely an artifact created to meet our human conceptions of what nature should look like, to satisfy our human interests? On the most fundamental level isn't restoration another manifestation of human domination of nature? Perhaps our work today, cloaked in the fashionable label of "ecological consciousness" is simply a continuation of that same age-old urge.

One of the "laws" of ecological systems is that they are complex, perhaps more complex than human beings can ever explain or understand through contemporary scientific methods. By imposing what we think the process of the oak savanna is, are we continuing to reconstruct nature for our own purposes, albeit more aesthetic and even creative purposes than grazing domesticated cattle on the oak savanna to provide us with meat? If "natural" means independence from human domination, how are we liberating natural processes by continuing to manipulate the oak savanna on this ranch by cutting Douglas fir and planting acorns?

These are more than questions of semantics, a philosophy student in the circle reminds us. Indeed, a philosopher who has considered these questions at some length suggests what he calls the principle of noninterference as a primary moral duty in his ethic of respect for nature. By putting aside our human interests and personal preferences for a landscape we acknowledge the ability of nature "to sustain its own proper order throughout the whole domain of life" (Paul Taylor, *Respect for Nature: A Theory of Environmental Ethics,* p.177).

Those questions were not resolved in conversation around the campfire that evening, but the conversation illustrated to me the importance of deep questioning in exploring the problems of developing greener lifestyles.

Most of people in the circle after our work day in the oaks expressed their sense of suffering and confusion. Our lives seem fragmented, unsettled, disrupted, much as the natural processes of the oak savanna have been fragmented by human impacts—especially over the past hundred years. Many in the circle said they want to live in harmony with nature, but questioned what harmony means. One young man wondered if the words *wild* and *wilderness* will pass from our language during his lifetime.

I express my feeling that I am in a process of recovery, that my culture, during the Age of Exuberance, has encouraged me to become addicted to the need for more—more education and more information, as well as more material possessions. I admit that I am addicted to "keeping up on the news" just as some people are addicted to going shopping for new clothes when they feel depressed. I feel one way to recovery is to recover my rootedness in the oak savanna, to become the oak savanna, to give voice to the oak savanna for what it *is,* not for what I want it to be. I want to be alert to the changes of the seasons. I want to watch the first wildflowers bloom and know when the gray whales are most likely to be seen along the coast migrating northward to their summer feeding grounds in the Gulf of Alaska.

One of the first premises of working in the recovery process is to remember that people in recovery are beautiful. We are facing our situation in all its complexity. We are living each day fully, looking directly at our need for hope, looking at our need for everything to be normal even though we know in our hearts that these are not normal times. We are facing up to the fact that during the rest of our lifetime, our relationship with nonhuman nature may never be "normal" again.

It is deep in the night when we realize we have exhausted our ability to discuss these deep questions in one meeting. Kaza suggests we have short sitting meditation. Folding our legs under us, we face outward toward the oaks we worked with that day, outward to the stars, outward from our thoughts into what Buddhist teachers call the great emptiness. Emptying our minds of thoughts, we open our minds to letting in the night.

GREENING OUR LIFESTYLES

*L*ifestyle is a loaded word, like so many of the words we use these days. On one hand, it means, a conscious sense of creating who we want to be. We make choices about our appearances, about the impressions we want to make on other people. During the 1970s, some sociologists used the term *lifestyle* to indicate the conscious effort by a group of people to create a "scene" as a focus for their lives. Sociologists wrote about *lifestyles* in the surfer "scene" or the hippie "scene" or the skiing "scene."

Lifestyle, in this book, is defined as a conscious creation of habits and ways of being in the world. A brief examination of the archaeology of this concept may help to illuminate a fuller understanding.

Lifestyle is a very modern concept. In most cultures, for most of human history, people did what they did because of custom, tradition, or social expectations, and if they deviated from expected behavior based on their social identity, their sex, status, rank or other criteria, strong measures of social control were directed against them. Lifestyle in modern society means, in part, conscious creation of our social identity. It also means mindful attention to the source of our philosophy, our understanding of our emotions and philosophical approach to life. Making our behavior conform to our philosophy is frequently difficult. As Arne Naess, the Norwegian philosopher who coined the term *deep ecology* reminds us, "many philosophers build castles in the mind, but live in doghouses."

Lifestyle, as used in this book, is based particularly on the insights of the German psychologist Alfred Adler, who argued that adults can never erase the hurts of infancy and toddlerhood—child abuse, rape, incest, neglect, negative labeling by peers, or alienation from nature. However, adults can develop values, passions, insights, and commitments that comprise a person's vision of how to make peace in an intransigent world and how to do the real work.

As used in this book, *lifestyle* means the total approach that adults take to the problems and dilemmas of living based on conscious decisions. To a certain extent, lifestyles are voluntary. We can make choices in our attitudes, in our approach to life and death, in our attempts to change our habits. However, there are certain conditions that limit lifestyle choices and certain cultural and political situations in which we play out decisions made from philosophical principles. We are limited by our physical conditions, that is all of us are differently able. Our reflections on gender and gender roles play an important role in lifestyle choices. We are also constrained by the historical situation of our society, by our age, and by our cultural and community affiliations.

Building a lifestyle is a continuing process for adults. Victor Frankl's logotherapy is one approach to developing meaning in the lifestyles of adults. He developed his insights from his own experience in German concentration camps from 1940–1945. He advises the therapist to be nondirective and nonmoralistic. He suggests asking what we find most meaningful and joyful in life. From our joys and sadness we begin the process of finding *logos,* meaning life.

How we frame our lifestyles depends, to a large extent, on our basic attitude toward life and death. Many people see their existence based on the image of the world as a battlefield. Good and evil are pitted against one another. Light and darkness battle for supremacy. People will be either saved or damned. In this view, we are always threatened. We must be militant, courageous, strong. We must be on the side of the righteous or we are surely on the side of the sinners. The attitude of many people with this approach is self-righteousness. This view encourages inflexible lifestyles; no deviation is allowed; no questioning is allowed; we must do what the authorities say. This approach has great appeal to many people. Decisions are simple. Do what is orthodox. Don't question authority. We will be saved because we know we are right.

A second approach, equally popular, is to see the world as a trap. Our task, if we take this approach, is to disentangle ourselves from the messy world, from the ambiguities and contradictions we constantly find ourselves in. We want to become detached from the ordinary, go beyond the petty daily struggle, become "enlightened." Enlightenment has profound meaning in many religious traditions and usually comes only after arduous trials, sometimes years of solitary meditation or "vision quests" in wild areas where physical and mental temptations constantly distract the seeker. The problem with this approach, in some of its current manifestations in our society, is that the world—including the devastation of whole ecosystems, of the atmosphere, of the diversity of life on this planet—is trivialized. People taking this path say, "Nothing really matters on the material plain. I want to transcend all this political discussion." Instead of becoming more attached to the world as it is now, at this time in evolutionary history, people who take this approach can only say "Reality is how you define it" or "I want to move beyond discussion of spotted owls and loggers."

A third approach to considering our lifestyles is what Joanna Macy calls "world as lover." "Instead of a stage set for our moral battles or a prison to escape, the world is beheld as a most intimate and gratifying partner" (*World as Lover, World as Self,* p. 8). Dolores LaChapelle, in her book *Sacred Lands, Sacred Sex,* elaborates on this approach by suggesting that we all engender life. *Engendering* is an inclusive, not gender-based term— not male *or* female but male *and* female. Engendering means contributing to life in the broadest sense. It involves our erotic, sensuous connection with life and death processes. If we embrace the world as lover, we are entering into the flow with trust and commitment to the flow, the Tao, the way things are. We can experience the world as extended self. As Joanna Macy says, "We return to experience, as we never could before, that we are both the self of our world and its cherished lover" (*World as Lover, World as Self,* p. 14).

The ecosophical poet Robinson Jeffers suggested that, in the post-exuberant era, we learn to "fall in love outward," with the great beingness of life. Lovers who fall in love outward do not "harvest" their love of a forest, a seashore, or nature. They participate with it, grow with it, suffer with it, engender with it.

Lovers are intertwined, erotic, passionate, demanding, caring, receiving, embracing, encountering each other anew each day, touching together, seeking deeper connections. The erotic affirmation of the phenomenal world, as Macy notes, is found in early Vedic hymns in Hindu traditions, in the ancient Goddess religions, in some strains of Sufism, and in Christianity in the tradition of bridal mysticism. By working for lifestyles in the eros of life and death, we can participate in the evolutionary journey without demanding that we—humans—be "above" or outside or superior to or dominating the evolutionary process.

Greenness, as used in this book, is a metaphor for consciousness practice. Falling in love outward, we become more mindful of the ways our actions influence the world around us, and we enrich our experiences without impoverishing the natural world. Greenness is used in this book in a much broader sense than supporting a "green" political party or supporting the platform of a "green" political candidate. In the choices we make—considering our position in life, age, gender, education, religious and ethnic group identification—we can see greenness as a continuum. There are many aspects of our mindful awareness of our actions.

Light green choices might include the decision to recycle more regularly or the decision to work consciously to reduce the amount of energy we use in our daily round of life—heating for our living space, fossil fuel for our vehicles, lights for the office. It might include the decision to develop a six-month plan to reduce the waste our household generates by a certain amount—say 30 percent.

Darker green means taking on additional responsibility, such as caring for some of the wastes generated by other people. For example, later in this book I will describe the Nuclear Guardianship Project as an example of a visionary approach to deep greenness. Deep greenness can mean engaging in various educational efforts, or participating in experiential workshops that are designed to open up participants to their connections to the long evolutionary journey of life on earth. Deep greenness means coming home to our broader self, to what ecologist Aldo Leopold called "thinking like a mountain" in his book *A Sand County Almanac*.

Recognizing the importance of the green metaphor in a society where literal language is frequently taken as the most realistic, but least evocative, form of discourse, Australian philosopher Warwick Fox suggests that the *Tree of Life* is a most appropriate metaphor for greening our lifestyles. As a metaphor, the Tree of Life evokes meaning on many levels of understanding. It represents all living beings as they evolve through time and can represent our connections as humans with the rest of creation.

The Tree of Life "fits the facts" as explained by evolutionary biologists and conservation ecologists. Sprouting from a "seed of life," the evolutionary tree continues to grow through time, branch, change, move without purposeful direction, without any "higher" or "lower" aspects. Furthermore, Fox says, "The image of leaves on a tree clearly suggests the existence of an entity that must be nurtured in all its aspects if all its aspects are to flourish. Damage a leaf badly enough and it will die; damage a branch and all the leaves on that branch will die." Visualizing the leaves on the Tree of Life we clearly "see" how all leaves (entities, species, beings) are interconnected because they are part of the same tree. At the same time the leaves (entities, our individuated selves as we experience ourselves during our lifetime) have some autonomy. Each leaf has some degree of "freedom," movement in relation to the wind, for example. The amount of sunlight that one leaf has during the day versus the amount of sunlight another leaf has because it is shaded by other leaves gives us an image of differences due to situation and experiences. While we recognize distinctiveness, individuation of different entities (individuated human individuals, for example, as seen as leaves on the Tree of Life), the metaphor of the Tree of Life also calls us to recognize impermanence, change over time. "Leaves come and go—and so does the tree itself (the cosmos), but over a much greater time span" (Fox, p. 262).

By recovering our connection to the Tree of Life, we can possibly reconnect, in our recovery process, with the roots of life, with our sense of place in the biosphere, in the cosmos. Reflecting on our connection, as humans, with the green Tree of Life, we see, in an ecological sense, that humans are an interesting (at least to us) variation (leaf) on the Tree.

Humans are creative, have big brains during this phase of their evolutionary change, show warmth and sometimes compassion toward some other humans, and sometimes toward nonhuman entities, but they are no more vital or important to the Tree (or to the forest, the ecosystem, or the biosphere) than other variations, for example the mycorrhizal fungi in the soil of the trees. Indeed, recent research indicates that the forest would wither and possibly die without the mycorrhizal fungi (Chris Maser, 1992).

In reflecting on greening our lifestyles, we see that reduction means reducing our sense of importance, our pridefulness and hubris. It means seeing ourselves within a nonanthropocentric or ecocentric perspective. As Christopher Manes, author of *Green Rage,* writes, a new language of nonanthropocentric perception may develop in us when we are "able to learn that language of ecological humility by responding to the insights of ecology and evolutionary theory, which means metaphorically learning the language of the winds, the frogs, the waterfalls, the earthworms" (*Wild Earth,* Spring 1991, p. 62).

This search for our ecocentric connections takes us far deeper than conventional therapeutic exercises that ask us to explore who we are in terms of family dynamics during our childhood or even our gender roles. The epistemologist and anthropologist Gregory Bateson, in his book *Mind and Nature,* summarized our dilemma when he wrote, "Most of us have lost that sense of unity of biosphere and humanity which would bind and reassure us all with an affirmation of beauty." This historical loss, which helped to set the stage for the Age of Exuberance, "was, quite simply, an epistemological mistake" (*Mind and Nature,* 1980, p. 19). When we ask, then, how we can dig deeper into our consciousness, to explore our interconnectedness with the Tree of Life, and how we can recover our rootedness in the "harmony of nature," we are asking for ways to see across boundaries.

Recognizing our connections with the Tree of Life, we also recognize that our actions as individuals—in households, communities, and societies—are restrained. Our freedom is limited by the laws of ecology. In order to cultivate deep green lifestyles, we need to understand the laws of ecology and the implications of these laws in framing our conscious choices for lifestyle.

ECOLOGY AND ECOSOPHY

*E*cology and *ecosophy* have the same root in their prefix: *eco*, from the Greek *oikos* or "household." Ecology, literally, is the study of the household. Alan Watts translates the word "ecology" as the "logic of the household" (*The Book on the Taboo Against Knowing Who You Are*, p. 86). The word was not coined until the 1850s, but the central insights of ecologists were revealed several centuries before that. Indeed, according to historian Donald Worster, who researched the history of ecological thinking in western society for his book *Nature's Economy*, "As long as ecology was kept in lay hands, it could continue to teach the gospel of organic community, whether or not this was subject to empirical validation" (p. 335). The task for philosophers and scientists in the late twentieth century is to help frame the discussion for laypeople so that empirical facts have ethical meaning that can guide our actions.

In 1971, the scientist Barry Commoner summarized the laws of ecology in his book *The Closing Circle*. He stated four "laws" that are limits on our actions as individual humans and collectively as a society. Even with recognition of the more recent emergence of chaos theory and general systems theory, these generalizations, stated as informal "laws of ecology" provide a framework within which we act. In the absence of supernational intervention or cosmic intentionality, these informal laws provide a basis for contemplating our human actions (*The Closing Circle*, pp. 29–44).

1. *Everything is connected to everything else.* There are multiple interrelationships in nature, and these interrelationships interpenetrate with each other. When humans create models of some aspect of nature, such as models of the flow of energy in a marsh, even with the most sophisticated computers they can only conceptualize some of the patterns of relationships in an ecosystem.

2. *Everything must go somewhere.* This is an informal statement of a basic law of physics, the law that matter is indestructible. In ecology there is no such thing as "waste." What is excreted by one organism is taken up by another. When we discard things, they don't just "go away." "Waste" from some of the operations developed during the Age of Exuberance, for example,

may be with our descendents for many generations. Wastes from nuclear weapons plants and from the use of nuclear materials in generating electricity will decay following a known "half life" of nuclear particles of various sorts, for hundreds and, for some particles, thousands of years.

3. *Nature knows best.* This means that human interventions into natural systems are likely to be detrimental to the integrity of the system. The implications of this law are so immense that they cannot be calculated for global interactions. We see some implications of this law in the effects of fluorohydrocarbons or CFCs on the ozone layer. We also see some of the implications of this law in the "greenhouse effect" brought about by releasing carbon dioxide into the atmosphere as a "waste" of industrial operations, burning fossil fuels in automobiles, and burning of tropical rainforests.

4. *There is no such thing as a free lunch.* Commoner says, "In ecology, as in economics, the law is intended to warn that every gain is won at some cost" (p. 42). Payment of the price can be delayed but not avoided. The environmental crisis—loss of top soil, decline in fish runs of many rivers, deforestation, desertification, salinization of agricultural lands due to irrigation, and on and on—shows that we have delayed payment for too long. The bills have now come due and our lifestyles, whether we want them to or not, will adjust to paying the "debt" to nature accrued during the Age of Exuberance.

Commoner recognized that the third law, "nature knows best," would be the most controversial for people who have been educated in the dominant linear mode of thinking during the Age of Exuberance. Humans, very frequently, like to see themselves as improving, controlling, and utilizing nature. We like the image of ourselves as stewards of the land, as happy gardeners tilling the soil, enriching the soil, making the desert blossom. This law suggests that our greener lifestyles may begin by accepting a more modest place in the world collectively as a species. When we attempt to dominate, control, force natural processes to suit our will, we tend to impair life processes.

For example, for the past eighty-seven years, since Gifford Pinchot became head of the U.S. Forest Service in 1905—and established the principle of "scientific management" of forests—industrial foresters have spoken of the advantages of "bringing the forests under scientific management programs." "Harvesting trees is just like harvesting a crop of corn in an Iowa cornfield," foresters said. Only during the past twenty years have forest ecologists begun to develop models that show that both the system of ancient forests and the system of prairie grasslands (which were plowed under to make way for a monoculture of hybrid corn in Iowa) are more complex than they realized. By stripping away the ancient forests so rapidly—all in the name of serving the needs of a growing human population and of bringing forests under "scientific management," industrial forestry may have upset the vital processes that allow the forest to express itself. Monoculture tree plantations that replaced complex, varied ancient forests are dying in many areas of North America where they were planted (Chris Maser, *Global Imperative*, 1992).

Learning the principles of ecology is a basic aspect of our education if we are to green our lifestyles. As ecologist Paul Ehrlich says in the introduction to his review of contemporary theories in the science of ecology (*The Machinery of Nature*, p. 13):

> The basic principles of ecology are accessible to any intelligent person who is willing to put a little effort into learning them. And there are many rewards for that effort. Familiarity with basic ecology will permanently change your world view. You will never again regard plants, microorganisms, and animals (including people) as isolated entities. Instead you will see them—more accurately—as parts of a vast complex of natural machinery—as, in the dictionary definition, "related elements in a system that operates in a definable manner."

Ecosophy is literally "the search for the wisdom of the earth." *Sophia* is from the Greek word for wisdom. For Greek philosophers this wisdom was not realized only from abstracted scientific theories understood by an isolated intellect. Wisdom comes when passionate love of knowledge and love of life, in the broadest sense, allows people to open to the wisdom of the moment. Ecosophical knowledge, then, can involve poetic, mythopoeic, musical, artistic expressions of our understanding of the laws of ecology.

Philosopher Alan Drengson, in his book *Beyond Environmental Crisis,* says:

> "Ecosophy" stands for the idea of ecological harmony, but it also refers to an actual state of ongoing activity, of vital, full aliveness, realizing the harmonies, fruits and bountifulness that flow from all of Nature, the Cosmos and from the Great Mysterious Source of all beings. It is a state of authentic existence through which the full and ultimate values of life on Earth are realized and made actual in history (p. 193).

In the anthropology of so-called "preliterate" or "primitive" peoples living in sustainable cultures in bioregions throughout the earth for millennia, as well as in some of the great religious traditions, we find basic ecosophical expressions. Lifestyles based on materialism, on high consumption, on waste, on acquisition of things, on hedonism, and on domination—domination of other people, of women, of slaves, and of "wild" animals and wild nature—are negatively evaluated by great teachers in the sacred bear religions of the northern regions (see Paul Shepard, *The Sacred Paw,* 1985) and by many teachers in Christian, Buddhist, Hindu, and Native American traditional spiritual practices. In all these traditions, greatness (of character and of living) and bigness are differentiated. Greatness is sought—greatness of generosity, greatness of character, greatness of deep spiritual understanding of our place in the cosmos, greatness of truth. Greatness refers to the quality of experience, the richness of life without quantifying it into some measure used by accountants. A great society maximizes richness of self-realization rather than economic output or gross national product.

Greatness is not measured, in wisdom traditions, by the acquisition of great amounts of material possessions. Indeed, material possessions, political power, vast wealth measured by the amount of money controlled are most frequently considered a burden to the path of understanding, the greatness of living well.

Bigness is seen as abnormal. After a certain point, big institutions, bigger populations, bigger cities, bigger houses become gigantism. Downscaling is inevitable. Exponential growth rates in populations, for example, always slow down and eventually stop. Exponential growth frequently reaches a peak and then rapidly falls because the system cannot maintain the rate of growth in bigger manifestations of whatever is expanding.

Cultural values, and especially values that are not directly "economic values" of money or monetary transactions, are more valued in the wisdom traditions than those marketplace values measured by such crude indicators as Gross National Product.

In the rising culture of the Age of Ecology, increasing concern is being expressed by many religious leaders for finding contemporary ways of relating these wisdom traditions to the environmental crisis, which is understood as a continuing and intensifying crisis of culture. The call for religious teachers to turn their teaching to caring for creation was sounded by the World Wildlife Fund in announcing the Assisi ecumenical discussions. In 1986 leaders of five major world faiths met in Assisi, Italy, and launched the New Alliance based on statements of caring for creation from the five religious traditions—Buddhist, Christian, Jewish, Muslim, and Hindu. In the tradition of the teaching of St. Francis—called by Lynn Whyte, Jr., in his landmark article published in 1967, "The Historic Roots of Our Ecological Crisis," the greatest spiritual revolutionary since Christ—religious leaders honored an ecocentric approach to teachings concerning the caring for creation. For example, since 1986 leaders of the Greek Orthodox church and other churches have issued statements on human responsibilities for creation. Furthermore, caring-for-creation statements have been issued by many Protestant denominations in the United States and Canada, and some denominations offer regular courses and training seminars on "green theology."

The search for ecosophy in making personal choices and in collective decisions made by our households, our communities, and our society will be based on intuitions of ecological consciousness. Ecological consciousness means our intuitive, experiential understanding of interconnectedness and concern for the quality of life. Paths to ecological consciousness are based on opening ourselves to change. Change in our consciousness consists of a transition to a more egalitarian attitude to life and the unfolding of life on earth. When we focus on our broader self-in-nature, the door is open to a richer and more satisfying life.

By cleaning up our internal awareness—by developing ways of being open to experiencing the richness of other beings, not only human beings— our participation in the ecological movement will be a renewing and joy-creating experience. In wisdom traditions emphasizing greatness rather than bigness—opulence, rich food, luxury, and affluence are appreciated, but not especially valued. Spartan denial—austere denial of basic human plea-sures—and feelings of guilt do not produce joy or caring behavior and therefore are not valued either.

Reliance on political changes or technological changes alone also detracts from the search for ecosophical lifestyles. Political actions are part of greening lifestyles, but the front is very broad, and reliance on political strategies and political organizations to solve the problems within existing political structures in the short term seems to place too much emphasis on processes that are dominated by the interests of politicians (who wish to be reelected), public relations campaigns (which distort information and are not motivated by deep ecosophical principles), and the interests of large bureau-cracies and agencies (including corporations).

Reliance on technological solutions places great responsibility—and power—in the hands of engineers and agencies that develop and market technology. Reliance on technology leads to a frequently elusive search for a "breakthrough" or a "new technological advance" that will solve problems without addressing the mentality and the institutions that cre-ated the problems in the first place. Great debates have occurred over the past two decades over "hard" and "soft" or "appropriate" technological methods.

Questions arise concerning the use of technological devices—motorized vehicles, computers, etc.—relating to how we begin greening our lifestyles. Reliance on "new" or "solar" or "soft" technology alone to solve the prob-lems, rather than changing our philosophical approach, is criticized. We do and will use technology in greening our lifestyles, but critical questions must be asked about it.

How simple is the technology? What are the environmental "costs" of widespread use of this technology? Who controls technological innovation? Is the technology mutable, that is, can it be easily changed as circumstances change? Recognizing that technology is never "neutral" but is always "loaded" with value assumptions and implications for division of political power in our community, we ask what social enterprise controls the technology?

The deep, long-range ecology movement recognizes that small-scale social forms and small-group empowerment foster and encourage wider and deeper personal identification with life that helps us become open to the "synergy" between personal and household well-being and the well-being of the earth. The needs and "rights" of a person are the needs and "rights" of the earth and vice versa.

Ecosophy involves the search for very practical knowledge on how to live well while working, simultaneously, with the broader context of the ecological unconscious. Humans seem to have a vital need to create meaning. The search for ecosophical principles for our lifestyles involves us in the great human quest, which is only partly cognitive. Intuitive openness to the ecological unconscious may help us find new narratives, helping us to be self-reflective in the Age of Ecology.

When Arne Naess articulated two "ultimate norms" for his version of Ecosophy T (as he calls his own philosophical approach to articulating ecosophy), he meant them as statements within which we can more fully articulate our lifestyles: Self-realization and Ecocentrism. Understanding by feeling, intuition, and intellectual effort of a broader, more inclusive meaning of *Self-realization* comes from exploring broader identification. That is, by sharing the joys and suffering of others, including nonhumans, the "others" become part of our self. Poet Gary Snyder calls this the "practice of the wild," and Buddhist teacher Robert Aitken calls it opening to the "mind of clover." Well-being, quality of life, and free nature become more valuable aspects of existence than merely striving for "more." *Ecocentrism* means placing the unfolding of the cosmos at the center of the historical drama. Humans are part of this unfolding, but they play a minor role.

In this sense, greening lifestyles involves us in the search for ecosophy.

With ecosophical wisdom, we can choose a path to take in our search for happiness and fulfillment so that our actions advance, not diminish, the self-realization of other human and nonhuman beings. As a community of people comes to "hold these truths to be self-evident," their ecosophy becomes a philosophical world-view inspired by a broader understanding of the conditions of life in the ecosphere. Ecosophy serves as an individual's philosophical grounding for an acceptance of the intuition of deep ecology.

GENERAL PRINCIPLES FOR DEEP GREEN LIFESTYLES

In *The Mind of Clover,* Robert Aitken writes that principles, from his understanding of Zen Buddhism, are written on something more fluid than water. By this he means that principles should not be taken as dogma but as a basis for dialogue and a search for deeper understanding in our commitment to strive for ecosophy in the Age of Ecology. In this spirit of inclusive dialogue, the following principles might best be seen as "tendencies" or considerations for thoughtful reflection. Sensing a need by many people for greener lifestyles based on deep ecology, Arne Naess and George Session presented a "platform" of statements in 1982. These statements were revised to permit clarification and elaboration of an ecocentric approach for the Earth Summit held in Rio de Janeiro, Brazil in June 1992:

1. The flourishing of human and nonhuman life on earth has intrinsic value. The value of nonhuman life-forms and ecosystems (watersheds, forests, etc.) is independent of the usefulness these may have for narrowly defined human purposes.

2. Richness and diversity of life-forms are values in themselves and contribute to the flourishing of human and nonhuman life on earth.

3. Humans have no right to reduce this richness and diversity except to satisfy vital needs of sustenance.

4. Present human interference in the natural world has been brought about by many factors—including domination of classes of people over other classes (men over women, wealthy groups over less wealthy groups,

etc.) and by ignorance and greed in the human mind.

5. Present human interference in the nonhuman world is excessive, and the situation is rapidly worsening.

6. Significant changes of life conditions for the better, with more likelihood of survival of many species (watersheds, ecosystems) in the longer term, requires drastic changes in social policies that affect basic economic, technological, bureaucratic, political, and ideological structures.

7. The flourishing of human life and cultures and richness of quality of human culture is compatible with substantial decrease of the human population. The flourishing of nonhuman life requires such a decrease.

8. The ideological change that is needed is primarily an appreciation of life quality, dwelling in a situation of intrinsic value—rather than adherence to a belief in and desire for more and more affluence, for an ever higher standard of living. There will be a profound awareness of the difference between greatness (of living well) and bigness (of wanting more regardless of the consequences).

9. Those who subscribe to the foregoing points have an obligation directly and indirectly to participate in the attempt to implement the necessary changes.

Statements 6 and 8 make it clear that political action is required. However not every supporter of the deep ecology movement must write or talk in public about political matters. How we live our private lives can be a public statement—to friends, to neighbors, to colleagues at work, to members of our church.

Arne Naess emphasizes that there is no value in complete agreement about a set of points as principles or platform of the deep, long-range ecology movement, but it has to be mentioned that there have been no fundamental criticisms of these eight points, and no fundamental criticism of the combination of six and eight among supporters.

Most supporters of deep ecology do not engage in writing articles or books. Deep ecology is not a movement among academics or intellectuals. Those academics and intellectuals who write books do so only to help further the dialogue among supporters of deep ecology and broaden the discussion of deep ecology among people who are sympathetic to the need for drastic changes in society based on ecocentrism.

There are many differences of opinion about what the "necessary changes" are. There is much room for individual styles, preferences, and cooperation among people who participate in different alternative social movements, religions, and communities. The unifying theme is caring for the place wherein we dwell because it is part of our self.

Deep greenness means acceptance of the need for radical changes not only in personal lifestyles, daily habits, but also in society, in social policies and the practices of agencies and corporations, and in the goals of our civilization, in international relations, and in our perspective on nature, community, and cosmos. In practice, it seems to me, all those who wish to explore greening their lifestyles—from light green to darker green, a radical change in consciousness and daily habits—must first be willing to change, to make a commitment to a movement larger than their narrow egos. In making such a commitment, our sense of self, paradoxically, expands, broadens, and is enriched.

Freedom means the willingness to restrict our freedom, and renewed commitment to freedom of the wild—freedom for nature and life processes—may be the greatest gift we can give to ourselves. By freeing ourselves from the illusion that by acquiring more—more money, more domination of nature, more power over other people—we may find the freedom to be ourselves in the midst of change and turmoil. In the following chapters many suggestions and principles for action are advanced within the general statement of greening our lifestyles. There are numerous, creative possibilities and options. Taking a path is what is important. Developing new habits, approaches, and mindfulness is encouraged.

None of us has complete consistency between our philosophy and our practice. Our practice is dependent in many instances on our life situation, the community in which we live, and the technological idiosyncrasies of systems upon which we depend. It is important, however, to translate philosophical principles into daily behavior and attitudes, because if we don't consciously do so, then consciousness and philosophy influence our actions only fragmentarily. The following list of tendencies was developed by Arne Naess. Some of the statements are overlapping; some are vaguely stated.

They are in no particular order. Some are abstract; others are specific. Some are reworded. They should be taken as suggestive, evocative. Some of these statements are extensively explored in various chapters in this book. All can be considered within the context of one's own process of recovery and discussed by families, by groups of people supporting each other in their move toward greener lifestyles, and in community meetings that focus on changes in public policy.

1. Use simple means, avoid unnecessary complicated instruments and other sorts of means.

2. Choose activities, including making a living, that most directly serve values in themselves and have intrinsic value. Avoid activities that are merely auxiliary, have no intrinsic value, or are many stages away from fundamental goals.

3. Be anti-consumption oriented. Maintain a high resistance to appeals of advertising to "buy now."

4. Endeavor to maintain and increase sensitivity to, and appreciation of, goods of which there is enough for all to enjoy.

5. Love not the new merely because it is new.

6. Make an effort to dwell in situations of intrinsic value rather than just to be busy for the sake of busy activity. When we are busy for the sake of being busy in order to avoid suffering, depression, and contemplation of fundamentals of life, we don't allow an opening for new understandings to emerge.

7. Appreciate ethnic, gender, cultural, age, and social-class differences among people and do not feel threatened by them.

8. Cultivate compassion for the situation in the third world and among indigenous and tribal peoples and attempt to avoid a lifestyle that is much more opulent than we need and many times more extravagant than minimal levels of consumption of the poorest people in poor nations.

9. Appreciate lifestyles that can be universal, that are not blatantly impossible to sustain without injustice toward other people, and that are not blatantly exploitative of nonhuman beings, species, or ecosystems.

10. Strive for depth and richness of experience rather than number of experiences or fashionable experiences.

11. Appreciate and choose whenever possible in one's life situation meaningful work rather than only making a living.

12. Lead a complex life, but not a complicated life, trying to realize as many aspects of positive experiences as possible during any time interval—hourly, daily, weekly, seasonally, or in broader time periods.

13. Cultivate life in community (*Gemeinschaft*) rather than in society (*Gesellschaft*).

14. Appreciate participation in primary production that is life sustaining and not exploitive, closer to the land such as small-scale, organic farming and forestry (e.g. forestry based on principles of ecosystem functions rather than based on desire to maintain a rate of return on investment for a large corporation).

15. Engage in efforts to satisfy vital needs but carefully examine desires.

16. Attempt to live in nature rather than visit beautiful places such as national parks; however, when traveling, maintain attention to principles of ecotourism.

17. When in areas considered ecologically sensitive or fragile, live "light and traceless."

18. Cultivate a tendency to appreciate all life-forms, not merely those that are useful, beautiful, remarkable, or obviously outstanding.

19. Never use life-forms merely as a means. Remain conscious of their intrinsic value and dignity even when using them as resources.

20. When there is a conflict between interests of domesticated animals and wild species, tend to protect the interests of the latter.

21. Make efforts in personal lifestyles and in community to protect local ecosystems, feeling one's own human community within the ecosystem moving in time as it tends toward a climax community.

22. Not only deplore excessive interference in naturally evolving systems as unnecessary, unreasonable, and disrespectful, but condemn it as insolent, atrocious, outrageous, and criminal. However, actions of people should not be confused with the intrinsic worth of people; do not condemn the people responsible for the interference, but show compassion towards them.

23. Try to act resolutely and without cowardice in conflicts, but remain nonviolent in words and deeds although realizing there is much dialogue possible on what words and deeds are considered or interpreted as nonviolent and what are interpreted as violent in different cultural situations.

24. Partake in and support nonviolent direct action when other ways of action fail or as part of a larger strategy of action.

25. Even if you find politics boring or distasteful, nevertheless engage in political activities as part of the necessary actions to bring about societal, community, and personal transformation, and to protect threatened and endangered species, endangered ecosystems, and ways of life that are less consumptive and destructive.

(Arne Naess, "Deep Ecology and Life Style").

LANGUAGE AND THE SEARCH FOR ECOSOPHY

When we consider principles and actions for greening our lifestyles, we need to include principles for our language, for the manner in which we converse about our experience and think about environmental policy, and for our modes of argumentation when discussing the emerging ecological consciousness.

I remember a slogan from my childhood that we recited on the playground when another student taunted us, "Sticks and stones may break my bones, but words will never hurt me." Of course words *do* hurt. Words can be used as weapons, labels, and legal categories that result in vastly different services provided to people who are given certain labels. Reconstructing some of our language is vital in developing nonanthropocentric, ecocentric expressions for the emerging green culture and for greener lifestyles.

As humans we share at least two universal characteristics. We experience—with our senses, our bodies, our minds—and we communicate. We communicate by touch, sign language, body language, and sound—including music. Language is only one mode of expression, but written language is the basis of this book and much other communication in our civilization. As any writer knows, communicating nuances of meaning through written language is difficult. Conventional modes of expression condition the way we "see" each other and "see" nature. Greening our lifestyles means, in part, that we change some of our habits of language. Changing some of our expressions is vital to reconstructing our identity and our thought. We have already begun this process with regard to some modes of labeling people in our society. Deconstructing references that are sexist, racist, and homophobic is an increasingly popular undertaking. Some feminists argue that sexism becomes ingrained in our thinking through sexist language. Nonsexist vocabulary has recently been included in standard dictionaries published in Canada and the United States, and nonsexist language is now required in many corporations, universities, and government agencies. The leader of a committee, for example, can be referred to as the "chair" rather than "chairman" or "chairwoman." Terms considered racist or prejudicial to some race or ethnic group are generally banned from use in print and broadcasting media.

AIDS activists have taught us the importance of deconstructing the labeling which has been associated with HIV positive condition, AIDS, and homophobia. When AIDS activists are told that HIV positive is the result of an "unnatural lifestyle" or of "perverted" behavior, they rise up with expressions of outrage. They point to the underlying ideology of fundamentalist Christianity which makes it possible for the rhetoric of hate to be used by some preachers and politicians to rally people against homosexual expression of affection. Some women's groups and gay liberation groups have conducted protests in front of churches where the protesters hear preachers using sexist language or preachers playing on homophobic themes. Meanwhile scholars, and others less scholarly, argue intensely over literal, historical and metaphorical meaning of biblical passages and over the historic origins of doctrines and beliefs.

Some victims of AIDS reject the disease model altogether and take a systemic or a metaphysical approach to their situation. Healing, for them, means more than killing a virus. Complex, not clearly understood, relationships between functioning of physical body, mind, and spiritual growth are involved in the healing process.

AIDS activists are alert to modes of expression which stigmatize those who are HIV positive. Groups such as ACT UP and Queer Nation have taken to the streets with slogans proclaiming new affirmation of "queer" and "faggot" and "fairy." Furthermore, the men's movement in the United States and Canada, taking note of the work of poet Robert Bly (*Iron John*), is developing a vocabulary of men's experience that fits changing gender consciousness.

The need for a deep-ecology language derives from the recognition that many of the terms used in the environmental movement to refer to nature are tainted with dualism and anthropocentric bias. Our language also contains a bias favoring the civilized over the primitive, the domesticated over the wild, the tame over the untamed. In constructing green lifestyles we need discourse that expresses ecocentric not human-centered principles. Humanity is no longer at the center of discourse about the cosmos, having brought much of the earth to the point of ruin and perhaps one-fourth of all the species on the earth to the verge of extinction. A new approach to discourse is long overdue.

Even terms frequently used to refer to green movements are outdated, based on discredited philosophy and rhetoric. These include terms such as "conservation," "natural resource," "preservation," "environment," and "environmentalist."

"Conservation," as used in twentieth century America, means "resource development." According to this ideology, nature consists of "natural resources" that are potential commodities for use by humans. Natural resources that do not have economic values for human use are conserved (i.e., protected) if these natural values do not conflict with economic uses. The conventional perception of "conservation" is that nature is "dead" of spirit, lacking intrinsic value.

In the rhetoric of the anti-environmental social movement called the "Wise Use conservation movement" in the United States and the "Share" movement in Canada, "preservationists" are attempting to "lock up" vast tracts of land and water, to keep the wealth of these areas from flowing into the human economy. "Putting People First" and "I'm More Important Than a Spotted Owl" are slogans illustrating the popular variety of humanism. The Wise Use movement has been exposed as a regressive anti-environment movement dedicated to disinformation campaigns and associated with the discredited rhetoric of former Secretary of Interior James Watt. (see Debbi Callahan, "The Wise Use Movement," 1992).

Although the words "conservation" and "conservation movement" have been somewhat co-opted by exploiters of natural resources and despoilers of nature, these words still carry positive connotations among many protectors of nature who identify with the word "conservationist." Some are promoting a "new conservation" movement that recognizes intrinsic values in nature.

Ike Livermore, former California Secretary of Resources under Governor Ronald Reagan, exasperated with the negative connotation of *con*servationists always being against something, proposed a new term "*pro*servationist." That idea died quickly however when *San Francisco Chronicle* columnist Herb Caen slyly asked what Ike would do with the word *con*stitution.

"Preservation" and "preservationists" are terms used to refer to those who, at the turn of the century, attempted to establish national parks or nature preserves based on higher values—noncommodity values. These included national heritage, scenic, recreational, scientific, historic, and even spiritual values. The ideology of the preservation movement did not, we now know, include insights from the science of ecology or evolutionary theory. Many of the national parks established during the period from 1872 to 1960 have lost some of their mammal species because the areas "set aside" were too small and have been severely impacted by human activities outside of park boundaries.

The terms "environment" and "environmentalist" are more contemporary, from the 1970s. Acceptance of these terms comes from recognition of the need to speak out, advocate change, seek new public policies that explicitly address industrial pollution, abuse of water, and myriad other changes brought about by human activities, which impair natural processes.

The term "environmentalist" is a label worn proudly by many, used with scorn by others. Like the term "fairy," "environmentalist" can mean "you are a social deviant, a pervert." In some communities in the western United States, the label "environmentalist" has replaced "commie" as the curse word hissed at public meetings and scrawled as graffiti. In other communities, developers promoting inappropriate, environmentally destructive projects will occasionally proclaim themselves to be "environmentalists" while casting their opponents as "environmental extremists."

The term "Environment" still contains the essential dualism of western thought. As philosopher Neil Evernden concludes in his book *The Natural Alien,* the aim of the environmental movement is to end the old separation between humans and the rest of nature. Not connections between A and B but interconnectedness, interpenetration is the basis of postmodern understanding of humans-in-nature. Humans are not above, outside of, superior to, or at the top of some hierarchy of evolution. However, environment also incorporates the older resource management concept into contemporary technocratic and scientific modes. When "nature" becomes "environment" it loses its sense as something that humans can approach only with humility, reverence, and limited understanding. "Environmental managers" now proliferate around the world. The increase in environmental managers and the combination of concern for environmental impacts of development and sustainable development as themes of discussion by politicians and many scientists show the continuing emphasis on what some writers call "old paradigm" thinking. That is, when we use the term "environment," we refer to nature as an abstract entity, passive, devoid of meaning. The phrase "environmental development" is more a contradiction in terms than an approach to occupying a niche in nature, and developing a mature sense of earth wisdom.

The buzzword for the 1990s is "sustainable"—sustainable growth, sustainable economic development, sustainable agriculture, and sustainable forestry. Sustainable has replaced "progress" as a basic tenet of post-modern ideology. For the past three hundred years, thinkers and politicians have propagated the idea that a progressive society provides more of everything for more people in that society—more civil rights, more economic freedom, more and better technology. The doctrine of progress assumes that newer is better. New technological innovations will replace outdated technology. New ways of manipulating natural resources will produce more goods for more people more efficiently.

While the subtext of many writers and politicians using the rhetoric of sustainability is still that more is better, that progress can and should occur, the intellectual development of the concept of sustainability will have to grapple with the underlying belief in materialism, progress, and economic growth. For the deep ecology movement, questions of lifestyle are nested in continuing the search for ecological consciousness.

The language of deep ecology refers to "consciousness" rather than only to the more narrow statement of "human consciousness." This is congruent with contemporary evolutionary theory, which suggests that dolphins are no more "advanced" than lichens or slugs, and no less advanced than peregrine falcons. In an ecological sense, humans are no more vital or important to the system of the forest, the ecosystem, or the biosphere, than spotted owls or mycorrhizal fungi.

As Christopher Manes says, a new language of nonanthropocentric perception may develop when we are "able to learn that language of ecological humility by responding to the insights of ecology and evolutionary theory, which means metaphorically learning the language of the winds, the frogs, the waterfalls, the earthworms" (*Wild Earth,* Spring 1991, p. 62). In the search for nonanthropocentric, nonhumanistic discourse, we are not limited by a chauvinistic attitude toward English or any European language. Languages of western civilization are not superior to so-called nonliterate, preliterate, or non-western languages.

The process of digging deep into consciousness and fully exploring ecocentric perceptions in the midst of this civilization is beset with difficulties. For example, when we use the term "life centered," are we using a fuller, more expansive definition of life or a narrower, more restricted definition? Most of the material in a living tree could chemically be considered "dead" matter. Yet we consider the tree as a living being. The tree is not isolated from its soil or from the air. In the forests of the Pacific Northwest, mycorrhizal fungi are in a sense part of the tree, communicating between trees.

Thinking across boundaries is necessary. Indeed Aldo Leopold's provocative phrase "thinking like a mountain" carries with it the connotation that the human mind is not projecting a humanistic bias or anthropogenic bias onto the mountain. "Thinking like a mountain" can be taken as a metaphor for considering the ecological processes continuing on the mountain, and it can mean something more metaphysical, thinking as the mountain being, as the consciousness of the mountain being expressing itself. Thinking like a mountain, thinking like an ancient forest, means taking a longer time perspective. The mountain moves, changes, responds to changes, changes again, senses growth on its slopes, perhaps has snow on its slopes, responds to fire, erodes in rain and wind.

An individuated human consciousness, a human being coming to the mountain, perceiving the mountain, may understand the mountain only as a "scenic attraction," a mountain recreation area, an area for scientific study. For some, the mountain may be understood as "sacred space," space that is not ordinary space, but space where the unknown and the known sometimes touch, space appropriate for ritual and through ritual to understand more of self-in-the-mountain.

When we approach language of "sacred space," language found in some American Indian religious thought, we run smack into metaphysical and legal difficulties that impede acceptance of a new discourse on nature. The majority of the members of the U.S. Supreme Court, in a famous ruling concerning the Siskiyou High Country, *Lyng v. Northwest Indian Cemetery Protective Association,* accepted the reality of sacred high country and agreed that "the logging and road-building projects at issue in this case [proposed by the U.S. Forest Service] could have devastating effects on traditional Indian religious practices. Those practices are intimately and inextricably bound up with the unique features of the Chimney Rock area, which is known to the Indians as the 'high country.' The threat to the efficacy of at least some religious practices is extremely grave." The court even went so far as to assume that the road proposed by the U.S. government would virtually destroy the Indians' ability to practice their religion—and by implication destroy the ability of all people to experience the 'high country' through walking on 'vision quests' or other 'religious' practices of opening the mind. However, the court ruled that the U.S. Forest Service could continue with its plans to build a road through the High Country. Having noted in its opinion that land, at the end of the twentieth century in North America, is alive and holy, the court used its power to rule that the U.S. government can kill the aliveness of the land if a government agency decides to engage in economic development activities such as logging, road-building, or damming rivers. (Brian Edward Brown, pp. 19-44).

Speaking out, giving voice to, participating with nonhuman beings, with the mountain, with the High Country, with the river is to express a being-with-the-process rather than abstractly viewing nature from the outside or as objective scientist. Indeed, contemporary philosophers of science understand that scientists change the process they are observing by their very observations. Both scientists and "environmental activists" are part of the natural system. When John Seed, an Australian writer, activist, and teacher, says "I am the rainforest speaking for itself, defending its own integrity," he is expressing an understanding long suppressed in western civilization. This affirmation moves us beyond even some of the most progressive terms currently in fashion in the reform environmental movement and provides an invitation to participate in the deep, long-range ecology movement.

FACING AMBIGUITY AND CHALLENGE

We will face challenges and ambiguities in changing our mental attitudes, changing to greener lifestyles in the Age of Ecology. Many people will make compromises. We are challenged to maintain our integrity when we deal with a lack of integrity in the social and political system within which we must find jobs and companionship and engage in social activism. There are no easy answers or solutions, no "magic bullets" to help us, but active participation in the process of change is a lot more interesting to many people than being passive observers, and in some cases victims, of change—of a radically changing economy, changing politics, changing realities about the situation of our homeland, the only homeland we will have—the earth.

A story told by deep-ecology social activist John Seed may help us understand the relationship between integrity and daily actions. He told this story in response to a question in a public interview by Ram Dass in a television series called *Reaching Out*. Ram Dass asked him, "Do you experience integrity in your game? You travel by jets and so on. How do you deal with the lack of integrity in the system?" Seed replied:

I try as hard as I can to have that integrity, but as you say, I traveled by plane to be here today, and I used all of this fuel. And the only thing that helps me in this is a metaphor from an archetypal cowboy movie from my childhood. All the cowboys were asleep and the fire's gone out and the clouds come over and there's a bolt of lightning and all the cattle start stampeding toward the cliff. The cowboys jump on their horses and they don't ride in the opposite direction. They ride straight toward the cliff, and they ride even faster than the cattle. Now their aim is not to go over the cliff, but they realize that it's only by keeping pace with the whole thing that they're going to be in a position to lean on that herd and turn them around before they reach the edge. So I use a computer and I know the chips were cleaned using CFCs, but there is no harmless way to live these days, really. Or if there is, way out in the woods somewhere, it seems pretty irrelevant to me. I'm prepared to get my hands dirty with sawmills and airplanes and anything at all, but I'm also, I believe, prepared to let go of them, like that, as soon as [possible]. They'll wither away after the revolution. That's all I can say.

To paraphrase Arne Naess, the more we contemplate our own smallness in the Tree of Life, the greater we become. In this paradox we may understand the new realities in the Age of Ecology. The more modest we become, more of what Aldo Leopold called "plain citizens" of the biosphere rather than lord and master, the more we come into our own sense of power. The more we bring together the mundane and the "sacred," the more we understand self-realization.

3

EXPERIENCING NATURE IN THE AGE OF ECOLOGY

n his book *The Voice of the Earth* (1992), Theodore Roszak describes the remarkable rediscovery by psychologists of the ecological unconscious. Some psychologists seem to be rediscovering insights known for thousands of years in many shamanistic traditions, in many different cultures, and expressed in image, ritual, and myth. There is more self to know than the history of any specific person reveals. Roszak concludes "making a personality, the task that Jung called 'individuation,' may be the adventure of a lifetime. But the person is anchored within a greater, universal identity" (p. 319).

Exploring the "ecological unconscious," Rosak says, "repression of the ecological unconscious is the deepest root of collusive madness in industrial society, open access to the ecological unconsciousness is the path to sanity" (p. 320). For therapists, the crucial stage in attuning to the ecological unconscious is in childhood, and this means, Roszak concludes, that adults in the process of recovering their roots will need to "seek to recover the child's innately animistic world" (p. 320).

The exercises and experiences described in the following pages include only a small sample of guided experiences that are currently used by teachers and therapists to help adults listen to the "more of self" of which Roszak speaks. Ecotherapists recognize that the most important task is to awaken us to listening for tones that are frequently lost in the noise of industrial society. Some of the following examples are drawn from the work of Joanna Macy and John Seed.

The basic theme of the exercises sketched in the following pages is openness. When we open the doors of perception, we can begin to hear the sounds of the cosmos. In many instances, in this historical era, that means hearing cries of suffering. As the great ecologist Aldo Leopold said over fifty years ago, we live in a world of wounds. In my own experiential class on deep ecology I take students out of the classroom and into clearcuts, to shopping malls, toxic waste dumps, nuclear weapons testing grounds. In these humanized landscapes we confront the "real work," the work of accepting the suffering of the world as our own suffering. We affirm our responsibility and we engage in consciousness practice.

In the following pages, I do not describe how to conduct these exercises. I want only to give their flavor. John Muir, one of the early leaders of the American conservation movement, expressed the essence of these practices when he wrote, "Going out is going in." Going out to clearcuts, visiting polluted waters, paddling down rivers that are "controlled" with dikes and levees is going into our larger *self* in this phase of human history.

Ed Abbey, author of many books on the American Southwest, constantly reminded his listeners of the importance of play. Playing in rivers, mountains, seashores, prairies, and deserts means getting into the place as it is without preconceptions, without hidden agendas, without any thoughts about social policy. Play is spontaneous, creative, intrinsically rewarding, and in the moment. Consider the following exercises in the spirit of play.

CLEARCUTS IN ANCIENT FORESTS

We are standing in the middle of a recent clearcut in northwestern California. In clearcut logging all the trees are chain-sawed. In this particular two-hundred-acre clearcut on a steep slope (one acre is the size of a football playing field), all the fallen trees were stripped and the logs were dragged upslope by heavy chains to a freshly cleared and scraped landing area. The logs were then loaded onto heavy duty trucks for transport out of the woods over freshly cut logging roads and thence to a sawmill nearly fifty miles from the site. Giant bulldozers have pushed broken branches, large ferns, and other plants from the understory of the old-growth redwood forest into piles called trash piles. All the trees and other vegetation have been cut or bulldozed into piles, even along the stream running through the site.

Seven environmentalists have been invited to participate in this outing organized by the agricultural extension officer of the state university. Foresters working for large logging companies and members of the local chamber of commerce and other local groups are also on this trip.

While the forester who planned this clearcut talks about "harvesting" mature forests to "make way for vigorous new trees," several activists sit together on the stump of an ancient redwood. Without talking, they form a circle on the stump for solace in the face of the pain of the forest. One woman, who has protested the chain-sawing of ancient redwood forests by sitting on a small platform hung high in a threatened redwood grove, begins to sing a song used in other gatherings in the forest: "Fur and feather, fin and skin, all in one and one in all." Tentatively, then more strongly, people sitting on the stump take up the song and blend their voices across the clearcut.

Other people on this tour look at the stumpsitters with exasperation—some with anger. "Damn tree huggers," one of the loggers loudly whispers under his breath as the stumpsitters finish their song. As if to ignore the feelings expressed in the silence after their song, the forester for the logging company continues his talk. "We are helping mother nature. Instead of waiting for slow regeneration, we plant five trees, which come from genetically enhanced seedlings raised in our nurseries, for every tree we cut. Raising trees is just like raising corn. We are raising a crop of trees to supply families with timber to build their homes and supply paper for our needs in this industrial society."

Is this all a forest means, I ask myself—a factory for growing trees? Will all ancient redwood forests be clearcut in the name of making them more efficient factories for fiber? Do we experience the presence of the forest as a great being when we clearcut the ancient forest and attempt to create a fiber factory in its place? "Clearcut," it seems to me, is a metaphor for destruction of forests. What we have clearcut from our minds is a sense of mindfulness, of awareness of our interconnectedness with the forest as a wild place.

Our search for wild nature grows from the same sense of displacement that motivated the romantics of the eighteenth century who rebelled against what the poet William Blake called the "dark satanic mills" of industrial civilization. Can we learn to experience what our remote ancestors intimately experienced—wildness in nature, wildness in ourselves? Is it possible or even desirable to experience wild nature—undomesticated, unmanaged, undeveloped, untouched by humans—at the end of the twentieth century? Some writers call for a return to "paleolithic consciousness," the first known period of prehistoric human culture. If our experience in nature is culturally mediated and our culture is rapidly changing, then what does it mean to experience nature? Our cultural experience is different in the 1990s from the situation of paleolithic hunters and nomadic herders. We may need guides and teachers to help us shed some of the assumptions we learned during the past several thousand years. We need to rediscover what Australian philosopher Warwick Fox calls consciousness practice.

Before discussing some of the principles of consciousness practice and describing some examples of guided experiences that can help to reawaken our sense of wonder, awe, mystery, and humility in nature, I will briefly describe how our experiences in nature became diminished and distorted, and how we became alienated from a sense of broader identification and compassion with nature.

NATURAL RESOURCE CONSERVATION AND THE GOSPEL OF EFFICIENCY

Especially during the past several hundred years in industrial societies, nature was seen primarily as a natural resource. Vast landscapes in North America were altered, humanized, bulldozed, and polluted in the name of economic growth and natural resource development. In *Nature's Metropolis*, William Cronon describes how this process transformed and diminished whole landscapes in the American Midwest. Focusing on Chicago, as a specific place but also as a metaphor for what occurred throughout North America, Cronon describes in detail the processes by which cattle were collected by the web of railroads, brought to the stockyards of Chicago, and dismembered into products that could be sold as commodities in the expanding city markets. Dismembering cattle into products is only one example of transformation of landscapes in the name of economy, efficiency, and markets. Biologically productive wetlands were drained, and the process was called "reclamation." Ancient forests were clearcut and the process was called "forestry." Planting tree plantations—row after row of the same species of tree—was called "reforestation" and "scientific management." Strip-mining the mountains was called "efficient resource development."

In daily household habits, more and more people sought comfort and convenience in their immediate environment, especially from the harshness of winter and the heat of summer. During winter cold spells we turned up the thermostats, confident that electricity or natural gas, transported hundreds or thousands of miles to our homes and offices, would always be available, always be cheap, always be in abundant supply to serve our desires, our whims.

I remember when my parents bought their first air conditioner. What a relief! We didn't have to swelter any longer during hot August nights in Kansas. Turn up the air conditioner, close the doors. Throughout the Midwest, a tradition that had lasted for generations vanished within a few years—the tradition of sitting on the veranda during the long summer evenings, catching the faint evening breezes, drinking ice tea, chatting with neighbors and friends passing by on the street. During the summer as well as the winter, people became more confined in their houses or apartments. Sometimes residents of the suburbs ventured forth to have a barbecue on the patio, but they sprayed insecticides to kill mosquitoes, flies, and ants before lighting the charcoal.

People living in cities and suburbs literally lost touch with the earth—with the soil that nourished them. They lost touch with wild animals—buffalo, deer, antelope. Few people could experience the sight of grizzly bears as they rambled about because grizzlies had become extinct through much of their range. Few could experience the sound of wolves howling in the distance because they too had been hunted to extinction.

In my own bioregion in northwestern California, I can hike in designated wilderness areas, but I realize that the wildness of those areas has been diminished during the past forty years. Even in the most remote sections of the Trinity Alps Wilderness Area, a designated wilderness administered by the U.S. Forest Service containing over 600,000 acres, I am never more than twelve miles from a paved road. I can see recent clearcuts on private lands and on lands administered by the Forest Service when I walk along some of the ridgetop trails in this wilderness area. In the eastern part, during hot summer days, I can see smog drifting into the mountains from the central valley of California.

During the past fifty years, most of us have lost touch even with the domesticated plants and animals that provide their seeds and flesh for us to eat. Many of us still eat the flesh of domesticated animals, but it is canned or frozen, provided by commercial slaughtering houses.

During the Age of Exuberance, some people tried to "get back to nature," but the style of outdoor recreation that became popular with urban middle classes during the post-World War II era was conducive to conspicuous consumption of toys—powerboats, off-road vehicles, luxury resorts in exotic desert and tropical settings, paved roads through national parks that allow elaborate motorized campers to penetrate into the heart of what had been pristine areas. The number of trips to national parks increased dramatically during the 1950s and 1960s. However, many of these new recreationists remained in their vehicles during park visits, or at best took short walks to designated scenic viewpoints. National, state, and local park agencies in the United States and Canada obliged multitudes of new park visitors by building more paved roads, installing full-service campgrounds, and providing guides who interpreted scenic areas as part of Canadian and American national heritage rather than teaching visitors about biodiversity and the natural values of wilderness areas. The U.S. Forest Service also built thousands of miles of new roads, many of them paved, to access timber on public lands and, in their words, to enhance the possibility of recreational access.

Increasing numbers of people explored roadless areas, especially in fragile desert areas, on a variety of off-road vehicles—motorcycles, four-wheel-drive vehicles, dune buggies, and all-terrain vehicles. Scientists documented that within a ten-year period starting in the 1970s, hundreds of thousands of acres of desert lands in California were damaged by off-road vehicles.

For many people, getting back to nature meant having fun, escaping from the conventional routines of life in the cities, buying more fossil-fuel-powered vehicles, and thoughtlessly trammeling landscapes. If riding motorcycles through the desert became boring or the scenery in national parks was not inspiring, the family could always take its vacation at Disneyland or the Epcot Center in Florida, where corporations mounted large displays extolling the glories of technology.

Schools were less helpful than the national park interpreters in engendering deep and joyful experiences in nature. When teachers discussed nature in science and philosophy courses, they taught from a materialistic perspective. Nature, they told students, is "dead matter." The science of ecology, if mentioned at all, was defined as "the relation between organisms and their habitat," a notion that falls short of even attempting to understand the complex interrelationships and bioregional systems found in nature. As students of science we were told to objectify nature, be detached observers of nature, design experiments using live animals, develop theories that have practical implications for "enhancing" productivity of natural resources.

Throughout society promoters of resource-development ideology told us how they would enhance productivity of fiber, trees, fodder, food, and cattle. Proponents of the "green revolution" (a misnomer in terms of contemporary connotations of the term "green") promised that selective breeding and increased use of fertilizers and pesticides would allow massive increases in food supplies for rapidly increasing human populations.

In sum, during the Age of Exuberance, few of our activities, even our recreational activities in parks and on seashores and lakes, brought us into intimate understanding of our modest place, as a species, in the Tree of Life. Many people ceased to engage in consciousness practice.

Leading voices in the American ecology movement have called us to experience ourselves deeply in wild nature for over a hundred years. We might recall John Muir's exhortation to "go to the mountains and get their good tidings." Henry David Thoreau's animism and Muir's pantheism came as a result of their consciousness practice. Muir, for example, spent many months walking in the Sierra Nevada virtually alone.

Although brutally suppressed and then ignored for a century by academia and by conservationists, American Indian teachers in many different tribes still teach ways of extending our identification. Stephen Boyd's book *Rolling Thunder* is one of many examples of the rising awareness of American Indian spiritual practices among non-Indians.

During the 1930s, Bob Marshall and Aldo Leopold wrote expressively of the need humans have for identification with big wilderness. Marshall trekked through much of the American West looking for remaining roadless areas and hiked through northern Alaska, meeting native peoples. During the 1960s, Ed Abbey's *Desert Solitaire* called out to a new generation of Americans who felt stifled by mechanized recreation and disgusted with our treatment of landscapes as disposable commodities. Abbey understood that walking through a landscape provided a more intimate experience of place than driving through that same landscape. "Get out of your vehicle," he cried. "Start walking in the desert. Your reward will be great."

In their haste to get back to nature, however, many well-meaning people underestimated the impact that our culture had on us during the Age of Exuberance. We had lost our sense of place in nature. Writing on the eve of Earth Day 1970, naturalist Loren Eiseley asked a question that is central to our human predicament:

> How is nature to be reentered; how can men and women who have been relatively unthinking creators of the second world, the world of culture, revitalize and restore the first world of nature, which brought us into being? [Humans have become] "a spreading blight which threatens to efface the green world that created [us]" (The Invisible Pyramid: A Naturalist Analyzes the Rocket Century, 1970, p. 137).

Eiseley prophetically concluded that we must be our own "last magician" seeking our way home in nature, "not simply by tools, but through the slow inward growth of the mind" (p. 155). "The task is admittedly gigantic," but unless we take even haltering steps to reconnect with primal nature, then our experience as a human species is so radically altered that it is possible that we will never be at home again on this earth.

CONSCIOUSNESS PRACTICE

Consciousness practice. is intense, mindful awareness of who we are in the first world of nature. The process of broadening and deepening our identification-in-nature is both personal—based on our individuated experience—and social—working "alone together" with groups that are consciously formed to give space for our meditations.

Consciousness practice takes time. It involves allowing our minds to slow down to the rhythms of nature—the time it takes the sun to set, the time it takes for flowers to come into blossom. In Zen practice the teacher advises students to watch each breath they take, to do one thing at a time.

Teachers of consciousness practice draw from nonliterate, non-Western, frequently nonpatriarchal, traditions. Human ecologist Paul Shepard suggests that our consciousness practice be the search for "paleolithic consciousness" in the postmodern era. Shepard attempts to summarize what he calls "emergent gestalts" of consciousness practice in these "experiences."

1. "Read the world as hunter-gatherers read tracks."

2. Give "voice" to the "livingness of the world."

3. Celebrate life transitions and milestones in social events.

4. Practice "Sacramental Trophism," incorporating "death as life" in meeting nutritional needs.

5. Assemble small vernacular social groups of 25 to 500 people in "The Fire Circle."

6. "Deal directly with the means of subsistence...."

7. Discover a sense of place.

8. Affirm the sacred presence, the mystery of being.

9. Escape from domestication and liberate ourselves from the doctrine of humanism.

("A Post-Historic Primitivism," pp. 87–88).

Consciousness practice fosters and engenders broader identification and compassion. Consciousness practice especially engenders cosmological and ontological identification. Ontological identification with *Atman*, the ultimate, the source, or the Tao is possible, we are told, through intensive and arduous practices such as *zazen* and *koan* practice in Zen Buddhism. Cosmological identification is easier to communicate than ontological identification because cosmology provides general accounts of how the world is, and our experience of "isness" can be expressed in scientific theories, music, or generally speaking in symbolic communication.

Consciousness practice has affective, cultural, and cognitive aspects. Affective aspects include fully experiencing our emotional responses to landscapes and human alterations of landscapes—clearcutting, destruction of habitat, extinction of plant and animal species, nuclear disasters. Cultural aspects of consciousness practice include recognition of the impacts that gender and culture, including religious and ethnic group traditions, have on our perceptions of nonhuman nature.

Cognitive aspects of consciousness practices include development of models and information about specific places as part of our process of healing ourselves in that place. Consciousness practice in this sense is linked to bioregional study. Bioregional means literally the region of life, lived space, and the interrelationships over time and space of different species, including the human species. Bioregional studies utilize some of the skills of geographers, geologists, historians, and social scientists. Bioregional studies are a combination of practice, art, and science and involve the student as participant in the lived space, whether that be a river valley, mountain, island, desert, or other type of bioregion.

During the past twenty years, many techniques and ways of consciousness practice have been developed and encouraged in North America. The new nature, nature transformed by humans, still has some more or less wild places. Some people will continue to seek wild places for vision quests, for fasting, and for solitude. However, consciousness practice is relevant in cities and suburbs as well as in wilderness. Indeed, given the fact that many of us will spend the vast majority of our time in cities, excercises that help us rediscover wild in the city may be the most useful.

Consciousness practice necessarily has political aspects. Some practice explicitly takes the form of political action, such as arising early in the morning to watch for an endangered species of bird roosting on property owned by a developer who is seeking permits to bulldoze the roosting area of the birds and convert it into a shopping mall. Some questions concerning political activism and consciousness practice are explored in Chapter 12 of this book. Out of broader identification we develop a sense of caring for the lived place and we are drawn to confront the assumptions of public bureaucracies and corporations or confront the ideology of "progress," scientific management of nature, and materialistic philosophy.

In order for us to react appropriately—without fear, selfish motivation, or despair—to the social, cultural, and ecological challenges of the 1990s, we must cross psychological barriers to new ways of perceiving ourselves in nature. This requires that we learn how to feel changes that are painful to our self-conceptions, our ideological beliefs, and our customary ways of behaving—to feel changes that occur in greater time frames of the earth's systems so that these changes have profound meaning to us in the present.

New forms of experiential education have the potential to awaken us from our collective suicidal path. The following examples of guided experiences are not exhaustive. More trainings are provided by the Institute for Deep Ecology Education. (See notes in the appendix for information on this and other organizations dedicated to helping people change their lifestyle to one based on deep ecology philosophy.)

WILD IN THE CITY

Lie naked on the pavement feeling plants struggling to grow through the cracks. Watch insects crawl across your belly. Smell the petrochemical exhausts from the multitude of vehicles. Remember the native vegetation that once inhabited this bioregion and envision the return of many species living in symbiotic and dynamic relationship in this watershed. Breathe deeply and become part of the flow of change into the next hundred years. (This exercise was suggested by a friend who lived as a homeless person in a large city while he was a teenager.)

COUNCIL OF ALL BEINGS

"I am spotted owl. I speak for all my sisters and brothers who need ancient forests in which to rest and hunt and build their nests. Logging is destroying our forests. I plead with humans to leave some forests for us." Eighteen people, each wearing the mask of a different creature, are sitting in council on a river bar in northern California engaged in a Council of All Beings.

The first Council of All Beings took place in a rural setting outside of Sydney, Australia, in 1985. Conceived by John Seed, an Australian, and Joanna Macy, an American teacher who has worked for many years in Buddhist tradition, Councils of All Beings have been convened in churches as a central part of the liturgy, in forests, schoolrooms, and conferences, in farm fields in Eastern Europe, in Japan, and in many places throughout North America. The Council of All Beings is one of many kinds of rituals that have been developed to affirm the interconnectedness of nonhuman and human worlds. It is a way to help us discard some of our cultural baggage and take on a new sense of identification.

Each Council of All Beings is special and different from other Councils because the people and the place are different, but the form of the Council has elements that are found in all Councils. Commonly a Council begins with sensitizing exercises that assist participants in remembering their rootedness in nature. The evolutionary remembering exercise, for example, guides participants through four and a half billion years of evolution in the long time frame, which helps participants understand their own lives in terms of the continually unfolding evolutionary process of life.

(Descriptions of these exercises and suggestions for conducting a Council of All Beings are found in John Seed's book *Thinking Like a Mountain: Towards a Council of All Beings.*)

RICH EXPERIENCE
IN TOXIC ENVIRONMENT

"Think of yourself as a plutonium particle going through its natural rate of decay. As a plutonium particle at Rocky Flats, you are stored in a storage container. Think about moving to a deep vault in eastern New Mexico, the proposed site for deposit of long-lasting radioactive wastes. You travel in a container on a truck. You might have an accident while on the truck, spilling onto the highway, contaminating human and nonhuman beings with a particle that can cause cancer or mutation. If you arrive as a particle, with other particles at the deposit, you are interacting with other particles seeking to express themselves. Some might leave their storage containers and enter the groundwater, continuing to decay through half lives over many thousands of years."

We are sitting near the fence at Rocky Flats near Denver, Colorado, with a group of students. We do not have authorized permission to enter the facility inside. If we trespass, we face possible arrest. We are meditating on our responsibility as nuclear guardians.

If we become nuclear guardians, we will share the responsibility with other guardians for above-ground, on-site containment and care for radioactive particles over hundreds and even thousands of years. We will be guardians of stored radioactive particles created during the Age of Exuberance. When the first atomic weapon was exploded at Alamogordo, New Mexico, in 1944, humans acquired a power never before available. Scientists working for the Department of Energy created plutonium for military uses. Uranium ore was mined, enriched by technology, transformed into a different form of energy, concentrated, and transformed into nuclear weapons. What responsibilities do humans have to far-future generations?

NUCLEAR GUARDIANSHIP PROJECT

The Nuclear Guardianship Project presents a guided experience called "the standard remembering" and a tentative "guardianship ethic." Joanna Macy and her associates in the Nuclear Guardianship Project found that the pilgrimage and hermitage or monastery is found in many cultures. Participants in the Nuclear Guardianship Project brought together images from many different cultures for a slide show on the Guardianship Project. Before viewing the slide show, participants are asked to think of themselves in the twenty-second century, looking back to the late twentieth century. The following script is used to open the slide show:

**The Standard Remembering of Our Ancestors
in the Times of Nuclear Peril**

I ask you to breathe and open
as we do when we remember times that are very far past.
Times that are very hard for us to imagine.
Hard for us to go back to the time
when the poison fire was on the planet
We in the 22nd century are accustomed to the danger.
But the people of that time,
mid 20th century were so innocent, dangerously innocent.
And as we remember the old stories,
we remember how it began in the press of war.
Oh our ancestors in the press of war
were seeking new and larger ways to kill.
And they opened the nucleus of the atom.
And with great effort and with great acumen
and with great applications of their brains,
they made and exploded the first nuclear weapon,
and the project, God forgive them,
they called Trinity in the desert of Alamo Gordo.
And the stories come down to us of a president called True Man
at a place called Pots Damn

receiving a telegram:
"Baby safely delivered."
And that baby was the poison fire.
And then in that very year, in that very month,
yes, the poison fire was first used as weapons.
Against great cities of a great people.
And we know the names, and you can say them in your heart,
we shall not forget them: Hero Shimah, Nagah Saki.
A quarter million people burned at once,
then people who sicken slowly,
for that is how it destroys,
slowly, hidden.
And then our ancestors of that time, the stories tell us
—this is hard—
they took that poison fire
to make electricity.
We know how easy it is
to share the power with the sun,
and with the wind,
and with the biomass,
but they took it from the poison fire,
and they used it
to boil water.
Oh the lords of arrogance were riding high then.
It was a dark time,
the times of nuclear peril.
And the signs of sickening grew.
For at every step along the way the poison fire proliferated.
And there were epidemics of cancer
and there were epidemics of viruses
and immune diseases
and deformity
and still births
and sterility.

Oh we know them well now.

And we know their source.

But for those ancestors

it was mysterious

whence came these sickenings of spirit and flesh.

And some,

sensing their connection with the poison fire,

with the huge accumulation of its wastes,

wanted to wish it away.

And the Governments tried to bury it—

There were places called Carl's Bad, Yucca Mountain

—deep holes half a mile down.

They wanted to bury it

as if the Earth were not alive.

And those who did not agree with the Governments said

"Not in my back yard."

Their pain and their despair were so great,

they wanted it out of their sight,

out of their minds.

We remember that in the story.

Because it was in those dark times

that the ancestors began to meet and take council,

groups coming together in their towns.

They looked into their hearts

and thought

"We can guard the poison fire.

We can overcome our fear of guarding it and be mindful.

Only in that way can the beings of the future be protected."

They remembered us!

How clear it is to us today.

But it was new in that time.

What inspired them?

What did they draw on in those closing years of the 20th century

to hit upon this idea to inspire themselves

and indeed then to carry it forward.

That was the question I asked myself.

And I went to the image bank,

and I collected images which they already knew in their time.

I'm going to show you on this very ancient mechanism,

and I'm using some music from earlier times as well.

Come around where you can see.

Go back in your mind to the late 20th century

to learn what they were thinking that allowed this to arise.

The Guardianship Project developed a tentative guardianship ethic which provides a basis for discussion of our responsibilities to far future generations:

1. Given the extreme toxicity and longevity of nuclear wastes, their generation by nuclear energy and weapons production must cease. The development of safe, renewable energy sources and non-violent means of conflict resolution is essential to our health and survival.

2. We all share in the responsibility for the nuclear wastes produced in our lifetimes. In taking care of these wastes, we are concerned with the well-being of present and future generations.

3. Future generations have the right to know about the nuclear legacy we bequeath them and to protect themselves from it. This right includes access to containers of radioactive materials for purposes of monitoring and repair.

4. Deep burial of nuclear wastes, which precludes containment repair and risks uncontrollable contamination of life support systems, conflicts with our responsibility to future life.

5. Transportation of nuclear wastes, with the inevitable daily risks of accidents and spills, should be minimized.

6. A large-scale research effort to develop technology for the least hazardous long-term treatment and disposition of nuclear wastes is of high priority.

7. In the interim, until responsible long-term measures are discovered and devised, it is our generation's responsibility to monitor all nuclear wastes and store them in ways that are retrievable, recognizing that "safe," permanent management of these wastes has yet proved illusive, and that total safety may ultimately never be attainable with respect to nuclear waste.

8, Responsible care of the wastes entails both citizen participation and citizen education. As a context we need a profound education about our relationship to the Earth and our relationship to time.

9. Policies pertaining to nuclear waste management must be arrived at with full participation of the public. Consideration of the interests of both present and future generations can be served only by lack of secrecy, free circulation of information, and open ongoing communication.

10. With respect to all parties, citizens, public interest groups, corporations, utilities, and governments, we choose strategies that are based on cooperation for the public good and the integrity of the biosphere.

11. The motivation and vigilance necessary for ongoing, interim storage of nuclear wastes requires a moral commitment on the part of citizens. This commitment, comparable to a spiritual vocation to act on behalf of the biosphere and future generations, is within our human capacity and can be developed and sustained through tapping the religious and cultural resources of our planetary heritage.

Both the immediate action and the ongoing training that Nuclear Guardianship entails have three simultaneous and interdependent dimensions: political, technical, and moral. Each is an aspect of Guardianship.

Political: Assuming our responsibility as citizens *to participate in decisions* about nuclear wastes. This requires familiarity with governmental and corporate processes currently determining the disposition of these wastes. And it requires involvement in these processes to represent the interests of present and future generations. It is not appropriate to leave this responsibility on the shoulders of decision-makers who are pressured by short-term considerations.

Technical: Acquiring knowledge about radioactive wastes and methods for their long-term care is requisite for political responsibility. Accessible materials on the nuclear fuel cycle, the biological, ecological and health effects of radioactivity, and best available modes for containment and transmutation are required for citizen study groups and schools.

Moral or Spiritual: Recognizing the moral challenge that results from having created nuclear technology. The spiritual strength to face the enormity of the problem we have created is available to us. It requires *rediscovering and reassessing our most deeply held values,* and cultivating those values that are life sustaining. The spiritual traditions of our species as well as contemporary insights into consciousness and value-formation provide rich resources for such training in Guardianship—the most crucial mission of our present generation.

To these ends the Nuclear Guardianship Project was initiated in mid-1988 in Northern California by Joanna Macy and colleagues and has spread to other parts of the U.S., Germany, Austria, Britain, Japan, and Australia. It has been developing and offering a variety of educational measures.

EXPERIENCING OUR OWN BIOCREATIONS

The movie *Bladerunner* is set in southern California in the near future. The vast, polluted, decaying city exists in darkness, dark skies, dark rain. The crowded streets are filled with a polyglot culture. Genetically engineered animals are sold for food in the shops. The hero, a policeman, is sent on a special mission—to find and terminate five replicants who have escaped from the space station where they are assigned to work. By law no replicants can be on earth, but these five have come to earth on a special mission of their own—to find their "father," the inventor who programmed them—and ask him to give them feelings, emotions. Replicants look like humans and can be distinguished from humans only through analysis of their tissue.

This film can be shown to church groups, to groups of students, and to groups engaged in discussions of environmental ethics and ecophilosophy. After viewing the film, the group discusses our responsibilities for and to our creations. When humans have the power to alter genetically living organisms, do we also have responsibility to include these creatures in our community? Are the inventors under any moral obligation to accept their own creations or help their creations to find their way in life? How do we distinguish between the natural and the unnatural when they look the same?

MOUNTAINS AND RIVERS SESSION

Lost Coast of California. Season when the poppies bloom. Eighteen of us gather at the mouth of the Mattole River to begin a week of the "practice of the wild." We are walking alone together along this rugged windswept coastline, focusing on our breathing, on being where we are in the joy of the moment. Our teacher, called a roshi in Japanese Zen tradition, is Nelson Foster, trained by Roshi Robert Aitken. He has led walking meditations in the Canyonlands of Utah, in the Sierra Nevada, and in the Arizona desert.

Buddhist teachings bring students to "see" the universe, the cosmos in its essential form. In the metaphor of the Net of Indra, each jewel on the Net reflects every other jewel. Seeing clearly one jewel, the student sees the whole. Mindful experience of nature—including nature manipulated by past generations of humans—leads naturally to emotional, personal relationships. Mindful experience can include rituals and making "earth prayers." Ritual and "earth prayers," done sensitively and with wise leaders and teachers, can help to remind us of our connections with broader nature and encourage broader identification.

"Earth prayers" can be derived from many different traditions including the Great Goddess tradition, Native American traditions, Buddhist traditions, and what ecologist Paul Shepard calls the "sacred paw," the cult of the Great Bear, which lasted for thirty-five thousand years, longer than any other known "earth prayer" cosmology known in human history. In the anthology *Earth Prayers,* Elizabeth Roberts and Elias Amidon collected poems from many cultural and religious traditions expressing joy in our experience of life and death as beings in the "great mystery."

The guided experiences discussed above help us become aware of, acknowledge, and integrate into our awareness our anxiety about the state of the earth and our deep love for our home. Earth–bonding rituals are expressed in many different religious traditions.

Besides rituals and what Theodore Roszak calls "ecotherapy," emerging green lifestyles are based on rediscovering sense of place and on working with the tendency of the specific bioregion wherein we dwell to heal ourselves while healing human-damaged landscapes.

Sense of place is discussed in the following chapter. In chapter 5, "Thinking Like a Watershed," some ideas are presented on the kind of work that is important in restoring the integrity of damaged landscapes.

CHAPTER

4

WE'RE ALL NATIVES

Snow is falling by the time I approach the last, steep, rutted mile of dirt road leading to the ranch house. It is the first week of April, and in these coastal mountains of northwest California, snow melts quickly in the Spring. The strength of the spring sun is stronger than the remaining cold of winter storms blowing from the north Pacific through the Gulf of Alaska. By afternoon the sun will be shining, and the snow will have melted, exposing the new oak leaves and blossoms on the trees in the orchard.

The ranch—the Home Ranch, we call it, although it has no official label as such on maps—is nestled at a strategic location on the east side of Redwood Creek valley. From the high meadow, the site of the original homestead buildings, one has a vista down the valley, into the deep inner gorge of Redwood Creek, across forests of oak, madrone, and young Douglas fir, across meadows and rocky outcroppings. The ranch contains two parcels of 160 acres each. Under the homestead laws of the nineteenth century, families were expected to live on a quarter section—160 acres. Land subdivision based on township and range lines has determined ownership patterns in the United States ever since George Washington and the Congress established the system in the Northwest Ordinance of 1789. It is a rational system of land subdivision—a numbered grid system comprised of squares six miles to a side called townships, and with 36 one-mile squares per township called sections—but this grid system is not congruent with ecological realities, with the complex relationships and changing patterns that characterize a naturally evolving landscape. The Home Ranch is located at the only reliable spring in upper Redwood Valley. The original homesteaders must have understood the land well, or at least they under-stood it much better than the city people who are now buying 40-acre parcels of dry hillside land in this valley.

The spring on the Home Ranch flows from the sedimentary rock, bring-ing life during the summer dry season, and flowing even during the pro-longed six-year drought of the 1980s. This is good land, indeed, very good land. It contains large natural meadows, groves of oaks, madrone, and fir, and good soil for gardening. This is the only place in the upper half of Redwood Valley where a household can raise a large garden, feed chickens, and graze some cattle. All the other land in the upper valley is too steep, or too dry, or the soil too thin, or the meadows not large enough to support a family ranch.

Richard is sitting in his bedroom when I arrive, listening to the sounds of chain saws and the crash of falling trees. Loggers are stripping the hill-side on the west side of the watershed. The west side is steep and contains mature stands of Douglas fir. Loggers are cutting roads with bulldozers, dragging the trees up steep slopes to log decks where they are trucked to the pulp mills on Humboldt Bay.

Logging is done on lands controlled by the U.S. Forest Service and on lands controlled by an unscrupulous lawyer-logger in Eureka, the county seat of Humboldt County. Much of the mature Douglas fir was logged from all the east side of upper Redwood Valley during the timber boom years of the 1950s. Douglas fir is a favorite wood for house construction, and some of the suburban houses near Kansas City, where I grew up, conceivably could have come from the old Douglas fir groves in this valley or one of the many other valleys in Humboldt County that were heavily logged during the 1950s and 1960s. In the 1980s and 1990s loggers began clearcutting groves of madrone, oak, and tan oak. No piece of land is left to rest for more than a few years before more trees are cut. Each week when I drive to the ranch I see new logging roads scarring the steep hillsides, new clearcuts, new skid roads where bulldozers have scraped down to bare rock as they drag trees to landing decks.

Flying over northwest California in a small plane at low altitude, one sees hundreds of valleys in these coastal mountains that have been clearcut.

From the air overlooking lower Redwood Valley, the few remaining groves of ancient Redwoods stand out as dark green remnants among the squared-off pale green sections that show where logging companies clearcut in the 1970s before Redwood National Park was enlarged in 1978.

Richard has lived in these mountains for over fifty years. He was born in traditional Yurok territory along the lower Klamath River. *Yurok* means "downriver" and the Yurok are one of seven distinct indigenous nations that inhabit the Klamath-Trinity river valleys of northwest California. He remembers the way it was before the clearcut frenzy began in the 1950s. "No one logged Douglas fir when I was a child," he said, offering me a cup of hot tea. "We thought Douglas fir was a trash tree. It is not sacred, like redwoods or pepperwood, and provided no food like the oaks, but we didn't clearcut or burn it. My people let it be. It has its own place. Why do these loggers tear up the land so much? Why can't they just let it be?"

Of course, this is a rhetorical question. Richard has witnessed the greed of some men, and the evil of others. He knows the complex conflict between the world views of Native Americans and European settlers in northwest California. He has witnessed the insistent drive for more money that drove some men and women to engage in massive clearcutting of ancient forests. Now the second and third growth, after the first cut was made in the nineteenth century, is being clearcut and some ecologists warn that the forests may never grow here again.

The dirt road passing through the ranch was bulldozed by loggers in the 1950s—up the ridge to Horse Mountain—as a haul road, connecting to a paved road built by the U.S. Forest Service to facilitate the rapid transport of logs from federally controlled lands to coastal sawmills. The road through the ranch follows, generally speaking, the track of the wagon road that was built during the nineteenth century to foster development of trade between the mining district on the Trinity River and the coastal regions of northwestern California. Richard has walked much of this older roadbed, looking for signs of Indian habitation. The tribes that used this territory for hunting—mostly elk and deer—and gathering acorns have been poorly recorded by archaeologists and anthropologists. Richard has found indications of sites of house pits and stones that he thinks were used for grinding acorns, but he hasn't been able to interest certified archaeologists at the local university in doing a thorough inventory of the upper valley.

Besides his Yurok ancestry, Richard has Cherokee and Scottish European ancestry. His wife was Hupa, and his children claim Yurok identity in tribal roles. He learned cattle ranching and farming as a child from his parents on the Hoopa reservation on the Trinity River. The Hupa were the only native peoples in California to retain their ancestral homelands when Indian reservations were established in California in 1872. He was taught basket weaving by the old people—the few old women who still knew basket weaving during the 1950s. They saw a talent, an interest, a commitment in him, and in traditional Yurok teaching ways they wove and talked— telling him the stories that are integral to Yurok weaving. Stories about Bigfoot, one of the legendary beings of the High Country. Stories about the designs to be woven into the basket, when to gather firewood (no wood to be collected in the winter when the land is quiet), where to gather basket material and when (burn the meadow after collecting bear grass in the high-elevation meadows of the Siskiyou mountains, where it grows in profusion), how to prepare material (soak spruce root before stripping the bark, then dry it in a shady place).

His parents took him to the Baptist church, one of the many missionary churches on the reservation. They did not want to be identified as Indians. They wanted their children to be assimilated into European culture and forget traditional Indian ways. In his own mind Richard labored to weave together stories of creation from the Bible and Yurok stories of the great creator and of multiple spirits in the land—Waga and Bigfoot among them. Yurok narratives include the story of the inland whale (retold by Theodora Kroeber in her classic book *The Inland Whale*), a story of love, fidelity, and loyalty.

When Christian missionaries find their way to the Home Ranch—as they do several times a year over the nine miles of rutted dirt road from the paved state highway—Richard tells them *his* stories of creation, humility, and responsibility to the land. Sometimes these missionaries condemn the "house sticks" outside the door of his house as "pagan idolatry." Richard tells them stories emphasizing the importance of the home place in Yurok traditions and the role that house sticks have in signifying the interrelation-ships between beings not seen and beings seen in ordinary time. The house sticks, generally of young Douglas fir branches entwined by vines, are pro-tectors of the home.

The ordinary and the unexplainable constantly interplay in human con-sciousness in this bioregion. David Rains Wallace, a contemporary writer with the eye of a poet but an intellect steeped in modern theories of evolu-tion, conservation biology, and biogeography, has called this region the "Klamath knot." Within the Klamath Knot, the strands of natural history are intertwined and as twisted and convoluted as the passage of rivers and streams that cut through the complex geology of the region. Wallace con-cludes that the Klamath province holds mysteries of evolving biodiversity that scientists have only begun to understand. Furthermore, he suggests that the systems on many interpenetrating levels may be affected by the very process of observing the system with human consciousness (*The Klamath Knot,* 1983).

The Yurok nation, one of five-hundred autonomous, independent, self-reliant, highly developed nations that existed peacefully on the land now called California when Spaniards first arrived two hundred years ago, was decimated by European settlers and the U.S. military. In the early 1860s, a military expedition was sent to burn Yurok villages on the Klamath River. The soldiers justified their mission as protecting the gold miners who flocked to the Trinity River region during the 1850s and the settlers who fol-lowed the gold seekers. Gold miners killed Yuroks and disrupted the rich salmon fisheries in the river. Diseases introduced by Europeans, murder by European miners, enslavement, and social disorganization brought about by Christian missionaries and secular European schoolteachers all took their toll on a civilization that had lived quietly and richly along the Klamath for hundreds of years (Jack Norton, *Genocide in Northwestern California,* 1979).

By the 1890s, some surviving Yurok began learning ranching and farming. The ranching culture, which Richard remembers from his child-hood, was an expression of new modes of adaptation for people who had spent centuries, perhaps thousands of years, dwelling in their homeland along the Klamath River. Traditionally salmon runs in the coastal rivers sustained the Yurok. Salmon, steelhead (an ocean-going trout), and sturgeon in the Klamath and the Trinity rivers as well as other coastal rivers, supplied a protein-rich diet supplemented with acorns. The only plant that the Yurok traditionally raised was a variety of tobacco that was smoked in sacred ceremonies. Europeans introduced cattle and sheep in the 1850s.

Richard established his first cattle herd as a teenager and pastured the herd on a friend's ranch in Oregon. Even when he was a student at the local university—on an Indian scholarship program—he went home in the summers to raise a large garden with his father, a garden that supplied tomatoes, corn, fruit, and beans for canning. The hillside farm-ranches of the first half of the century in these coastal mountains were sustained by thriving sheep herds. Wool was the most important cash crop for the ranches. Sheep were grazed on mountain meadows where the native Roosevelt elk had been exterminated and where almost all the predators—including bear and mountain lion and bald eagle—were ruthlessly hunted and exterminated. After the logging boom of the 1950s, during which most of the ranchers sold the mature Douglas fir on their land, many of them, White and Yurok, abandoned their ranches because of a depression in the price of wool and cattle. Only a few families continued to ranch—those who were able to consolidate their holdings into large acreages.

Richard bought his first small ranch soon after he graduated from college. One of the first Indians (a label he prefers to Native American) to graduate from the local university, he worked as a schoolteacher and then as curator of the native basket collection at a local museum. He bought the Home Ranch a decade ago. He intended to try to keep the old lifestyle that he had known as a child. The old homestead in Redwood Valley called to him. Remembering the lessons he learned as a child, he planted an orchard before he built a house. Apples and cherry trees—but not peach or pear—can produce abundant, sustaining crops in these coastal valleys. The miners always planted apple trees when they staked their claims along these rivers during the nineteenth century, and even now while wandering along the Trinity or other rivers mined in the nineteenth century, one can find an old apple tree—alone, clawed by bears, broken by storms, but still flowering in the spring and still bearing solid, substantial apples in the fall.

When he built his house, Richard sited it to face the garden on one side and the view across the valley on the other. When money was available, he fenced most of the ranch for cattle. Later he bought a team of Belgian work horses—almost an endangered breed because of the decline in horse farming—determined to return to the old ways of farming on steep hillside farms. But the horses were too big for the land. Their hoofs dug into the fragile soils, and the pastures, during winter, did not provide enough grass to support them. The grass in the pastures had to be supplemented with increasingly expensive store-bought feed.

Living on a ranch in the 1990s and trying to maintain even some of the old ways is not easy. Richard has a woodstove for cooking, heating, and hot water. He prefers candlelight, but his son, who does most of the physical work on the ranch, wanted to watch TV, so they bought a gas-fueled, electric generator—Japanese-made. He refused to have a telephone for the first five years he lived on the ranch, but his aging parents wanted to keep in contact with him and demanded that he acquire a cellular telephone.

He continues basket weaving, especially during the winter. Weaving is part of life. Baskets, to traditional Yurok, are alive. Old baskets must be taken out and used, given air, talked to. It is not possible, in this brief passage, to express more than a fragment of the rich meaning of baskets in traditional Yurok culture. As a Native American on the official roll of a rancheria, Richard is given gathering privileges for basket-making material on lands managed by the U.S. Forest Service. He resents having to ask a government agency for permission to collect materials in areas where his ancestors collected such materials for hundreds of years in a sustainable way before the U.S. government took them over. It has become difficult for Richard to find materials traditionally used in weaving Yurok baskets because of changes in land-use practices. His favorite sites—for collecting spruce roots, willow, maiden-hair fern, bear grass, and other materials— have been clearcut, or have been invaded by exotic plants, or have had access blocked by private landowners or the U.S. Forest Service.

Much of the traditional homeland of the Yurok has been clearcut by

Simpson Timber Corporation. Also Simpson Timber and the U.S. Forest Service have sprayed large areas of the lower Klamath watershed with herbicides. The traditional Yurok Basket Weavers' Association and supporters from environmental groups have held numerous protest demonstrations in front of the local offices of Simpson Timber Corporation and the offices of the U.S. Forest Service, but the corporation maintains it will contain aerial spraying of herbicides. Richard and his son have experienced aerial spraying on the forest lands on the slopes of Redwood Creek opposite their ranch. Richard's son developed lymph gland problems in the years since spray began drifting across their ranch. Although it is extremely difficult to prove cause-and-effect relationships when exposed to herbicides, Richard is convinced that contamination by herbicide spraying contributed to his son's health problems.

Sometimes he thinks of giving up. He talks of selling the ranch to developers, moving to the suburbs of a city. It is much easier living in the suburbs of a city than in rural areas. In the suburbs one is close to social and medical services, and telephones. Electricity is supplied by the grid system of a giant energy production corporation. One can pick up milk at the corner store rather than milking a cow, have access to many channels on cable TV, be closer to friends and possible part-time jobs as they become available. "But I don't know anything but stories from the old Yurok elders I knew as a child. What would I be in the city? I wouldn't be myself. I'm part of this valley," Richard says.

I too feel part of Redwood Valley. I worked, as an activist in several different groups, for the establishment of Redwood National Park in the lower eleven miles of Redwood Valley. I have spent numerous weeks each year walking through portions of lower Redwood Valley or working on the Home Ranch. I tried to buy a 160-acre parcel adjacent to the Home Ranch a few years ago, but the bank turned down my loan application. I didn't earn enough money to qualify for the loan, and I had no business plan to make an income off the property. I did not want to log the ancient oaks off the property to make mortgage payments. I didn't want to subdivide the parcel into 40-acre ranchettes, because I knew the scarcity of water during the summer dry season. I just wanted to build a small cabin on the land, take care of the land during my lifetime, maybe plant oak seedlings in an area where a small fire burned several years ago. I felt part of the valley and wanted to put my roots into the valley.

Instead of selling to me, the bank allowed the unscrupulous lawyer who has systematically abused other portions of the valley to log the ancient oaks and madrones. He sent bulldozers to scrape delicate meadows, creating a new road system. Now we hear he is trying to sell the property to some people in the San Francisco area who want a "rural retreat."

We're told there are many people from the "city"—meaning any large urban area—who want to buy rural retreats. They have the money to make a large down payment on logged-over parcels. If they respect the land, they will need to learn about the land. The land, to me, holds numerous complex and mysterious relationships that are only partially described by scientific ecological theories. The land is alive, animated, changing in its own ways in response to natural geological changes as well as changes wrought by humans coming from European traditions over the past hundred years. We need, in my opinion, people who will love the land, feel part of the place, discover what American Indian shamans, as well as contemporary ecophilosophers, call the "sense of place"—if settlers are going to understand what it means to dwell richly and sustainably for many generations on the land.

We put a great deal of emphasis on owning property and on what we call "property rights" in America. Many people put a down payment on a mortgage for a parcel of property and then claim their "right" to abuse that land to satisfy their whims, desires, or schemes to make a profit off the land. In my view, any new settler, as well as many people who have lived in a rural area for many years, would do well to understand the place wherein they dwell before claiming any "rights" to use the water for development, to mine, log, graze domesticated livestock, kill predators (such as mountain lions and bears), or cut more roads across the landscape.

I feel part of Redwood Valley, but I know that I will never own property there. I can still speak for the valley as I know it, however. I can lobby to maintain its integrity as an entity, a being. The common good of a community, to me, is not restricted in value to the total tax dollars assessed on timber logged-off watersheds like Redwood Valley. The common good includes maintaining the integrity of the land for itself over the long term.

WHERE WE ARE IS WHERE WE'RE AT

A nyone seeking to enter the life of a place walks into that place in a certain historical situation. Misunderstanding that historical situation and the forces that created the place can have tragic results, for the new settler and for the land. As I write these lines, for example, developers have gone to the county planning commission seeking to rezone portions of Redwood Valley, near the paved state highway that transverses the valley, into five acre parcels. Developers want to pave the lower six miles of the road leading to the Home Ranch to make easier, quicker access for new settlers who want a "country setting" for their homes with convenient access to jobs in the city.

When the road is paved, the remoteness of the ranch will decrease, a remoteness that has helped preserve some of the possibilities for survival of bear, grouse, deer, and occasional eagle. Already some hunters use the road as easy access to poach. Some people bring packs of dogs out to the valley on the dirt road to train the dogs to hunt bear. The hunters put radio collars on their dogs so they can direct them and track their movements.

Building new roads or paving existing roads into semi-remote, wild places, rarely contributes to increasing the richness of life in that place. It may take generations for new settlers to learn to know and intimately feel the presence of a place. Richard learned from his ancestors but has had to adapt to the historical condition of Redwood Valley in the late twentieth century.

We all have a responsibility to care for and participate in the restoration of the North American continent wherever we dwell on it. That means we are embarking on a journey home. Home is a specific place, for me, not a generalized, abstract construct. I hear people urging us to become "planetary citizens," and I hear terms such as "global village," but our daily lives must always be lived in specific places like Redwood Valley. "Global Village" is, to me, an oxymoron.

During our lives we can experience, attempt to understand, identify, with only a small part of the earth. Some New Age thinkers suggest that humans are becoming the eyes and ears of the earth, the consciousness of the earth. Such statements, it seems to me, continue to place humans at the center of the cosmological drama. In all likelihood there will be no global political solution to the environmental crisis of the 1990s. And even if the United Nations agreed to any global action plans, these plans or treaties or agreements in the short term, during the next decade, would only remotely and in the most abstract way apply to the Home Ranch or help to restore the natural processes of Redwood Valley. It seems to me that our responsibility is to work, to dwell, to live wherever we are and to heal our relationship with that particular place on the earth. Until our lives become part of a specific place, our identity part of a specific place, we can relate only abstractly to the whole earth.

WHERE WE'RE NOT IS NOT WHERE WE'RE AT

Some of us are embarking on the journey home, a journey of discovery of our sense of place in specific bioregions on this earth. All the while, there are others who argue that humans have a destiny to begin huge projects to develop, to "terraform," other planets (i.e. "greening planets" by transforming them into a habitat for humans). We read of scientists who propose that "our next home," as a species, will be Mars. One scientist suggests that Mars is a "corpse" and bringing it "back to life" would be a "miracle," yet he expressed the hope that humans could accomplish such a miracle ("Our Next Home," *Life*, May, 1991. "Can Mars Be Made Hospitable to Humans?," *New York Times*, Tuesday, Oct. 1, 1991, p. B5).

True believers in the ideology that produced the Age of Exuberance celebrated the 500th anniversary of Christopher Columbus' first voyage to the "new world" by asking for public support and financing to continue the hubris of the past five hundred years. They want to "develop" Mars for human settlement during the next five hundred years. The project could, to these scientists, engineers, and others who propose it, provide a new vision, a new challenge for humanity. Terraforming Mars would be the largest engineering project ever undertaken in the history of civilization. The project could be undertaken only by huge bureaucracies and would require enormous allocations of money, scientific expertise, and centralized control. Proponents suggest that such a project could provide a stimulus for technology, boost the economies of nations participating in the project, and elevate national morale. They see it as a project that would bring life to another planet, furthering the highest human purpose in the solar system—life seeding.

From an ethical, and a deep ecology perspective, the proposal is even more provocative and disturbing. The project to terraform Mars is the largest, most extravagant, and logical extension of the mind-set that created the Age of Exuberance—excess, deficit spending, huge public works projects built without concern for ecological integrity of specific places—and the excessive use of technology to control, dominate, subjugate, and simplify vast areas of the North American continent. There are many social services in this nation that desperately need scarce funds. Scientific talent is needed to address such issues as AIDS and cancer, ozone depletion and global warming. Yet proponents of the Mars project want to embark on a mad scheme to totally humanize another planet.

Philosophical questions concerning the Mars project are even more provocative than economic questions. Is the destiny of the human species to "seed" other planets? If, as suggested in this book, the human species is a leaf on the tree of life, do we have a right or responsibility or obligation to direct the evolution of the tree of life? In order to "seed" life on Mars, what life-forms will be declared as "unnecessary" on Earth?

How many places on this earth would be disrupted, developed, and altered in the name of serving the needs of the Mars project? Would the overriding vision and power of the vast bureaucracies necessary for the Mars project be used to invade valleys and mountains deemed necessary to support this project on Earth? By going to Mars, is there anything that we, as humans, can learn about becoming natives of earth, natives of local regions on this earth, as full of life and adapted to our small homeland, valley, mountain or stretch of seashore as the red squirrel is to Mount Graham?

We witness the arrogance of some scientific and government institutions when the leaders of these institutions define some overriding "national interest" which somehow is used to justify destroying local habitat. On Mount Graham in southern Arizona, a consortium—including NASA, the University of Arizona, and the Vatican—is constructing a huge telescope to probe interstellar space. Some critics suggest that the project on Mount Graham could also be used in developing the "star wars" missile and satellite weapons system. Biological scientists have determined that Mount Graham is the home of a rare and endangered red squirrel. Only a few of the squirrels live on the mountain. The mountain is their home. Construction activities, wildlife biologists say, will disrupt their home and reduce the possibility of maintaining a viable population of red squirrels on the mountain.

Many humans have been caught up by the vision of "new lands," "new visionary prospects" over the five hundred years since Columbus' momentous voyage. Yet these conquests led to massive disruptions to the habitat of nonhuman life-forms, genocide against indigenous peoples in the "new world," and they transformed complex ecosystems into monocultures of a few crops for human use—sugar cane, tobacco, cattle, sheep, wheat, corn, rice (Crosby, *Ecological Imperialism*). Must we repeat the mistakes of our ancestors?

BIOREGIONAL HOMES

B ioregional studies are multifaceted mindful observations of the immediate region within which we dwell. They involve us in daily, seasonal, yearly, and longer-term cycles in change and evolution. Metaphors and descriptive theories are used to frame humans within the larger, ecocentric frame. By understanding some of the ways of nature, through the narrative stories of modern science, we "see" humans in a more compassionate way. Dualism is understood as an illusion. To work for the long-term well-being of any human beings, we must work with the ecocentric cycles, which have intrinsic worth and "right" to existence beyond any short-term "instrumental" worth they have to humans. When we become ecocentric, we can look at humans with love and respect and work to develop human communities that are ecologically sustainable. As Bruce Byers, director of environmental studies at Naropa Institute in Boulder, Colorado, writes, "On an endangered Earth, anthropocentrism can be misanthropy if it promotes further ecological degradation" ("Deep Ecology and Its Critics: A Buddhist Perspective," 1992).

Bioregions have "soft" boundaries and are not political entities. A bioregion is the area a person or community is most intimate with in the whole of the earth. Bioregional studies include personal experiences of connecting with the energy of our home place and understanding of the geological history of our home place, the soil of our home place, and the contemporary human geography, vegetation, and history of human land-use in our bioregion. Bioregional studies are fundamentally the study of person in place. Author and farmer Wendell Berry has said that if you don't know *where* you are, you don't know *who* you are. Berry identifies with his Kentucky farm country. Writers such as Wallace Stegner, Edward Abbey, and Dave Foreman identified with the American West as "placed persons."

Bioregional studies foster sensitivity to the contours of the land in one's home place, to the vegetation and seasonal changes, the smells, tastes, moods, and feelings of the place wherein one dwells. Placeness involves the senses, emotions, and intellect in the ongoing richness, including the richness of death and decay, of a particular place. With such placeness comes intimate affection and understanding and love of the bioregion as part of one's self. The placed person naturally takes responsibility for his or her home place.

In bioregional studies with my students in northwestern California I begin with the Humboldt Bay region, including all the streams flowing into Humboldt Bay. I ask students to listen to what scientists say about the complex faults underlying the Humboldt Bay region where the Pacific plate, the North American plate, and the Gorda plate meet at a triple-junction. A fissure across the Pacific Ocean basin called the Mendocino escarpment and fracture zone is the locus of many, many earthquakes in our bioregion. This is earthquake country, and the rate of geologic uplift of the mountains is one of the highest in the world.

We take field trips to work on stream restoration projects, learn about the forces that cut the valleys, human changes in the valleys—road building, ranching, logging—that have changed the load of material, called sediment, in the streams. We look for animals in the forest and learn from biologists about the "edge effect," wherein creation of an opening such as a clearcut can affect the whole forest, including the survival ability of animals that live in the deep woods by reducing their range and living space and disrupting their foraging areas and feeding habits.

We make a pilgrimage to our decommissioned local nuclear reactor—now in the process of "cooling down." The radioactive fuel rods are no longer used to generate heat to generate steam to turn turbines to generate electricity for distribution by a system of wires to subscribers in this area. The radioactive rods are stored in vats of water, going through their "half life," decay of radioactive particles. The rods are stored at the reactor site near the mouth of Humboldt Bay in an area that geologists tell us is riddled with surface faults.

In our pilgrimage we both honor the power of the nuclear reactor and make a ritual of our approach to the fence surrounding the reactor. Students write poems, sing songs that they created, even perform dances that symbolize the decay of radioactive particles. Driving back through town after our pilgrimage, we try to imagine ourselves a hundred years in the future. If we just arrived in town, a hundred years hence, how would we "make sense" of the development patterns—of shopping malls, traffic jams, pulp mills, hillsides clearcut and covered with brush, cattle grazing and "industrial parks," on filled-in wetlands? That was all part of the late twentieth century strategy that politicians called, in the old days, "economic development."

Bioregional studies—grounded in studies of ecology and conservation biology; grounded in concern for "seeing" our lives in larger perspectives; grounded in longer time frames than are usually considered; grounded in deep questioning; grounded in the search for ecosophy; and, grounded in our authentic, intuitive responses, with careful consideration of our emotional states of being—help us transcend the dualism of materialism vs. spirituality, of conservation vs. preservation, of people vs. spotted owls.

Poets and artists during the Romantic era of the eighteenth and nineteenth centuries went to the English countryside and to the Swiss Alps to experience wilder nature, more wild at least than the nature of smog-filled industrial cities. Some poets wrote of their *sublime* experiences in nature.

Few people during the late twentieth century describe visits to toxic waste sites or to overgrazed areas of designated wilderness as sublime, but such experiences can be powerful and empowering and can broaden our identification. When we understand our human energy as part of the ongoing flow of energy in the cosmos, we are then able to seek harmony with all energy.

"Healing the wounds" of our childhood is important within the context of ending our denial, accepting our responsibility toward our bioregion, and grounding our actions in what is happening during our lifetime in the larger frame of ongoing change in natural processes on the earth.

In his book *The Klamath Knot,* David Rains Wallace suggests that the age of myth has not ended, but is beginning. Myths are narratives that bring forth what is true. We need strong, powerful new myths concerning human beings in the context of ecosophical wisdom. Through our deep experiences in our home region, we develop ecosophy. Without a vision of the good life based in the realities of our home region, how can we hope to encourage our children to become native?

As natives of our home bioregion we can still appreciate the earth as the once and future home of our species. Our actions on the home front, it seems to me, should be devoted to becoming natives of our own bioregion wherever that is—in Redwood Valley or Appalachia, the Canyonlands of southern Utah, or the Los Angeles River basin. Our work is grounded in intimate identification with our home place.

From a deep ecological perspective, humans have no right to diminish the life quality of whole ecosystems or of species that are native to specific ecosystems. It is time to come home, to pay attention to the lifestyles of the small, quiet, even humble beings who co-dwell with us in specific biomes, specific valleys, mountains, plains, deserts and coasts. Becoming native to our own lives, to the place wherein we dwell, is a noble, vital, enthralling, passionate, and entirely appropriate endeavor—by far more appropriate than terraforming Mars.

And so I come again to Redwood Valley. I return to the Home Ranch for the summer solstice. As the long evening shadows fade into twilight, Richard brings out one of the drums given to him by an old woman on the Klamath, which in turn was given to her by a shaman before the great burning of the Yurok villages by the U.S. military. Richard calls up one of the old prayers and chants in Yurok, the ancient words. After the prayer we sit quietly in the meadow, watching the stars. Why "develop," terraform, colonize Mars, I ask myself, when we can participate in a world "not half yet made," as John Muir said. It would take many lifetimes for me to understand this small mountain valley.

The next morning I drive back to my home on the coast. I hear the sound of chain saws whining as I descend the dirt road from the Home Ranch to the state highway. I feel anger, frustration, despair, even grief as I see two new logging roads bulldozed since I drove to the ranch two days before. I want to reach out and stop the loggers, but I know that it will take much more than just stopping logging on this particular day. It will take the development of a mind-set that appreciates this valley for its own sake. I know that all those who understand the intuition of deep ecology have experienced the kind of suffering I feel when I see inappropriate human actions. I know that people we recognize as voices of the land, supporters of the deep, long-range ecology movement experienced this suffering—Henry David Thoreau, John Muir, Mary Austin, Rachel Carson, Ed Abbey, Annie Dillard, and many, many more. During this last decade of the twentieth century we work to stop the destruction.

CHAPTER 5

THINKING LIKE A WATERSHED

I'm sitting with my friend Bob on the banks of Jacoby Creek, a small, coastal creek that drains into Humboldt Bay. This creek, like hundreds of others in the Pacific Northwest, has been greatly altered during the past century by the interaction of human activities—especially logging and cattle grazing in the stream system. The creek is very slowly healing by periodic flushing of sediments from eroding hillsides into Humboldt Bay during major storms. Bob has been walking this "hydrological unit," as scientists call a watershed—the cup of ridges, gorges, and bottomlands that enclose the creek. For nearly two decades he has been walking, sitting sometimes, working on erosion control and revegetation projects, thinking about and meditating on the processes of this small watershed.

Bob discusses his work in Jacoby Creek watershed:

> Sometimes I will be working by the creek, or hiking along a trail and suddenly I become aware that I am part of the wildness of the place, the rippling flow of the creek. If you watch the creek awhile, then look at the land, you can see the land rippling. Along the bank there are snags and stumps from the logging days. I probably would have had some part in taking down the forests if I had lived here one hundred years ago. I feel myself as part of the future of the creek, the whole watershed, following its own tendency to heal itself. There's a poem "Crossing Brooklyn Ferry"—do you know it? Walt Whitman calls to the future from the past. I hope I

can call to people in the present and tell them what a wonderful future we can have.

I can only start the repair process. Hopefully, I can make a lot of people aware of the potential and possibilities for the creek. But for the creek physically, in my lifetime, I can work for the remaining wild places along the creek. I can do some work to stabilize portions of the streambed which have been eroding at faster than natural rates due to human activities in the watershed over the past hundred years. I've planted willows along the banks, helped stabilize streambanks from erosion in a few small sections, dug out some road crossings, and pulled out some invading foreign plants: pampas grass, Scotch broom, and English ivy. But this small watershed, and virtually all the watersheds I've seen in northwestern California that have been fooled with, will take both a concerted community effort and a long time to heal, longer than my lifetime.

My real work here is to learn from the creek, not direct the future or even presume to restore it. When you think about it, restoration is benevolent hubris. We can't restore this creek, or any other, to the condition it was in before European settlers began logging. Imagine what this watershed, its estuary, and Humboldt Bay, were like. This temperate rainforested valley was teeming with wildlife, towering climax forested vistas from ridge to ridge, bank to bank runs of spawning steelhead and salmon, elk, grizzly bears, seals, and otters all abundant here—maybe even an occasional condor soaring overhead. Only a century ago this valley was wild, and I see my best role as helping create the space to allow as much of that wildness to return as possible.

Bob calls himself a "friend of the watershed" and is a co-founder of the emerging Jacoby Creek Land Trust. He is not a property owner in the watershed—or anywhere else—but he works daily with property owners. He started working on the process of healing this watershed during a year when he lived in a rented house along the stream. During all seasons of that year he took hikes up the stream.

I often took my six-year-old daughter with me. She asked questions: "Why does that landslide go into the creek? Are there fish in there? How long will it take the trees to grow back?"

I saw what was happening during my walks. I didn't understand why these events were occurring. I could still feel the wildness of the land even after massive recent clearcuts. I saw rock quarries which had obliterated drainages. The stream in storm flow is a light mocha brown from the eroding hillsides, cattle overgrazing along the stream, and species of plants which I knew were not native to the area becoming established. I felt an obligation to use my knowledge and training as a biologist for an unrecognized, little-financed purpose—making known and correcting the abuse of our long-term commonlands which we call "private property."

During the early 1970s, when the federal government was giving grants to local governments, Bob and a friend, Alison, obtained a one year grant to study this watershed with a team of six people. They studied water quality, fisheries, erosion control, and native revegetation. They also gathered information on the watershed land-use history, soils, archaeology—all the information they could find in government reports, projects written by graduate students at the local university, and older accounts written by European pioneers.

A woman who lived up the creek took beautiful pictures for our final report. The photos were gems: a stretch of headwater stream lined with mature alder trees in winter for the front cover, and an arc of shorebirds entering the estuary for the back cover." Their report, *The Jacoby Creek Watershed Study*, became a popular source for local residents and students and a base-line study of the condition of the watershed. "The biggest stir we created in the community at that time was that we documented levels of coliform in the water of the stream which far exceeded state standards for water quality." The study was used in educating local residents and as a source for people presenting testimony before the county planning commission and the Jacoby Creek Water District. The district was considering subdivision plans without adequate sewage treatment provisions.

We named, in the study, some of the small tributary streams running into the creek for the first time. Names seem to help people to identify with the place. Instead of referring to their small stream as a "class 2, intermittent stream," the way it was labeled in state documents, they could say "I live on Snag Creek, or Steep Creek, or Rebel Creek." We named the headwaters the *Barunda,* a sacrosanct place. The long-term goal is to give the Native American Wiyot name back to the stream. I think names of places should be a changing and evolving part of the local language. Mostly names given by European settlers denote property. They aim to demystify place.

After this first project on the watershed, Bob participated in other projects, most centered around concern for rapidly declining salmon and steelhead fisheries. In 1989 he met a landowner who had recently bought some creekside land, who engaged him to stabilize his failing streambank.

With his daughter, and a shifting group of volunteers, Bob resloped the bank to a stable grade; then he revegetated the bare slope by burying large willow logs, planting cuttings, and mulching. After this treatment the vulnerable inside meander was covered with hog wire. Then his team of workers planted trees such as maple, spruce, and redwood, which would eventually give strength to the streambank.

Groups of students from the local university helped to create a demonstration riparian area. One task they worked on was bringing logs down to the base of the stream where the mountains meet the coastal plain. The logs were put there to help make habitat for all kinds of creatures. Fallen trees, carried downstream by periodic flooding, used to be deposited on the floodplain. Most people don't know that a forest existed on the floodplain before it was cleared and all the stumps pulled for agriculture. The logs help to tell the story to schoolchildren who regularly visit the area.

Bob and his team of volunteers also pulled out poison hemlock, an invasive weed that had held the ground stable against cattle grazing. Bob does not call this "restoration work." "I am leery about trying to make a science out of restoration. I think that human participation in the recovery process needs to be considered somewhere between a religion and an art—a sacred work based on provincial knowledge passed along from master to apprentices, an accumulation of generations' love of the land."

Through the first creek project, Bob has worked with landowners who are not pro-development. After the discovery of high levels of bacterial pollution in the stream, a building moratorium was placed on a part of the watershed by the regional water-quality control board. These concerned citizens then went on to be elected to the Jacoby Creek Water Board, which has responsibility for some aspects of water distribution to households in the floodplain.

After working for over a decade in the watershed and in spite of a lot of good things happening to benefit the watershed, Bob sees little material evidence of positive and healing processes on Jacoby Creek. The intensity of logging of the upper watershed by timber companies has continued unabated. Bob feels that state regulatory agencies responsible for forestry, fish and game, and water quality all have narrowly defined bureaucratic purposes that keep them from dealing effectively with the degradation of the biological and physical entity that comprises the watershed. "The spaces between their regulations are large enough to drive a loaded lumber truck through," he says.

> The best thing that has come of my work is a spirit of caring by some of the property owners who live in the watershed. Whether I talk to old-timers who were engaged in logging, or their relatives, or with property owners who moved here from places they saw trashed, abused, degraded, I think that none of them want to see the places they love destroyed again. I mean, they transfer some of the sense of loss and feeling of concern from the place they remember in their childhoods to this place. In the past property owners were primarily concerned with how much their property would sell for, but now a growing number of people who live in Jacoby Creek are concerned with nonmonetary values. They care about the place. They don't see the forest as primarily a resource to be logged and developed for monetary values. I see many property owners who

want to take positive steps about preserving the landscape they love. However, they don't want to be overtly political. Some people in the watershed see the efforts of some environmental activists as being counterproductive and polarizing.

Most likely Jacoby Creek won't be the focus of national environmental groups. It is not a famous place, not a grand, spectacular valley. There are few trees in the valley over a hundred years old. It will be at least a hundred years before any forests in the valley really tend toward climax again even under most favorable conditions and if humans can restrain themselves from logging the young trees for that long. But for those of us who live here and know this place, there is still a quality of wildness in the valley. I believe if people can understand the state of the watershed now as compared to what it was a hundred years ago, and the direction present use is leading, then maybe they can begin to understand how interconnected the whole system is—and I mean the system of the Klamath-Siskiyou bioregion and earth.

Bob sees his role as a person who provides information, stimulates landowners, mediates between different groups living in the Jacoby Creek watershed. "When we got property owners together who valued the landscape, they saw they were not alone in caring about the place. They saw the value of cooperating with each other. The Jacoby Creek Land Trust grew out of this group. The goal of the land trust is to find a way over the long term of the community to save the open space we treasure."

The land trust approach is a way local people can govern land use without having a government agency step in. This approach appeals to many people who distrust government agencies. The land trust, which legally is a conservancy, can acquire conservation easements, development rights, and even hold title to property. Through deed restrictions, roads and structures, including houses, could be prohibited in ecologically sensitive areas and timber could not be logged.

Besides the land trust, another group formed, which is proactive. This group, the Jacoby Creek Protection Association, has sued the State Department of Forestry over timber harvest plans that threaten increased erosion and impair the habitat of the few remaining salmon and steelhead in the creek. The activism of property owners and those, such as Bob, who identify with the watershed is frequently not as dramatic as confrontations in front of bulldozers. There are times when concerned people must stand in front of bulldozers or demonstrate in front of the offices of big timber corporations to protest such practices as aerial spraying of herbicides. But long term healing of human damaged landscapes begins only when people who are dwelling in a place start respecting and working together both in reactive and proactive ways, and develop land-use plans for whole watersheds. When people share a common, ecocentric sense of purpose and community in the land wherein they dwell, then they begin healing themselves as they work with the tendency of the land to heal itself.

People become involved in helping to further the healing tendency of a place out of a sense of being true to their feelings, their broader and deeper sense of identification, out of a sense of community and out of fear that what they care for, indeed love, is vulnerable to destruction by short term economic development.

In the early 1990s nothing is certain about the future of this watershed—or many like it in the Pacific Northwest. More logging plans have been submitted for the last hard-to-reach stands of mature trees on steep headwater areas, and more subdivisions have been proposed for the floodplain and on the ridges that provide spectacular views of Humboldt Bay. Some property owners want to log their property to pay off debts, pay for their children's education, pay for comfort in their older years, or even to "get more sunlight" for decks, gardens, lawns, and solar panels. Still, a spirit of concern is growing in the valley—not as fast as most environmental activists might want—but still growing.

The water of Jacoby Creek pumps life into Humboldt Bay—its nutrient-rich waters support microorganisms, plants, and animals in the estuary. If the levees, built by engineers years ago in the now-discredited notion of channelizing small streams for flood control—for conversion of flood plains and wetlands to farmland, pasture and development sites—can be breached or removed, the stream would be free to meander again, to find its own course. The biological productivity of the estuary would begin to return.

Bob's vision for the future of the Jacoby Creek watershed can be magnified thousands of times by people working in small watersheds across North America: "I believe that richness of life will return; humans again will be guided by a thoughtful mythology that people are only one among many codependent species. I dream of humans becoming native again, indigenous to the flow of time, contributing to the richness of biological diversity. I probably will never own property in the legal sense, in this place, but this watershed is part of me, and I intend to help the healing process as long as I live. My vision of the longer term—how long? centuries—is reestablishing viable connections between this watershed and others around it with corridors where little human use occurs. Somehow I think a complex biological diversity will return when humans realize that their actions—which take place in a short time period but have long-term consequences—influence the richness of present and future human lives as well as the whole system."

ECOSTERY: ANOTHER VISION OF DWELLING IN PLACE

Bob's work in a small, coastal watershed in California is an example of work that needs to be done in hundreds of small watersheds in California and thousands across North America. This community based watershed work needs to be supported by appropriate social organizations and by public policy. In the following sections of this chapter, suggestions for new social organizations and suggestions for changes in public policy affecting how we relate to large river systems are discussed. In the broad sense of lifestyle, as used in this book, our actions include not only our daily habits and our attitudes, but also the kinds of social organizations we support. The ecostery and the land trust are two examples of social organizations worthy of investments of time, energy and contributions. Both the ecostery and the land trust empower participants in their daily lives and in their dealings with large public agencies such as water quality boards or the U.S. Army Corps of Engineers.

The ecostery concept derives its origin from monastic forms of land-based communities. During the Middle Ages in Europe, and in some Buddhist cultures in Asia, the monastery served the purpose of economy, spiritual growth, and personal security. The monastic form is associated with hierarchy and patriarchy in European history, but such characteristics are not inherent to this form. The underlying principle of a monastic form in Europe was the rule, usually outlined by the founder of an order, such as the rule of Saint Benedict for the Benedictine Order. The rule is a general set of principles or precepts that guide members of the order. Monastic form has possibilities for decentralized, more or less self-sustaining communities, committed to the work of bioregional restoration over long periods of time without the demand for profits or centralized power. Alan Drengson, a professor of environmental philosophy at the University of Victoria, has suggested the term *ecostery* to refer to such a form of community, which could be appropriate for the 1990s and into the twenty-first century. Drengson sketches some of the characteristics of ecostery.

Ecosteries can be formed by local groups and individuals in both urban and rural areas. "Normally, ecosteries will be formed as nonprofit societies or corporations, and they will be accessible to the public. . . . Ecosteries will promote environmental research and education, restoration and preservation of land; they will be devoted to the cooperative cultivation of ecological wisdom and harmony."

Drengson considers "ecosophic practices" as the rule for ecosteries. "Ecosophic practices are based on learning the wisdom of the Earth. Ecosophy is the wisdom of dwelling in a place and the wisdom to dwell in a place harmoniously with Nature."

The word *ecostery* was formed by combining elements from *monastery* and *ecology*. "Monastery," says Drengson, "implies a place where spiritual discipline and practice are the central purpose. In the case of ecosteries, the focus will be on Earth spirituality, since a major dimension of the environmental crisis reflects a spiritual crisis, a breakdown in the spirit of community in the larger sense, which includes not just humans, but also other beings."

Ecosteries will be non-partisan and non-sectarian. Drengson sees the ecostery movement as an important part of deep, long-range ecology movement because it emphasizes lifestyle and practice while other parts of the movement emphasize political change and changes in social policy.

Drengson says, "The philosophy of the Ecostery Movement will cultivate practices which give humans contact with their own wild nature and with Nature's wildness. These practices will be holistic and trans-disciplinary. They will bring together all human pursuits from art to engineering, in a comprehensive, visionary way in practical and ceremonial activities. By means of first-hand experience, and ecosophic spiritual disciplines, humans can deepen their sensibilities to Nature. Through deepening our sensibilities to Nature and to each other, we will be able to restore and renew all relationships on every level, so that they become harmonious and manifest mutual understanding. From this understanding will be generated an environmental ethic that is not an externally imposed code, but an internally realized respect and compassion for all beings" ("The Ecostery Foundation of North America (TEFNA): Statement of Philosophy," *The Trumpeter,* Winter 1990, pp. 12–16).

THINKING LIKE A BIOREGION

Jacoby Creek is an extremely small watershed compared to other rivers of California—the Sacramento, Klamath, Trinity, Eel, and Smith rivers, for example. And these river systems are small compared to the Columbia, Fraser, Colorado, Missouri, and Mississippi. The conquest of the West for the past two hundred years of American history has been a saga of "internal development," and much of that development has meant taming the great rivers of this continent with water resource development projects—dams, levees, dikes, and channelization projects (conversion of naturally meandering rivers, streams, and tidal inlets into permanent rock- or concrete-lined ditches). From the first canal projects on the Potomac during Washington's presidency through the building of the Erie Canal, the expansion of the railroad system across the continent in 1869 through the Roosevelt New Deal programs to tame the Columbia, the Colorado, the Tennessee, and the Missouri, the river systems of the continent have been used by humans as a source of resources for industrial civilization. In the process of this development great biological diversity has been destroyed or severely damaged. The magnitude of these changes is only now beginning to be understood by ecologists.

In the American West, this process led to what one writer has called the "Cadillac desert." Marc Reisner concludes that the federal development projects of western rivers cost the integrity of the river systems, a cost not accounted for in the taxpayer dollars that paid for the physical structures—dams, canals, and pipelines. These projects were "a vandalization of both our natural heritage and our economic future, and the reckoning has not even begun" (*Cadillac Desert,* p. 503).

Ninety percent of the wetlands in California have been destroyed—due to diking, dredging, draining and filling—the habitat for millions of migratory birds has vanished. The salmon runs of the Sacramento, the Columbia, the Klamath are almost gone. Now, at the end of the century, those who speak for the salmon and steelhead, or for the habitat of any threatened or endangered species, or for endangered wetlands, river habitat, and wild places, must confront massive government and quasi-government agencies—the Tennessee Valley Authority, BC Hydro, Bonneville Power Authority, Army Corps of Engineers, U.S. Bureau of Reclamation—and with agencies "owning" rights to water or electric power generated from these massive projects.

In California the "water wars" continue to be fought between large farmers, water districts, urban users, fishers, and environmental groups. Officials of the state of California recognize the need to maintain in-stream flows for the health of the riparian system, including the health of rapidly declining, and even threatened and endangered species of fish. Increasing human population in California cannot be used as an excuse for drawing off water from the Sacramento River system or any other river system, when the draw down threatens the life support of that system. Water conservation measures both in urban areas and on farms will need to be intensified. Less water will be available to large agricultural corporations, and more water, especially during years of lower than average rainfall, will have to be allocated to in-stream flow to maintain habitat for threatened, river-dependent species.

Water allocation in the gigantic Central Valley Project of California was changed by Congress in 1992 to require more in-stream flow for the benefit of wildlife and fisheries. The water reform act of 1992 is only the beginning of changes which need to be made in federal state water policy. Continued political efforts to change water laws will be made by reform environmental groups to guarantee, even during drought years, sufficient water to serve the needs of diverse life forms in watersheds. Concurrently, individuals and groups of property owners will continue their efforts to protect the integrity of places from development schemes by using land trusts and conservancies. Under U.S. federal law and California state law, trusts and conservancies are becoming powerful tools for speaking for the integrity of place and for the rights of far future generations of nonhumans who will inhabit that place.

Land trusts and conservancies can become powerful countervailing forces to government development agencies and corporations. The Tennessee River Gorge Trust, established by interested landowners in 1986, for example, took on the powerful Tennessee Valley Authority and has protected 12,000 acres in the Tennessee River Gorge north of Chattanooga that was proposed for a dam site. The Trust continues to raise money to buy key properties in the gorge and to manage the properties for values other than the production of hydroelectric power (*Sierra,* March 1992, p. 58).

Land conservancies can be national, statewide, or very local and as reactive or proactive as their members want, as long as their conservation activities are judged to be nonpolitical and of public benefit by the Internal Revenue Service. A land conservancy can negotiate with public agencies, engage in educational efforts, save historic structures and historic landscapes such as gardens, manage land through conservation easements, participate in the planning process for regional and local plans, and engage residents in healing damaged landscapes through use of volunteers. People who never expect to "own" land can feel part of the process of helping a place by participating in conservancy activities.

An important connection is shaping up between agricultural groups and conservationists jointly using the tool of conservation easements. Institutes such as the Land Institute in Kansas are experimenting with use of perennial grasses and other sustainable agricultural practices. Sustainable farming practices need to be protected from the vicissitudes of the commodities and real estate markets.

An example of grassroots activism to begin the restoration of a watershed by removing an aging dam can be seen on the Olympic peninsula of Washington, where local groups are proposing the destruction of the Eleyaha Dam. This small mountain river once supported a run of salmon that was described as so thick one could not see the water during their spawning run. Removing this dam could symbolize the movement to restore free-flowing rivers or portions of rivers in many bioregions in North America.

EMERGING PUBLIC POLICY AND LAND-USE PRACTICES FOR THE NEXT CENTURY

Public policy during the 1990s will likely be focused on stopping certain destructive activities on public lands and private lands that were widely accepted during the past century but are no longer appropriate. For example, given the current condition of forests in America and the small amount, relative to the total, of ancient forests on public lands, extensively researched arguments have been advanced for virtually ending large scale commercial logging on national forest lands throughout the United States. Proposals have been made to "rest the West." After a century of extensive development activities on public lands—cattle and sheep grazing, vast mining operations, logging and road building, oil and gas development—resting the American Great Plains and the Great Basin, as well as the mountain states and the Pacific Northwest, seems a reasonable proposal. "Rest the West" may be a slogan worth using as a basis for drastic changes in public land policies, a phrase to replace "multiple use" or "land of many uses."

Frank Popper, a geographer who has studied human settlement patterns and changes in the northern Great Plains, argues that depopulation has already begun in the approximately seven to nine million acres he calls the "Buffalo Commons." Declining population in the northern Great Plains offers the opportunity to restore the Buffalo Commons. Nine million acres of prairie and grasslands could, over the next hundred years, become grazing area for buffalo and antelope again. Dams could be removed on the Missouri and on other rivers of the Great Plains. Riparian habitat could reemerge along the rivers, and migratory flocks of birds could again flourish. Changes in the northern Great Plains are occurring now because of the convergence of many factors: overuse of the underground water sources, decreasing economic viability of family farms, declining productivity of soils to produce crops including forage crops, and the desire of many people to live in towns and cities rather than on isolated homesteads.

Phasing out most grazing on public lands of the American West could be done in a manner that protects the lifestyles of most existing small scale ranchers who wish to remain on the land. As ranchers die, or leave the land, grazing leases would expire, and no new leases would be given. Children of ranching families who identify with the land, the bioregion within which they live, could find work restoring, watching over the tendencies of restoration, just as Bob and his friends are caring for Jacoby Creek.

Structural changes are already occurring in the timber industry throughout North America. Automation, changes in ownership patterns of timber lands, changes in regulations of private timber lands by states and provinces—as well as failure of tree plantations in some regions of North America—may lead to taxes on wood products to provide funds for restoration work, higher prices for lumber, and a search for alternatives to wood products. Government incentives, which encouraged rapid rates of cutting in national forests in the United States and provincial crown lands in Canada, are likely to end. Timber, according to some analysts, should be treated as a nonrenewable resource much as we treat natural gas or oil or precious metals.

The challenge for many rural communities in Montana, Idaho, California, Oregon, and Washington, as well as British Columbia and southeastern Alaska, is to find ecosophic community lifestyles that are compatible with a sustainable culture and a sustainable economy. Diversified economies can replace the current unsustainable practice of cutting forests. Mechanisms in existing government programs to create training for jobs that benefit a green century—replanting forests, farming organically, restoring fisheries, developing sustainable forestry on private lands—can encourage people living in rural areas to assume responsibility for the continuing well-being of their bioregion.

Creativity and flexibility are required. Political activism is required. In California, as an example, groups interested in fisheries worked quietly for most of the 1980s "restoring" coastal rivers. Different groups—including those representing Native American, sport, commercial, and conservation interests—formed the California Salmon, Steelhead and Trout Restoration Federation. They raised funds for the physical rehabilitation of a few coastal streams, but engaged in little lobbying, litigation, or political campaigning. They made few political waves, preferring to work quietly, removing log-jams and improving habitat to allow salmon and steelhead to return and increase in numbers. However, by the early 1990s, despite the best efforts of volunteers, fish runs in all the major rivers of California were at historic lows. The Pacific Fish Management Council, a regulatory agency established under federal law, considered in 1992 banning all commercial fishing for salmon in the waters off northwest California, Oregon, and Washington.

In the early 1990s supporters of fisheries lost their innocence. They realized the futile effort of "restoring" decimated fisheries without confronting the timber corporations engaged in massive clearcutting of whole watersheds and government agencies such as the Bureau of Reclamation, Corps of Engineers, and the California Department of Water Resources. Grassroots restoration activities will not help fisheries unless the political decisions are made to consider whole watershed systems including the Trinity, Klamath, Sacramento, and San Joaquin in California.

Economic growth in California to a large extent has been based on interbasin transfer of massive amounts of water, to the detriment of rivers as living beings, and to the detriment of the beings dependent on the living rivers, including the fish. Speaking for the fish means confronting intransigent adversaries in politics. No amount of grassroots work by volunteers can help the salmon and steelhead runs, and no amount of "public education," discussing in public forums the ecology of fisheries, will help the fish, not until the decisions of agencies that control the massive system of dams, channels, and distribution of water are changed to favor the fisheries. In order for this to happen, the present status quo economy based on resource extractions and allocations must be confronted and radically altered.

Changing decisions concerning how this civilization approaches living rivers means accepting the fact that the development pattern—of settlement, agriculture, forestry, mining, massive urban aggregations—of the American West during the last century was an aberration and that continuing the programs and mental attitudes that fostered that pattern of development is no longer desirable and could not be sustained even if it were desirable. Then we can move on in the search for an ecocentric social policy that is well grounded in science and acceptable to communities that are seeking ecosophic lifestyles and economic stability.

Can we ever hope to live in harmony with nature unless we dream of whole systems and their richness of life, unless we change our personal lifestyles and also engage in political action?

Water, as many wisdom traditions tell us, is a great teacher. Dwelling in a watershed, working for the watershed as part of our larger identification, provides us with daily teachings in the search for ecosophy.

I met a person several years ago who had devoted most of the past decade to working for the Los Angeles River. When he first told some of his friends that he was working for the Los Angeles River, they laughed at him. They thought he was making a joke. "Los Angeles River" was an oxymoron to them. The "river" was channelized in a concrete levee from near its source to its mouth near Terminal Island in Los Angeles Harbor. It was dry much of the year, and some politicians proposed using the concrete riverbed as a supplemental road during rush hours on the freeways. This friend of the Los Angeles River said, "No, not a dead river at all. It is a living river. Look where willows grow through the cracks in the concrete. Look at those few sections of riverbed that are not concrete, and you will find life." And because of decisions concerning water quality that required several state and local agencies to upgrade sewage treatment in areas of Los Angeles and put the tertiary effluent into the river, there is now enough water in the river to kayak near the civic center of Los Angeles. Life is returning to the Los Angeles river system.

This friend of the Los Angeles River says that his own practice of finding meaning in his life involves caring for the life of the river. He proposes that community groups—Hispanic, Asian, groups in middle-class, predominately white suburban areas—all share the river as a living system. By cooperating to clean up the river, letting the life return to the river, their joint actions can be a focus for cleaning up relationships between people who share the river. Sharing means sharing with nonhuman beings, not only among humans. Sharing means accepting what is given by water, participating in the joys of life in and along the river, participating in the circle of life. Only within the ecocentric circle of all beings can sustainable human communities be developed.

SUGGESTIONS FOR NEW NATIVES

■ If you are considering buying property in a rural area, find a sympathetic green real estate agent who knows the area and is sympathetic to biocentric, bioregional perspectives.

■ If there is a local bioregion group in the region you are considering as a homeland, read its newsletter and if possible attend some of its gatherings. In the southern Appalachian region, for example, *Katuh* is a well-respected bioregional journal; *Talking Leaves* covers community building events in the Willamette Valley of Oregon; *Econews* covers Northwestern California.

■ Educate yourself in the land-use history, ecology, and environmental issues of the region. Is there a group that is tracking decisions concerning toxic waste dumps or nuclear reactors or chemical factories in your region?

■ If you are interested in forming or joining a land trust or land conservancy, contact the national organization for land trusts for model language for conservation easements on property and model charters for land trusts. A reliable real estate agent might be able to tell you how to contact a local land trust. Well-established land conservancies sometimes can provide advice for those seeking to establish new conservancy groups. The State Coastal Conservancy in Oakland, California, provides technical assistance to groups interested in establishing and operating a land trust. The Peninsula Open Space Trust in the San Francisco Bay

Area and the Santa Monica Mountains Conservancy in southern California are well-established models for land trust and conservancy groups forming in large metropolitan regions. The Mountains Restoration Trust, located in Malibu, California, is experienced in transferring development credits as a technique for preserving natural areas. While not a conservancy in the legal sense of the term, the Mount Diablo State Park support group in the East Bay region of the San Francisco metropolitan area is a model for protecting a large open space in a suburban region experiencing rapid population growth.

MAKING A HOME

My local newspaper recently carried a story about an entertainer who built a huge house in 1992 in the hills of the San Francisco Bay region near Fremont, California. According to reports, the entertainer, twenty-seven years old, built a 15,000-square-foot house, costing $6.5 million for himself, his wife, and his only child. The architect commented that the owner is young and willing to experiment with the latest in technology and design. The owner's willingness to try new things shows in his house just like it shows in his MTV videos. "This is all state-of-the-art stuff," the architect said. The house is described as including a fiber-optic lighting system in the bedroom that will create the illusion of starry skies, a twenty-eight-foot pond containing brightly colored carp, and a video wall sculpture consisting of nearly two dozen color monitors that can project single or multiple images.

By contrast, I have a friend also in his late twenties who became an ecoactivist (his own label) after he had worked for several years as a carpenter and plumber on extravagant houses built in the Reno, Nevada area. When he became a committed ecoactivist, he quit his job as a plumber. Lacking a regular income, he shared a storage unit with a friend for nearly a year. He slept in a sleeping bag he bought at a local thrift store and used a small camp stove to heat water for tea and soup. He then moved to Santa Cruz, California, to continue his work on environmental issues and lived in a tent in the woods near town, riding his bike to the office of an environmental group each day to organize population action campaigns. He perfected the art of dumpster diving—going into large metal trash containers usually placed behind supermarkets and restaurants—and ate most of his meals from still edible residuals thrown out by people who were fussy about their food.

These are extreme examples—most people live somewhere in between. Most people I have encountered say they want their own house, that is, a home. Home means having one's own space where one has a sense of security, a sense of personal expression. The conventional image of a homeowner is someone who has a stake in the community, a solid citizen, a respectable person. However, making a home means more than seeking social status or social prestige in a community. Making a home in whatever kind of dwelling unit—a house, a condominium, an apartment, a trailer, a mobile home, a camper on a motorized vehicle—means having some sense of control of the physical space where we eat, sleep, relax, study, engage in hobbies and work, exercise, meditate, and entertain guests.

In America the favored type of dwelling unit has been, and for millions of people remains, the free standing house. The house is the physical location of the home. A house can be an artifact, a physical object. A home is a place of emotional attachment. People may have a house where they "hang their hat," but still feel homeless, detached, without emotional commitment to the context of the house—the relationships with people in the household, with the neighborhood, with the community, with the geographical features of the site (soil, slope, drainage, vegetation, exposure to sunlight), and with the bioregion (relation to the nearest wild area, and the kinds of birds and animals which visit the local area during different seasons of the year). Becoming attuned to the ecological and social contexts of the house are essential elements for "being at home."

Homelessness is a psychological condition as well as a physical condition. Homelessness is only partially related to having a house. Some people may not own a residence, or have long term roots in a particular area, but they may still feel at home in the region wherein they dwell because they know the moods of the neighborhood. If they wander the streets of a city, they feel at home in their city. If they live in a rural area, they may feel at home in the mountains, or deserts, or prairies of their bioregion. Being at home means to be at home with the moods and rhythms of the valley wherein one dwells, or the moods and rhythms of the desert or the prairies or mountains wherein one dwells.

The distinction between household activities and dwelling in our home place is important when considering homelessness in America. People without a roof over their heads are usually referred to as "homeless people" in the media—a new category of people in our society. To call a person "homeless" raises multiple negative images—unemployed, incompetent, dirty, lacking a sense of social responsibility, careless in habits. These images indicate a lack of compassion for the suffering that homeless people experience—suffering from cold or extreme heat, lack of sanitation facilities, lack of a place for food storage and preparation, lack of personal security and a safe place for one's belongings, and vulnerability to personal attack.

The increasing visibility of homeless people on the streets of large cities and small towns, sleeping in public parks and on the streets of some relatively affluent neighborhoods, is described in the press and by some sociologists as a social problem. Gender, race, and age are important criteria differentiating how homeless people are treated—by the police, by casual bypassers, by public and private social welfare organizations—and how they cope with their homeless condition. Generalizations for one person without a house may not apply to other people without a house. For example, homeless women without children, we are told, are treated differently from homeless men. Stephanie Golden, in her book *The Women Outside— Meanings and Myths of Homelessness,* concludes that homeless women arouse intense negative feelings in many "respectable" homeowners. The "bag lady" is a prototype of the outsider, despised, feared, avoided, mysterious, without location in conventional imagery of the urban landscape. However, the mental landscape of being homeless is only partially explored by recent sociological studies.

The deeper, ecocentric meaning of homelessness is "lack of sense of place." Even for those people who have a roof over their heads, the mental landscape across the continent—of the large metropolis, of the small city, of the rural forest and farmland areas dominated by corporate industry—itself is alienating. As Paul Goodman and Lewis Mumford warned half a century ago, alienating people from the earth—the actual, real soil of the earth—is destructive to human fulfillment. Lewis Mumford in a series of books, including *The City in History,* demonstrated the difference between city and metropolis. The scale of a metropolis overwhelms the landscape. The city is different from the rural areas and from wild areas, but in the small city the social organizations, public rituals, and symbols are based on an understanding of the dependence of that city on the surrounding bioregion. Public rituals honor the bringing in of harvests, the return of the fishing season, or the change in seasons and the rhythm of life and death in natural cycles.

Ecophilosophers such as Gary Snyder and Wendell Berry write eloquently of rediscovering the ancient wisdom of making a home in our bioregion—learning the names of local plants, attuning to the changing seasons, and adjusting our behavior to the order of things as they are rather than imposing a humanized sense of order on the landscape. In this chapter, I discuss primarily our practice in the physical space of the house, or, in the jargon of the United States Census Bureau, the "dwelling unit." Following the themes of this book, I focus primarily on the choices and possibilities of homemakers—men and women, adults and children, older people and younger people—to make their daily habits in their place of residence part of their ecological consciousness practice.

Many people are already engaged in recycling, reducing their use of excess packaging, reusing. Many communities have laws and regulations that require some recycling or water and energy conservation. Many books and articles have been written on strategies to reduce consumption and waste in households. I draw upon this literature but encourage that changes in behavior toward the house (which is shorthand for any dwelling unit) can be part of our deepening understanding of our place in nature. I especially discuss the process of forming volunteer ecoteams whose members help each other to make changes in lifestyle.

Many housing units—indeed millions of housing units in the United States and Canada—are considered energy inefficient, poorly designed, and built with materials that are considered inappropriate by standards used in the 1990s. The vast differences in styles of building, size, location, and conditions of different structures makes any generalization problematic at best.

The different situations of people living in high rise apartment buildings in a cold climate and people living in suburban communities in the desert southwest call for different solutions on an individual household level. As with other comments in this book, the following comments are best considered suggestive, and possibly provocative, rather than definitive or dogmatic.

Consciousness practice in daily life, in the household, can enrich our attention to living. For example, a simple mindfulness practice taught by Thich Nhat Hanh, a Vietnamese Buddhist teacher who has frequently toured the United States, is based on an ancient technique.

In his teaching, Thich Nhat Hanh holds up a piece of newsprint and asks, "Do you see the clouds and the forests in this piece of paper?" He asks his students to move in their minds into the process of becoming newsprint. Where was the newspaper printed? What city? How was the newsprint transported from the paper mill to the printing factory? What was the process of stripping pulp fiber into pulp? Was the pulp created with chlorine processes or oxygenated delignification processes? Was dioxin a byproduct of the pulp process? Was the dioxin—a deadly chemical—spread into the water and air around the pulp mill? Where did the wood come from that went into the wood chips used in the pulp mill? What kind of habitat of plants and animals, perhaps endangered species of plants and animals, was disrupted in cutting and transporting the wood that went into the wood chips? How old were the trees when they were cut? What seasonal changes did the trees witness? How many winter storms swept across the forest during the life of the trees? How much rain fell from the clouds? Can you sense the rain, the clouds, the long years stretching over centuries perhaps, before the trees were cut, chipped, made into wood pulp? And what of the future? Where will the newsprint go from this room? Will it be recycled? Will it end in a landfill dump? How long will it take for the forest to grow to maturity again to replace the fiber in this piece of paper?

The above example of mindfulness practice from Thich Nhat Hanh can be applied to any of the topics discussed below.

DOWNSCALING

Downscaling is one word that summarizes changing lifestyle choices to address economic, social, and environmental issues of the 1990s. It means simplifying household tasks, reducing the amount of physical space a household occupies, reducing consumption of household products, and reorganizing our personal space and time in the household. In other words, downscaling means recovering from the excessive and wasteful and, for some, hedonistic, patterns of behavior of the Age of Exuberance. It means, for example, finding a smaller dwelling unit that serves the needs of the inhabitants without imposing a sense of sacrifice or deprivation. In an era of downscaling, houses and apartments are not places for ostentatious display of artifacts or wealth. They are places of rest, retreat, and—for increasing numbers of people—work. Work stations have become a standard part of the house, not only for writers and artists but for many self-employed persons in many types of occupations who have found it too costly, inconvenient, and inefficient to maintain work space separate from their residences.

Downscaling begins, for many people, when they begin to realize they have too much clutter in their lives—too many things, possessions, automobiles, recreational vehicles, appliances, furniture. In addition, more and more people are beginning to realize how much toxic material they have stored in their dwelling unit—paint, solvents, oil for the automobiles, herbicides for the lawn, pesticides for the roses, fungicides for the bathroom, cleaning substances, rat poison, radon in the basement, potentially hazardous chemicals in the wall board, insulation, carpeting, and ceiling. During the process of downscaling, responsible householders safely dispose of accumulated toxic materials.

Downscaling means moving away from excess of consumption combined with concern for the health of the neighborhood. An ecohousehold is a household in which members are reducing their consumption, conserving water, reducing energy use, and reducing excess waste, excess packaging, and extraneous gadgets. Downscaling combined with developing an eco-household is a process that can be fun, interesting, and creative, but it is rarely simple or easy. It requires breaking old habits and establishing new ones. New chores by members of ecohouseholds include separating materials for recycling, composting garbage, tending a vegetable garden or herb garden rather than emphasizing an exotic display of roses or other ornamental plants, watering the garden with gray water (wash water from clothes, dishes, showers, and baths), monitoring energy use and turning off lights in rooms not occupied, turning down the thermostat, and arranging ride sharing for commutes to work and for shopping excursions.

Members of ecohouseholds become mindful of actions that are harmful to their own health, the health of other household members, and the health of their bioregion. The dramatic decrease in smoking in the United States shows that deeply ingrained habits, habits that once were thought not only acceptable, but also fashionable and stylish, can change within a few years. There is widespread acceptance of "no smoking" bans not only in restaurants, airplanes, and workplaces, but also in households. It is not considered impolite in the 1990s to ask a guest who smokes to smoke only in designated places, usually outside the house. It is no longer considered good etiquette to provide ashtrays to guests in one's home.

The following example concerning water use in households illustrates how environmental concerns can shape daily habits in households. In some areas of the nation, years of drought have increased water awareness. In the early 1990s, after six years of drought in parts of California, mandatory water reduction requirements led many people to install low-flow shower heads in bathrooms, to use gray water to water plants, and to change landscaping to plants requiring less water. Gray water used sparingly on hardy native plants can maintain the garden with less effort. Gray water can be captured by hoses or pipes connected directly to sinks, showers, bathtubs, and washing machines.

GARDENS AND LAWNS

As sketched in earlier chapters, greening our lifestyles is the metaphor for themes discussed in this book. The green, well-watered lawn is a symbol of the American suburb. However, a paradox is presented:

greenness of lawns in some regions of America is associated with wasteful use of water, monoculture, overuse of herbicides and pesticides, wasteful use of space, extravagance, humanized landscapes, and overconsumption of energy.

Even in desert regions of the American Southwest, many householders attempt to keep a green lawn during the summer. Television advertisements play on the dream of a perfect yard. Many ads promote fertilizers, herbicides, pesticides, and power lawn mowers to help the weary homeowner cut the grass. The lawn and the perfectly tended rose garden, maintained with nonorganic herbicides and pesticides, are in some ways the prototypical symbols of success in the Age of Exuberance. In the age of Ecology, increasing numbers of householders are greening their lifestyles by browning their lawn and using gray water from the kitchen sink for a vegetable garden to replace the rose garden.

Furthermore, householders are reconsidering their relation with their garden. In many western traditions and some oriental traditions, the garden has been a part of the household for thousands of years. An enclosed garden, usually centered around a small pool or fountain, was found in many Middle Eastern dwelling units, thousands of years before the time of Christ. Gardens supplying seasonal vegetables, herbs, and some grains are found in many historic cultures around the Mediterranean basin. The garden and lawn in North American suburban culture during this century, however, became something different from the traditional uses of the garden. They became objects of conformity and of conspicuous display. Numerous cities passed ordinances requiring householders to cut their lawns to a certain height. Weeds were defined as unsightly intrusions into the *perfect* lawn. Cutting the lawn became a kind of weekend ritual for householders in the suburbs. The flower garden became filled with hybridized species of roses or other ornamental plants.

What principles could be used for greening our perception of lawns and gardens? Based on the principle of less waste and the principle of biodiversity, lawns could be planted in native vegetation for the specific region wherein the household is located. Lawns can—and in some cities are required to—go brown during the summer in order to conserve costly water.

Householders can refuse to use commercial pesticides on their lawns. Householders can dig weeds by hand, or, better still, plant a mixture of native wildflowers in the yard.

Many types of dwelling units, including some apartments and trailers, have space for a small kitchen garden. Window-box gardens planted with herbs can be adapted to fit windows in apartments and houses. The garden is a way to grow some of the food of the household, but perhaps equally important, even the smallest garden reminds us of our connection with living beings, which we must kill to eat. Even sprouting grains in a glass container in the kitchen can be a kind of gardening. The garden can be an integral part of life in the household rather than an object of display or wealth.

When the householder sees the garden as a food production area as well as a small retreat from other busy household activities, then gardening becomes part of the richness of living in rhythm with the bioregion within which we dwell. The garden can be a delight for the household and draw participants from the stresses of humanized urbanity. It can be a place of hope and love, a place of sustenance in the deepest sense. The garden in this sense is a place where people and nature are cooperating in a special way. Nothing forced, nothing dominated. Revisioning gardening as a process of coming into harmony with our place will require a new aesthetic and new sense of peacefulness.

ENERGY USE

Dwelling units, especially freestanding houses in suburbs, have evolved substantially over the past century. Indoor plumbing and electricity supplied by a grid system changed household energy use and changed the way we think about energy. Many people thought that technology and centralized organizations had solved the problem of limited energy by providing them with unlimited, inexpensive sources of water and power.

We now realize that only the sun can provide unlimited energy—at least unlimited in terms of human life on the earth. Energy production, distribution, and use always have "costs," some of which are reflected in the bills paid by household consumers, some of which are not—loss of habitat for endangered species, for example, when a dam is built to create a reservoir of water for use in hydroelectric production.

Most of the discussion on household use of electricity and fossil fuels has focused on issues of efficiency of use and reduction in total amount of electric energy and fossil fuels used. This theme can be stated in a few simple statements:

- Turn off the lights when not in use.
- Turn down the thermostat.
- Install more efficient lighting and cooling and heating equipment.
- Reduce water use by installing low-flow shower heads, putting dams in the toilet, installing drip irrigation in the garden or using gray water from the sink.

Following these guidelines may help reduce the electric and water bills and, at least for a short time, may help encourage energy awareness among members of the household. Modifying behavior as members of a household group is the most practical approach to household energy use.

When new dwelling units are constructed, prospective buyers can demand that they include contemporary passive solar systems, heavy insulation, and energy monitoring systems controlled by computers. For those who must live in aging housing units built over the past century, however, modifying behavior is the most practical, cost-effective, and socially responsible way to address the problem of energy use. By reducing use of electricity, water, and fossil fuels, we collectively send a message to corporations and government that we don't want any more big and expensive power plants based on fossil fuel, large-scale hydroelectric dams, or nuclear fission. When attitudes change from believing in a "technological fix" to accepting responsibility for our own actions, then the energy problem is solved simply. The message is clear. Households would rather change lifestyles and redistribute current available electrical supplies, water supplies, and fossil-fuel supplies than invest in massive expansion of supplies based on big technology, including development of nuclear fusion.

TOXIC HOUSEHOLDS

Reports commissioned by the EPA, investigations by citizen action groups, and research published by university scientists have combined in the past decade to heighten awareness of household toxic problems. Concern for personal health and for the health of the environment has led many people to reexamine their dwelling units from attic to basement. In some well publicized examples, such as the Love Canal in the state of New York and Times Beach, Missouri, whole neighborhoods or whole towns have been declared unsafe for human occupancy because of toxic problems. In other places, homeowners discovered they were living downwind or downstream from major sources of pollution, including nuclear facilities, uranium mines, and pulp mills.

Furthermore, many products that were routinely used in building millions of dwelling units during the past thirty to sixty years have been determined to be hazardous to human health. Other hazards were discovered in appliances and in building sites. These include asbestos (found in ceiling texture, ductwork, linoleum, siding, insulation, or plaster), lead (found in paint used before the late 1970s), chlordane (a toxic pesticide, now banned, injected into the soil around and under many houses), electromagnetic field pollution (generated by appliances, wiring, motors, transformers, and high-voltage transmission lines), radon (a gaseous isotope of naturally occurring uranium in the soil which can become trapped in buildings), and other chemicals including volatile organic compounds, some cleaning products, and formaldehyde. Some of these substances can be detected only by experts with the use of special equipment. Some of these substances should be removed and safely disposed by people trained in removal and disposal techniques.

It is ironic that many people sought refuge in their homes from outdoor pollution—smog, auto exhaust, pesticides and herbicides, and industrial pollution—only to discover hazards in the indoor environment. Cleaning the household sometimes produces anxiety in household members because of the disruption of a place previously considered "safe." In addition to the stress, it is costly in time and money.

Every dwelling unit is unique and requires a unique plan if the household members decide to live in a healthier environment, but a few general guidelines can be helpful.

FORMING AN ECOTEAM

Some people are downscaling in a willy-nilly fashion—because of changing financial circumstances, changing needs of household members, new laws, rising costs of maintaining a household, and mixed advice from friends and family. It is possible to make changing circumstances into an opportunity to take a conscious approach to changing the household into an ecohome by forming or joining an ecoteam. An ecoteam is a combination of recovery group and technical support group in which members can offer psychological support for behavior changes, information and advice on tough problems, and continuing feedback on success in meeting group goals.

Many people want to retrofit the equipment in their house or apartment, but changing equipment, such as installing more efficient light bulbs or low-flow shower heads or using recycled paper, is only half of change. The other half, and one some people find more difficult, is changing behavior or the daily routines of all members of a household. Many people feel at a loss on how to begin and how to proceed. Sensing a need to help people organize their household changes, David Gershon and Robert Gilman designed a six-month program to begin restoring households to environmental balance.

In the *Ecoteam Workbook,* the authors define an ecoteam as a small group of people working with each other, and supporting each other to make changes in their own household or among several households. An ecoteam can consist of members of a household, or members of different households in the same neighborhood/community/social organization, or members of different households who work in the same office/workplace. The ecoteam can function as both a support group and a group where information can be exchanged—where ideas, successes, and failures can be discussed. How the group functions depends on the needs of its members.

Although the ecoteam may be composed of people from different households, it is important that all members of each household agree that changes are needed and agree to cooperate in making changes.

Change is difficult. Routines and habits, sometimes maintained over many years, require attention in order to change them. Individuals can and do change their behavior, but when individuals act alone they are acting without the support and encouragement of others. Teamwork can be both enjoyable and rewarding.

Gershon and Gilman suggest that members of the ecoteam clarify their goals before beginning a six-month project. The first goal of the team I formed in my household was to plant more native plants, eliminate the use of household pesticides, including snail and slug bait, and consider the garden as an extension of wild nature rather than cutting and hacking vegetation to conform to the standard of neatness of lawns in my community. The second goal was the safe disposal of toxics. We collected all herbicides and pesticides as well as oil and paint cans in the house. We had to create a locked toxic waste dump in the storage area of the house, however, because our local waste disposal center will not take household toxic wastes. The community makes arrangements with a firm that specializes in toxic household wastes to come pick up this material twice a year. The last time this service was offered in the community, nearly four hundred vehicles arrived at the disposal site the Saturday morning advertised in local papers. The safe disposal personnel were overwhelmed with the response. They did not have enough containers for the wastes and sent most of the people home with their household toxics, telling them to come back in six months when the service would be offered again.

There are many projects in which ecoteams can work. Ecoteams might investigate what services are available in their community, including services for safe disposal of toxic wastes, advice on insulation problems, volunteer groups that might assist in conducting an energy audit of the house or apartment, availability of low-interest loans for retrofitting homes, and other useful information for changing habits and technology in house or apartment.

Members of an ecoteam will want to clarify when and where the team will meet, set goals and priorities for each member and for the team as a

■ Do you want to bring domesticated animals with you, including but not limited to dogs, cats, goats, sheep, horses, and Vietnamese potbelly pigs? Will these domesticated animals disrupt the lifestyles of native plants and animals? For example, in some areas in southern California where new housing developments have sprung up in the chaparral hillsides, coyote and mountain lion habitat has been intruded upon. Instead of learning to coexist with mountain lions and coyotes, some new residents shoot at them or demand that the authorities remove them.

■ What are the recreational habits of members of the household? Do teenage children, for example, bring ORVs, ATVs, dirt motorcycles, and guns with them to the site, and will their use of these devices harm the native animals and plants?

■ Will water runoff, for example, from the addition of fertilizers and watering of lawns in desert regions affect the balance of nature in that micro area and water quality in natural streams? Much of the valley in which Palm Springs, California, is situated, for example, has been turned from dry desert vegetation to lawns, golf courses, and pavement (streets, side walks, parking lots), such that some native species habitat has been reduced to several small areas that are currently managed as nature reserves.

■ How fragile is the site? Three criteria for determining a site's fragility are: 1. rarity—ecological, geological or visual uniqueness, 2. vulnerability —susceptibility to damage by humans, including the building process itself, and 3. recuperability—recovery of the site unassisted by humans.

The suitability of a project or structure can be determined after evaluating the fragility of the site, the impact of the project on the environment, and after analysis of the purpose or need for the project. Bennett and Wakeman explain that a project's suitability can be weighed on an ecocentric to anthropocentric scale: "A ski cabin to entertain friends has an anthropocentric purpose. Human needs are the primary concern and the place would require parking for several cars, multiple sleeping accommodations, and a sizable common area. We can assume the structure would not be minimal, human energies would not be directed to preserving the site, and significant damage would result if built on a very fragile site. On the other hand, a resilient site might handle it" (p. 3).

Attitudes from the Age of Exuberance concerning private property "rights"— to develop, drastically alter and change areas due to our whims, fantasies and shallow desires—are a major cultural and psychological deterrent to ecocentric approaches in siting and building appropriate structures. We have seen, along the California coastline, instances where new owners of coastal lots fought local planning commissions, the state Coastal Commission, and natural forces themselves, for the right to build dream houses on hazardous coastal sites. People appearing before the Coastal Commission have demanded, as property rights, permission to block historic public access to the beach across their property, to build monster homes, and to build horrendous rock seawalls on public beaches (in a sometimes futile attempt) to keep the ocean's waves from crashing through their living room windows. These examples demonstrate narrow visions on the part of people who want to "get away from the city" or "make a statement" or "have a weekend retreat."

Consideration for the human community is another important consideration. When people are so afraid of their neighbors, or others who might pass by, that they require special security measures—large electrified fences, elaborate alarm systems, night-lighting throughout the property, reduced vegetation to maintain a line of site, and guard dogs—then we know that a fortress mentality has developed that inhibits their ability to become more attuned to the natural processes of the bioregion.

Ecocentric awareness encourages an egoless, expanded sense of self by adapting to the tendencies of the *place*. Ecocentric means not imposing a narrow, historical, cultural definition of "beauty" on the place. It means living in voluntary simplicity, without urban baggage obscuring our understanding of the vital needs of the place where we dwell. The primary consideration of an ecocentric approach to dwelling in a natural place is concern for learning the lessons that a more or less natural site can offer and learning how we can become guardians, protectors, and defenders of these sites.

Bennett and Wakeman ask us to move beyond shallow, culturally instilled ideas of taste, style, conformity, conventionality, beauty, and neatness. They ask:

> Can we rise above our human and cultural limitations to design in a way that is ecocentrically responsive and responsible? The answer seems clear: If (and only if) our heart is in the right place. Only if we think and feel and act as a part of nature. Only then, architect will turn poet.

CHAPTER 7

The Empty Nest
is Full of Life

As I write this chapter, I think of Eric. Eric is nearly four years old. He is by any criteria a bright, energetic, alert, and active male child. He will, with luck and with careful parenting in a household filled with love, and with education, possibly become a self-realized adult, making many contributions to his community. But Eric's parents are now divorced. They were both nineteen when he was born. They both admit that they were not psychologically or economically ready to have a child. They never thought of family planning and took no precautions to prevent pregnancy. When Eric was three years old, his father lost his job as a cook. His mother took a job as a cook's helper. With only a high school education in an economy in which employers increasingly demand highly educated and skilled workers or unskilled workers who are paid only the minimum wage required by law, Eric's father may have difficulty finding another job that can support his child. If Eric's parents are like many other couples across North America, they will both find other partners. They both claim they do not want to become parents again, but neither is committed to long-term or permanent contraceptive solutions. Neither is practicing abstinence and neither regularly uses any form of contraception, so it is likely both will parent additional children.

Demographers tell us that due to what they call "population inertia," that is, the continuing thrust of population growth, even if the birth *rate* were to decline in North America, the large number of people in their prime reproductive years will lead to an increase in population and thus more demands for social services and more demands on raw materials from forests and farms and other resources.

During the 1980s, demographers also noted what they call a baby "boomlet." Women in their thirties and early forties who had no children previously or only one child previously became pregnant—sometimes after working with newly emerging reproductive technology in order to become pregnant. My friend Carol is in this age category, but she made a different choice. She has a PhD in environmental education. She is divorced and remarried and has never had a child, nor has she ever had an abortion. She delayed having a child while she was in graduate school and then, during the difficult last years of her first marriage, did not want to become pregnant. She and her current husband are committed to each other. They have built a home together. She has been pregnant—several times—and each time had a miscarriage.

Now in her late thirties, she had to make a decision. Did she want to go through fertility tests, perhaps in-vitro fertilization, in an attempt to become pregnant? She knew she only had a few years left before it was no longer possible for her to conceive. Carol is a godmother for several children. She is an aunt to the children of some of her siblings, and she takes that role seriously. Her life is rich with community work, with her work as a teacher, with her husband, with experiences in nature. She has engaged in a lifelong spiritual journey and has focused on the Goddess, Mother Earth, for spiritual understanding for many years. She also saw most of her friends, women in their thirties and early forties, become pregnant during the last several years. These women extol the joys of motherhood.

Talking about children, sharing babysitting chores, becoming politically active in campaigns demanding more government assistance for child care facilities, for education, for single mothers—these seemed to be the central life interest of many of her friends.

Jerry, Carol's husband, did not have a strong desire to father a child, but he says he feels pressure from his parents and siblings and some of his male friends to become a father. Their relationship is an exclusive sexual relationship; neither has sex with anyone else.

After long discussions about the consequences and the alternatives, Carol decided she did not want to have a child in this lifetime. As a couple, she and Jerry decided that Jerry would have a vasectomy. Carol decided that she gives much of her time and energy to many people, to children of her friends, to students, to friends. Given the situation of the world at this time, she decided that not having a child would be one of her gifts to future generations. Her decision not to have a child in this lifetime was a conscious, heartfelt decision. She says it helped her mature as a person. She creatively turned the term "childless woman" into a different sense of parenting. She directs her sensuous, emotional, caring skills to caring for a small part of this earth—the coastal watersheds near her home.

Soon after she decided not to have a child, Carol submitted to a biopsy, which confirmed the presence of a small tumor in one breast. She agreed to surgical removal of the tumor but not to any radiation or chemotherapy. In her meditation on her cancer and her life changes, especially the coming of menopause, she came to see her breasts as a metaphor for the blocked streams in her bioregion. As part of her healing process, she began to walk through the small coastal streams blocked with debris from logging operations. She studied the history of logging in her region. Healing these watersheds by physically clearing logging debris from the streams and working in political processes to change logging practices became part of her evolving sense of place, her evolving self-realization. She began to understand the relationship between healing the earth and healing her psychic and physical wounds.

Carol realized that although having children can be fulfilling, and certainly is a natural and frequently an expected outcome of marriage and sexually intimate relationships, there are many joys in life, many ways to participate in the life of the community without having the title of "parent." Indeed, in the situation we find ourselves in during the 1990s the decision to become a nonparent may mean that one has as much love and commitment, if not more, for the future of humanity and for the future of nonhuman nature.

When a man and a woman make a conscious decision *not* to have a child, they are taking one of the most significant actions that any couple can make to deal with the current tragic destruction of biodiversity on this planet, which has been brought about, in part, by human overpopulation. This decision addresses a question that is central to the subject of this book: How can people expect the world around them to change unless they are willing to assume responsibility for their own reproductive behavior?

The decision not to become father or mother requires us to examine our sexual urges, the expectations we have been taught in our culture, our desire for immortality through passing on our genes to our offspring. It requires us to address our fears—of loneliness, of being different from our peers, of sexual inadequacy, of the meaning of our lives. It requires us to address our responsibilities to future generations.

In this chapter I will discuss arguments for not having children and some of the joys of nonparenting. In these arguments I am particularly considering the situation of persons dwelling in wealthy nations—persons of all races, ethnic groups, and religious traditions. Reducing the birth rate of people in wealthy industrialized nations—especially in the U.S.A., Canada, most western European nations, and Japan—is important because each child born in these societies is likely to have a much greater impact on resources than a child born in the poorest and least industrialized nations on earth.

Anne and Paul Ehrlich present a simple formula to illustrate the importance of birth control and social policies encouraging population stabilization in nations such as the U.S.A. and Canada. They call it the Impact Equation. I(impact)$= P$(population) A(affluence) T(technology). We have great affluence in the U.S.A. and Canada. Even the poorest one-fourth of families live with much greater affluence than the majority of people in the poorest one-fourth of nations. And we have massive technological projects. Higher per capita consumption in a region of high affluence (relative to the average among people currently living in all nations) makes each additional child a greater load on the system. In the U.S.A. and Canada, for example, the A and T multipliers for each person are very large. The total impact of a given nation can be lowered by decreasing A or T or P. However, the other two factors must not be increased or they will offset the decrease in the third factor.

Furthermore, throughout this book I have focused on lifestyles of people in industrial nations, especially in the U.S.A. and Canada. The situation of poor women in many third world nations who are oppressed by a patriarchy, who do not have access to education, who have no money for nor access to safe and reliable contraceptive devices is much different from the situation of people living in the wealthiest nations, even people living with less than average income in those nations. Evidence indicates that many women both in third world nations and in wealthy nations prefer to limit their own reproduction. Raising the status of women, changing attitudes of husbands who frequently demand that their wives continue having children, and providing reliable contraception and education to women have been effective in reducing birth rates wherever these policies have been adopted and implemented equitably and consistently through the society.

The conscious decision to be a parent or a nonparent is one that can be made earlier in life rather than later, that can be based on philosophical principles, and that can be made responsibly within the context of the community wherein one dwells. In earlier chapters I have outlined ecosophical principles that can help us make conscious lifestyle choices aimed at greening our lifestyles. In this chapter I want to consider the decision not to have children rather than a decision to engage in what is frequently called "family planning." Family planning frequently means spacing births by delaying conception, for which there are many practical reasons. However, the decision to parent only one child during one's lifetime or to become a nonparent requires as much of a commitment as a decision to delay parenthood.

When a man and a woman make a commitment not to have any children, then that man and woman are making a political statement. Stephanie Mills, a writer and bioregionalist, provides an example. She created somewhat of a media stir in June 1969, when she announced in her commencement address at Mills College that "the most humane thing for me to do is to have no children at all." Reflecting on her decision in 1989 in her book *Whatever Happened to Ecology,* she admitted to some ambivalence. She played the role of anti-hero, she says, and perhaps inspired a few other women to choose not to be mothers. Life involves making choices, and making the choice to be a nonmother for political reasons takes courage in this culture. Mills concludes that our culture offers little support or even spiritual direction for nonmothers; however, she concludes there is an eco-logical demand for them. The decision not to have children is not a casual decision. It goes against the grain of our society. It is much easier to go along with the expectations, even demands, from one's parents, peers, and church, as well as the general culture and one's biological urges. It is partic-ularly easy to avoid making a conscious decision to be a nonparent in a soci-ety where denial concerning the issue of overpopulation is so prevalent.

In discussions with students, friends, colleagues, and groups of people in my travels around North America, I see a kind of glaze appear in many people's eyes when I mention population as a problem. Some feminists, progressives, political conservatives, and members of certain Christian denominations take an almost militant pronatalist position. *Pronatalism* means encouraging parenting by arguing that couples have a moral obliga-tion to procreate, or that rising birth rates are good for the economy. I recog-nize that pronatalist attitudes are deeply ingrained in our culture, and that is why the decision to be a nonparent is a political decision.

As noted with other aspects of green lifestyles, we need appropriate words to express positive connotations for the emerging roles in a greener community. The word "nonparent" seems negative and empty. Worse still, the English language includes words that demean women who do not bear children. "Barren woman" implies a woman incapable of giving life, with-out life. Indeed the lack of a similar word for an infertile male may indicate the greater importance of motherhood than fatherhood in our culture. Men can still be considered virile even if infertile or with low sperm count, as long as they are not impotent. The childless and the unmarried are frequent-ly lumped together as a class of people who are forlorn, unhappy, and lone-ly. The implicit message is "have children" in order to have social acceptance.

After some liberation from traditional gender roles during the 1960s and 1970s, the social trend during the 1980s and early 1990s seems to be back to traditional families as an ideal for heterosexual intimate relationships. In my view, nonparents must be aggressive in asserting their own social worth *as* nonparents.

More and more men and women living in North America are making the choice of nonparenting. There may exist certain connotations that non-parents are "selfish," that they "dislike children," that they are "misanthrop-ic" (for example, that they care more for spotted owls than for people), and generally that they are "nonproductive members of society." However, all of these negative characteristics are independent of parenting. Throughout his-tory nonparents have been saints, heroes, shamans, priests, nuns, monks, creative artists, philosophers, warriors, explorers, inventors, scientists, and have served their communities in a wide variety of ways. Nonparents can lead very fulfilling lives. The choice to abstain from having children is a socially responsible decision and a socially acceptable lifestyle. The choice to rear children, on the other hand, is a decision that carries with it many more far-reaching ecological, practical, moral, and economic implications.

RIGHTS AND RESPONSIBILITIES OF PARENTING

The choice to rear children carries with it awesome responsibilities. These include the responsibilities of parents and society to provide chil-dren with adequate food, clothing, shelter, love and attention. The develop-ment in each child of a sound, ethical, socially acceptable value system is also a duty of parenting. In this Age of Ecology, parents also have a respon-sibility to bring up their children with a healthy, biocentric respect for nature—for being native—to nurture in their offspring a socially responsible land-ethic. The responsibilities of parents to increase the possibilities for the health of their children and of the world include a duty to introduce their children to wilderness and provide them an opportunity to explore wild nature. In the Age of Ecology, parents are now responsible for working as diligently as they can to protect the environment with rich biodiversity for the health of their children and for future generations.

To assert that every person has a right to a healthy environment without asserting that every person has the responsibility to make choices that col-lectively will increase the possibility of a healthy environment is to have only half the equation. The situation of rapid population growth in the world demands that all people carefully consider their options—on whether to bring new children into the world and, if so, what limits are most appropriate for their family situation. Mindless cultural pressures for having children—and for keeping safe sex and birth control "in the closet"—need to be resisted emphatically. Positive recognition needs to be given to those individuals and couples who are content to be part of the "family of man" without raising their own individual families.

CONSEQUENCES OF NONPARENTING

Making a choice to be a nonparent, that is never to produce a child, means taking responsibility for the consequences of that choice. Nonparents who fear they will be lonely in their old age because they will not be surrounded by their children and grandchildren can remember that many biological parents are lonely in their old age because their children have died or are not able to be near them or are unable emotionally and financially to support them.

Few decisions are so intermingled with mixed emotions, cultural expectations, ideological arguments, and biological, sexual urges than decisions concerning birth control. Religious and cultural traditions tell us to procreate. "Go forth, multiply and subdue the earth" is a basic tenet of Judeo-Christian religions. We've heard the conventional arguments:

"Procreation creates a bond between men and women; it is a basic human urge."

"The problem is not with children born in wealthy nations, the population problem is a problem of the third world, where 80 percent of the world's people live."

"I have a right to the choice to have children; no one, no government can take that right away from me."

"I will be a responsible parent, unlike my parents or many of my friends or people I know or read about who abuse their children. I will care for my child."

These are frequently asserted rationalizations and justifications for having children. None of them addresses the issue of the environmental impact of having children. None acknowledges that parents cannot ever entirely determine the way their children will act as adults or the situations that their children will face. None addresses the positive aspects of nonparenting.

Nonparenting provides a person more time for pursuit of many interests, including more time for self-realization through spiritual exercises. Many eastern and western religious traditions recognize that the way to spiritual self-realization is very difficult. We can't have it all, now. We can't have everything we desire in this life. One thing at a time. Those who choose a spiritual path are frequently admonished to stay constantly focused on the task. Nuns and monks in Christian and Buddhist traditions, for example, commit themselves with a diligence to spiritual practice, and their practice would be compromised by the responsibilities of childrearing.

Nonparenting also gives one more time for self-actualization, for engaging in the practice and appreciation of art and music, sport, travel, and hobbies, for exploring nature, for participating in social causes and activities, even for participating as members of "extended" families. In the Age of Ecology, nonparenting does not be need to be linked to a spiritual calling or other vocation—it is seen as plain good citizenship.

Greening our lifestyles requires reduction in consumption. Downscaling a household is easier without the responsibility of childrearing. A couple can live with comfort in a smaller dwelling unit than a family can. Without children, one has more time to educate oneself about ecological problems. Nonparents can, if they choose, devote more time to service to environmental organizations and programs, as well as to service to the human community. Nonparents can become positive role models for younger people who sense the social pressures of family and peers to have children.

It is imperative that individuals and society be pro-choice on methods of preventing unplanned pregnancy. Nonparenting through abstinence, safe sex and use of contraceptive devices is responsible behavior. Contraceptive devices, particularly condoms, have become more available and accepted, particularly since the outbreak of the AIDS epidemic. Some school districts distribute condoms to their students and provide instructions on how to use them for the prevention of pregnancy and disease.

Discussions of various methods of birth control are important, but the fundamental question for potential parents is one of intent. As a male or a female, what is my intent? Do I want to have a child to experience having a child? Do I want to father or mother a child because in my family and community I am expected to have a child? If I don't have a child, a few children, am I considered inadequate or inferior or deviant? Why do I want to have a child? Do I intend to have a child or several children because I yearn for security in my old age? Do I hope my children will work for me as I work for them? Will I be making the world a better place by bringing more people into it?

I encourage couples and individuals to work through these difficult questions in the context of their own religious and cultural traditions. If nonparenting is too demanding a standard within one's religious and cultural traditions, then one child per lifetime could be a standard to discuss. That doesn't mean one child per couple—marriages in our society frequently end in divorce or separation, and when people find another partner they frequently want to bond to each other by having a child together. Thus out of serial couplings can come a succession of children. From a global perspective, if each person were to bring one child into the world, the rate of population growth—and consumption—would decrease, and then level off in about fifty years before beginning to decline.

Industrial societies can look at examples from third world nations. The Nyimba of Nepal, for example, allow a woman to have many husbands at the same time. Typically a woman marries several brothers and moves into their household. The woman is expected to treat each brother fairly and any children resulting from the relationship are considered children of all the brothers. The Nyimba tolerate other types of intimate relationships. For example one man may marry several women and the family unit is expected to decide how many children they can support depending on the family income.

Historically, in some cultures, perhaps one-fourth of the males never sired offspring. In Tibetan culture before 1959, for example, as many as one-quarter of all males went to monasteries as teenagers and remained in monastic, celibate orders for the rest of their lives. In many hunting-and-gathering societies, males lived in "men's houses" during the teenage years when sexual urges emerge. Many cultures also had prohibitions against sleeping with women during menstrual periods and before going on hunts. There are also examples of cultural traditions where intercourse was forbidden or discouraged for some months, or even years, after the birth of a child.

Religious groups and social organizations of all sorts can take positive actions that will reduce the birth rates and promote more functional families and a healthier environment. The choice for nonparenting, including adoption, can be encouraged. Delaying the age of marriage is itself correlated with lower birth rates. Couples who want a "nuclear family" can be encouraged to have only one child. Once the decision is made not to have children, many opportunities for richness in life experience become apparent. Nonparenting is a significant gift to one's community and is worth significant community support.

END PIECE FOR ACTIVISM

We can support raising the status of women in society and providing them with opportunities for education and equal opportunity with men for jobs, professional advancement and freedom from fear of violence.

We can support the right of men and women, teenagers and adults, to have birth control information and contraceptives at low cost. Those who take a pro-choice position on abortion can continue to demand that women have a right to abortion during the first trimester of pregnancy.

Those who make a conscious decision to be nonparents, following the tradition of social movements in North America, may engage in political actions to dramatize and legitimize nonparenting as an acceptable social role. Nonparents need to support each other, to be nonapologetic about their decision. Many actions can be taken.

Nonparents and others who support and encourage choices for voluntary population controls, can oppose pronatalist statements and programs of churches and governments. For example, Mother's Day and Father's Day can be utilized as occasions for public demonstrations and education on issues of population control and family responsibilities, and for de-mystifying the inbred cultural imperative for having children. A positive political statement for establishing a "Nonparent Day" on an equal status with

Mother's Day and Father's Day would help further public understanding of this issue.

These types of actions follow in the tradition of actions taken by oppressed peoples in the U.S.A. and Canada over the past century. During the past decades, for example, groups of men and women have engaged in demonstrations in Catholic, Protestant, and Mormon churches opposing the positions of these churches on ordination of women, on homosexuality, and opposing the statements of some church leaders concerning people who are HIV positive.

Some church groups for centuries, even for thousands of years, have convinced some of their members of the advantages of nonprocreation, of becoming nuns or monks. Certainly, in the midst of the greatest environmental crisis the Earth has known since civilization began, religious groups can support the choice for nonparenting without a requirement for a monastic lifestyle.

In American politics at least, the debate over abortion has overshadowed discussion of underlying issues including the issue of availability of information on birth control, availability of contraception devices, and availability of counseling concerning sexuality and nonparenting.

The debate can be opened by including discussion of social policies that allow for human needs, including sexual needs, while reducing the number of births. For example, acceptance of homosexual and lesbian couples, some of whom may choose to adopt unwanted children, would provide one channel for parenting without procreation.

Both parents and nonparents can expose the "traditional family values" rhetoric of many conservative religious leaders and politicians. "Traditional family values" is often used as a label which covers pronatalist, anti-homosexual positions. The "traditional family values" label is used generally to promote fundamentalist Christian positions which subject women to the domination of men, as well as pro-growth and pronatalist positions. In the Age of Ecology, biological parents need to be held accountable for the costs of their children to the community as well as for the increased stress they place on the world's ecosystems. Never before has the relationship between quality of life and quantity of human lives been more critical from a standpoint of nature's ecology.

8

FOOD AND SUSTAINING ECOSYSTEMS

Our patterns of food consumption and production have as much impact on the quality of our lives as any habits we have. Food is a necessity of life, but food preparation and consumption also provide us with many rich aesthetic and social experiences. What we eat, how we eat, when we eat and with whom we eat are topics that depend on personal preference, medical advice, nutritional needs, and cultural tradition.

The anthropology of food reveals wide differences among cultures concerning what is considered edible and what is considered unfit for human consumption. But it may be noted here that the introduction of home refrigeration units had a major impact on the lives of Native American communities and their cultural practices. A complete discussion of attitudes of different religious and cultural traditions toward food is beyond the scope of this chapter.

The rise of the fast food industry, convenience food, and meat-rich diets are part of the history of the Age of Exuberance. For example, the frozen TV dinner was widely accepted only when seemingly abundant electricity during the 1950s allowed expansion of freezer storage in stores and homes, and when growing numbers of people desired to reduce the time spent in preparing food so they could use that time for leisure activities.

Due to evolving understanding of nutrition, changes in the way we integrate eating into our schedules, and increased concern with both health and the social and environmental implications of food production and distribution, several movements centered on food have arisen during the past three decades—the health food movement, the vegetarian movement, and the environmental movement—that seem to be converging in some ways in the 1990s.

This chapter includes an overview of some of the food trends in North America, a discussion of some general principles for greening our food buying and consumption habits, and suggestions for enhancing the quality of life by becoming more careful in our food buying and consumption habits.

QUALITY OF LIFE, SOCIAL JUSTICE, AND FOOD CONSUMPTION

During the 1960s, 1970s and 1980s many nutritionists and medical researchers focused on the impacts of sugar, salt, cholesterol, and food additives such as nitrites on human beings. This trend came in the wake of increased interest in the "health food movement," a loose term covering nutrition for people seeking to avoid chemical additives, wanting vitamin and other food supplements, needing special diets, as well as for those desiring to watch their weight. The vegetarian and vegan movements were based on philosophical concerns. People who objected to killing and unnecessary suffering of animals advocated diets containing no meat or fish and no dairy products. Vegan diet goes beyond vegetarian diet and is based on ethical principles compatible with deep ecology, including the principle of dynamic harmlessness. Vegan diet includes avoidance of animal products from cattle, sheep, pigs, poultry, and fish. Vegans also avoid dairy products, including milk, cheese, and butter.

Vegan diets were developed during the early 1940s in England, when the Association for Vegans was formed. The founders were concerned with ethical questions concerning suffering of domesticated animals and the suffering of wild animals hunted for sport and eaten after a chase, such as deer and other animals, as well as birds. Vegans did not know the existence of (high-protein) soya when the movement was founded in England, although soy grain products had been known for thousands of years in parts of Asia. Vegans had available many nut products, including peanut butter and other types of nut butters, as well as a variety of beans, wheat and other grains, and fresh vegetables. Nutritious diets were developed by vegans to help each other create recipes based on vegan principles and the availability of food by seasons.

Tom Regan, a philosopher, developed a sophisticated argument for what was called the "animal liberation movement" based on the ethical principle of reducing suffering of sentient beings. Regan's book, *All That Dwell Therein: Animal Rights and Environmental Ethics* (1982), explored factory farming and the treatment of domesticated animals. He documented how young calves are locked in small enclosures and force-fed milk for a few months, then slaughtered to provide veal. Chickens are fed amphetamines so they will lay eggs faster and then slaughtered after being kept in small, lighted cages throughout their lives.

Vegetarian and vegan diets were given scientific credibility as "healthy" diets when the surgeon general of the United States, the National Academy of Sciences, and the American Heart Association began agreeing that we should eat fewer fatty foods and more complex carbohydrates such as grains, fruits, and vegetables.

Health and environmental concerns were combined during the 1970s with the widespread recognition of the environmental and health impacts of increased use of pesticides and herbicides on food crops. These impacts include the possible adverse health effects from consumption of residual amounts of pesticides and herbicides. DDT was banned in 1972 in the United States, but former dumpsites remain contaminated, and residues are still detected in some bird eggs in distant areas (and even in the early 1990s, DDT may still be sold and used in some third world nations).

Other hazards of pesticide and herbicide use include adverse effects on the health of farm workers exposed to these chemicals in the process of planting and harvesting crops. While the EPA and chemical-producing corporations argue that pesticides and herbicides are safe "when used as directed," researchers have documented that workers frequently cannot read labels because they speak and read only a non-English language and the labels are printed only in English.

The trend toward eating with the environment in mind came to include, during the 1980's, concern for impact of food production on ecosystems. For example, in 1985, the Rainforest Action Network in San Francisco and Earth First! documented the connection between destroying rainforests in Central America and America's affection for hamburgers. Researchers showed that rainforests in certain Central American countries were being cut and burned and converted into pasture for cattle. The cattle were usually owned by wealthy ranchers who sold their cattle to a supplier in Miami. In the Miami slaughterhouses, lean beef from Central America was mixed with fatty beef and formed into hamburger patties and frozen, then distributed throughout North America to fast-food restaurants. Protests directed toward one large fast-food chain with leaflets describing the hamburger connection showed that customers could quickly understand the environmental connection of their eating habits if provided with clear, easily readable, brief material. Within months after the nationwide protest and boycott was launched, a major fast-food chain, Burger King, announced that it would no longer use beef from Central America in its hamburgers.

Jeremy Rifkin, in *Beyond Beef,* provides evidence that cattle raising on a global scale takes up nearly 24 percent of the land mass of the planet. At the beginning of the 1990s an estimated 1,280,000,000 cattle lived on the planet and consumed as much grain as would feed one billion humans. Rifkin charts the central place that cattle have had in western civilizations and in African and some Asian civilizations for thousands of years. Conflicts have occurred during those thousands of years between those who raise cattle and those who farm the land. He describes the rise of cattle empires in North America during the second half of the nineteenth century and the rise of cattle addiction in a few wealthy nations—United States, Canada, and England.

Rifkin discusses the effects on health of rising red-meat consumption during the first half of this century, including rising rates in "diseases of affluence"—heart attacks, certain forms of cancer, diabetes. The ecological effects of cattle production on a massive scale include conversion of tropical rainforests to cattle pasture, desertification, and overgrazing of large portions of the American West—nonessential agricultural practices that sacrifice wildlife habitat for unhealthy, red-meat diets. Rifkin shows that the slogan of the beef industry—"Real Food for Real People"—is hollow rhetoric. A more appropriate slogan on meat products might be "Warning: This Product May be Dangerous to Your Health and to the Health of Ecosystems." Rifkin suggests that reducing beef consumption by half on a per capita basis in wealthy nations could dramatically reduce ecological impacts on millions of acres of lands, and that changes in the cattle industry could reduce water pollution and damage to fragile wetlands and other sensitive habitats.

Anxiety over pesticide residues was heightened in 1989 by the revelation of the possible carcinogenic effects of Alar, a chemical used to hasten ripening of apples. Consumer anxiety led to removal of this chemical from the market, although corporations producing the chemical continued to claim it would have no harmful effect on human health. The question of "detectable chemical residues" is complex, and experts disagree on what tests are necessary to detect residues. Even the lack of detectable chemical residues does not mean that the food production processes raise no other environmental and health concerns.

What has emerged in the early 1990s is a greening of food buying and consumption habits that combines health, environmental, ethical, and diet concerns. People working to green their food buying and consumption habits also are concerned with packaging of food products. More and more consumers are questioning excessive packaging. More consumers are using cloth containers to carry their food from markets to home, and questioning the use of styrofoam containers and nonrecycled paper containers for food served at fast-food outlets.

More consumers also are seeking to understand the broader context of food production and distribution. They are asking that food be produced in ways that minimize impact on the environment and that do not harm the health and safety of farm workers or workers in food-processing industries. They are asking their grocers questions not only about environmental effects of food production but about social effects. Just as some consumers will not buy goods produced by prison labor camps in China because of alleged human rights violations by the Chinese government, some consumers boycott food grown on farms where workers are exposed to pesticide contamination, or food products produced in food-processing plants where workers are exposed to health risks.

Consumers are asking many questions concerning labeling of food products. Consumers are mystified by the names of chemicals included on the labels of processed foods. While labels may include total calories in the product, it can be difficult to determine what percent of the calories are from protein, fat, or complex carbohydrates, and what this means in terms of recommended daily intake.

The Nutrition Education and Labeling Act of 1990 instituted sweeping reforms in food labeling regulations that will give consumers uniform information about serving sizes, and standardize terms such as fat free, low fat, and low cholesterol. The act applies only to food regulated by the Food and Drug Administration (FDA), but the Department of Agriculture (USDA), which has authority over meat and poultry and processed foods containing meat and poultry, agreed to go along with the labeling changes so that consumers will have uniform information on all products.

The new labels are considered an especially important source of information for health-conscious Americans. Medical research continues to show a firm association between diet and the development and prevention of certain medical conditions, such as cancer, high blood pressure, and heart disease.

The most significant change is that labels will now list the amounts of nutrients—such as fats, carbohydrates, sodium, protein, and fiber—in the context of a daily intake of 2,000 calories, which is roughly the need of an average adult woman. The USDA added a second set of figures for a 2,500 calorie diet for men. The USDA initially resisted the changes, and the American Meat Institute criticized the regulations as "fattening the labels."

Increased attention to personal health, environmental, and social impacts of food production and processing are important aspects for "eating greener," but equally important is the quality of good food. Based on their search for a bioregional identity and their desire to be close to the production, processing, and consumption of their food, more people are rediscovering the joys of raising at least some of the food they consume. This may mean, for people living in apartments without access to community garden space, sprouting grains for home consumption or planting window box gardens with herbs. In suburban households, equal attention is being given to growing a vegetable garden along with decorative flower gardens.

GUIDELINES TO CONSIDER IN CHANGING FOOD CONSUMPTION PATTERNS

■ *Be informed.* This involves recognizing the difference between the hype of advertising and accurate information from reliable sources. Many experts will disagree on the health and environmental effects of food products, and changes in evaluation occur all the time. Consult a variety of sources and compare conclusions by different experts.

■ *Eat less meat.* I was raised on beef in Kansas during the 1950s. As middle-class residents of the suburbs, it seems we were expected to eat meat at every meal—steak a few times a week, pot roast on Sunday and hamburger a few times a week for lunch or dinner. Besides beef, we ate large quantities of poultry (usually deep-fried chicken) and pork, including pork chops, bacon daily for breakfast, and pork roasts. In the culture of the middle-class, midwestern suburbs, I never remember any serious questioning of the health or environmental effects of eating so much meat. It was the norm, the generally accepted community standard, for healthy and affluent families.

■ *Avoid excessive packaging.* Packaging consciousness has advanced along many fronts during the two past decades. Consumers now use fewer paper products, ask for paper bags made of recycled paper, and often take their own cloth bags to stores. Styrofoam packaging and packaging in certain types of plastics has been questioned as well as excessive packaging of fruits and vegetables to prolong their shelf life.

■ *Collect and eat plants native to your own bioregion in season.* This guideline encourages bioregional studies. When do the blackberries become ripe? When can pine nuts be collected? What mushrooms are edible, and when do these mushrooms reach their peak of taste? If meat or fish is included in your diet, hunt or catch wild game in a legal, ethical manner and prepare it with reverence.

- *Eat locally.* This may, for some people, mean buying some produce at the weekly markets of organic vegetable growers. For others it may mean owning shares in a local subscription farm. Consumers pay farmers in advance of the growing season to grow organic vegetables and fruit, and subscribers have first choice of produce in season. Not only do consumers have confidence that the food from the subscription farm is the freshest available, they also are in closer touch with the process of food production.
- *Tend toward vegan diet.* Wider availability of high protein soya products, including soya milk and soya margarine, in the past decade has made a vegan diet easier to maintain on a daily basis.
- *Where possible, produce some of the food eaten in the household.* Seasonal gardens, small greenhouses attached to dwelling units, even sprouting grains in a jar in the kitchen are some actions that help people become aware of the practice of producing some of their own food. Children in school classes can learn to sprout grains in the classroom and can taste the grains they have sprouted.
- *Eat joyfully in the company of friends.*
- *Eat with reverence and grace.*

CHAPTER

9

ORGANIZATIONAL REFORM

In my informal interviews with college students and in discussions with participants in deep-ecology workshops over the past two decades, I find many people who say they desire to dwell in a small community with other people who are committed to spiritual and green values. When asked what would be some of the characteristics of such a community, many people answer: organic gardening, small scale community, caring for the land, having a bioregional sense of place, peacefulness, less stress than living in the city, personal growth, and inclusiveness (welcoming people of different genders, sexual preferences, races, ethnic groups, and ages), in other words, an ecocommunity based on ecophilosophical principles. In this chapter I discuss both our yearning for community and the need to work for change within the current structure of bureaucracies in North America and within existing social organizations of all types.

Humans are social beings. We need to live in communities of other humans. Considerable research indicates our basic human needs are most adequately fulfilled in small-scale communities where members share in the work of the community. Besides sharing food and shelter, members of a community share visions, dreams, and fellowship. The community nourishes each individuated person toward fuller self-realization. A person individuated as a unique personality expresses talents, choices, decisions, and spiritual growth within the community. In healthy communities, the wise elders know the twists and turns that a person can take that distract from the process of personal development and broader identification with the cosmos. These elders, as well as shamans, encourage healing processes and development of maturity in individuals and in the community as a whole.

The term *community* comes from the Latin *communitas,* meaning "fellowship and community" and was derived from the Latin *communis* which means "common." This is also the root of the English *communion* (sharing spiritual awareness) and *communication* (sharing information or messages). In a human community, members share many kinds of communication.

To ecologists a community is defined as the interactions between a number of plants and animal species on a given specific site. For example, an ecologist might discuss characteristic relationships in a forest community or a desert community. Climatic conditions, soils, geological conditions, geographical location (for example, the difference in available sunlight in the Arctic region vs. along the Equator), and prevailing wind patterns are some of the factors that influence the biotic community as it changes, evolves, adapts over time. The German sociologist Ferdinand Toennies, in a famous definition of human community, used an organic analogy to refer to human community. He defined an "organic community" as consisting of "natural, spontaneous, organic relations of people as they develop in the course of living, growing out of mutual affection, acquaintance, custom, and tradition." "Society," on the other hand, Toennies defined as the formal organization of relationships between humans, including contracts, legal obligations, and deliberately planned agreements. Another German sociologist, Max Weber, in his monumental work on the history of modernism, concludes that the dominant type of social organization in modern society is not an organic community, but rather bureaucratic organization. Bureaucracy as a form of social organization is characterized by hierarchy, written contracts, specified job descriptions, and reliance on experts to establish the justification for decisions within the bureaucratic framework.

While many people search for community, in the organic, spontaneous sense of community, most of us live our daily lives within society and specifically within the boundaries of bureaucracies—in schools, corporations, government agencies, churches, and voluntary organizations that have bureaucratic forms of organization. Most bureaucracies in modern society, including corporations and many churches, are proponents of anthropocentric philosophies. The bureaucratic form of organization is, in fact, an efficient method of furthering an anthropocentric agenda.

SURVIVAL AND SOCIAL CHANGE
IN ORGANIZATIONS

As individuals or members of small intimate groups we attempt to meet our survival needs—as citizens, as members of groups, as employees—by working with or within bureaucratic organizations. When we reflect on our lives and our participation in large organizations, we may come to ask deeper questions concerning our existence. Writers such as Franz Kafka have explored the terrifying sense of powerlessness, meaninglessness, and despair of individuals caught in the clutches of faceless bureaucracy. More and more people are deciding, at some point in their lives, to leave bureaucratic organizations because the basic thrust of the organization does not fit their moral principles, or because they no longer trust the leaders or the process of the organization. Many others stay in organizations, with the intent to work for reform from within. Revitalizing organizations can be difficult, however, and sometimes reformers are rejected as heretics. In this era of rapid social change, there will be many opportunities for heretics, saints, ecowarriors, and leaders who can inspire resistance to oppression and inspire people to commit themselves to the "real work," as deep ecology philosopher Gary Snyder calls it, that will extend over many decades.

While some people are willing to take the risk of founding a new business or nongovernmental organization, many others will seek the rewards of working in an existing bureaucracy and will seek to reform the organizations they work for and the voluntary organizations, including churches, in which they participate. Attempting to green bureaucratic, hierarchical organizations is a daunting task and frequently involves taking personal risks, including the risk of being ostracized by others, and risks to one's career, even to one's life. We have examples, however, of people who took those risks, who found others to join them in a support group, and who see themselves as part of a movement of reform and revitalization within existing organizations and structures.

The politics of organizations are frequently complex, and each person or small group of people who work within an organization must assess— from an ecocentric perspective—their own willingness to deal with uncertainties of achieving success in moving the organization toward more harmony with nature, and their overall commitment to greening their lifestyles. Revitalization movements in organizations need leaders, martyrs, saints, and people who will work daily to advance and confirm the values of right livelihood instead of the values of greed, power politics, organizational survival, and corruption. Revitalization needs to occur in all organizations— corporations, government, public agencies, educational and religious institutions, and even nonprofits.

CHANGING CORPORATE VALUES

Some corporate leaders in the early 1990s began to realize that they must address environmental issues in order to survive in the changing social and environmental situations we face in this decade. "Changing Course" is one example of the response of some corporate leaders. This is a report that resulted from discussions among members of the Business Council for Sustainable Development, an ad hoc group of European, Japanese, and American corporate leaders organized by Swiss corporate executive Stephan Schmidheiny. The group supports a value-added tax on energy and an end to price subsidies for coal and electricity. The group embraces a recommendation that all goods and service prices be adjusted to reflect environmental costs, including costs of production, use, recycling, and disposal. Increased costs reflecting the environmental costs, according to these corporate leaders, will reduce consumption and provide an incentive to search for environmentally gentle alternatives.

The model of change in business organizations based on perceived change in the business climate of the 1990s—consumer demand for simpler products, lower-priced products, more durable and reliable products, organic food, environmental harmony in production and distribution of products, and environmental ethics—is a top-down kind of change. Management committees, sometimes after consultation with workers and after reading surveys of consumer values, make decisions on restructuring the organization and redesigning the products. Downsizing, restructuring, and redesigning have become the slogans for competitive companies in the 1990s. For the most part these decisions are based on conventional criteria of survival of the corporation. It has not yet been shown that these changes can be made within compassionate, ecocentric guidelines.

CHANGING BUREAUCRACIES
FROM WITHIN AND WITHOUT

If companies and public agencies do not provide the services requested by citizens or if these organizations are ineffective, corrupt, or insensitive to the greening values of the 1990s, then the organizations will become obsolete and citizens will either ignore them or make a dramatic statement to catch the attention of corporate leaders and politicians and the general public. When a private citizen in Los Angeles captured on videotape with his personal video camera police officers beating an unarmed black man and took that videotape to a local television station, he was taking authority away from uniformed officers and empowering every ordinary citizen to stand as a witness against abuse by authorities.

Change is not always easy or peaceful. While activists adhere to the general principle of nonviolence, the leaders of organizations have been known to use intimidation, harassment, manipulation, and even violence to quell dissident members. Persons or small groups of people who seek to change an organization from within—for example, to keep an organization from reaffirming conservative values or turning toward fascism—may be labeled disloyal, reprimanded by the authorities of the organization, or excluded from the organization. Where workers feel intimidated by their bosses, they may need to find support outside the workplace, telling reliable environmental groups, for example, about pollution from a factory that managers refuse to acknowledge openly or do anything to stop.

Reports by members of public conservation agencies such as the United

States Forest Service, Bureau of Land Management, National Park Service, and Environmental Protection Agency indicated that in the early 1990s there was a repression of progressive, green attitudes in employees of these agencies. Instead of greening the policies and practices of these agencies, agency leaders were actually suppressing scientific studies that showed the extent of overcutting of forests and destruction of wildlife habitat.

Some employees formed their own organization, the Association of Forest Service Employees for Environmental Ethics, to protect both their civil rights and their rights as employees of public natural resource agencies. They also began to work collectively as advocates for progressive environmental policies in the agencies.

Collective action by employees of organizations can keep the leadership of organizations from picking off individual employees, labeling them as disloyal because of their green attitudes, and finding excuses for firing them. Of course, the ability of some organizational leaders to maintain their own power at the expense of those seeking social change is well known.

STRATEGIES FOR PEOPLE
SEEKING TO CHANGE BUREAUCRACY

During the turbulent years of the 1990s the best strategy, in all situations, is to maintain one's center, "keep cool," to use an old slang expression, stay clearheaded and focused on the issue of green change without diversion to other agendas. Remember a couple of sociological truisms:

Most organizations want to continue existing. When their previous mission is no longer relevant, they try to find new ways to justify their existence. After the end of the Cold War, for example, the CIA began developing a new mission statement that included a new purpose: to keep track of environmental changes such as greenhouse warming and deforestation in third world nations, and social responses to those changes.

Most organizations resist ideological changes. Basic conservative inertia keeps organizations from making drastic changes quickly. For example, numerous Christian denominations debated the issue of slavery for over fifty years before the Civil War. Some denominations split over the issue of slavery. Similar splits may occur in church organizations and other private organizations over green issues—including the issue of birth control—during the 1990s.

Large changes in the society are sometimes required before an organization will open to change or before a crisis of sufficient proportion occurs that will allow reformers to come into power positions in an organization. Until such times, individuals and small groups can pursue other community goals, present ideas and models for other people to work within the organization, or to work in ways that subvert the organization.

Strategies for change include forming a change movement within an existing organization, precipitating a situation that requires the leadership or membership of an organization to choose decisively one alternative or another—if the majority chooses a non-green decision, for example, the minority has the option of forming their own organization. Distraction of an organization's leadership or massive withdrawal of membership in voluntary organizations makes the organization impotent to achieve its stated purposes.

In public agencies, legislative pressures can force agency directors to change policies and practices—either positively or negatively from an environmental perspective. Provision of funding can make programs work, while budget cuts can emasculate otherwise effective programs. Appointments of strong administrators who are advocates of the agency's purposes can bring new vitality, camaraderie, and creativity to an agency. On the other hand, appointments of administrators who are fundamentally opposed to an agency's programs can demoralize a dedicated staff and cripple an agency. The strengthening or weakening of environmental regulations, and their implementation, is in the hands of our elected government officials—and ultimately, the courts.

Massive protests by workers—strikes, work stoppages, and pressure by employee organizations on management—can win concessions from reluctant management. This has been proven time and again, from the labor strikes of the 1930s to the civil rights demonstrations of the 1960s.

REFORM IN THE CHURCHES

Reform of religious organizations is perhaps most important for those attempting to reform major institutions in liberal-industrial society. Perhaps only religions and churches have the power to move us into post-modern world views where we accept the sense of sacredness of all life, not just human life, on earth. Reforming Christian churches into an ecocentric perspective involves the work of church scholars, philosophers of religion, religious leaders, and a multitude of active, hard-working, and persistent members of churches who demand that Christian church leaders shed their metaphysical blinders and accept the "ecological unconscious," as Theodore Roszak calls our being in the cosmos, as the grounding within which the church occurs.

Thomas Berry, a Catholic-trained thinker, points the way for reforming Christian thought in his book *The Dream of Earth.* Berry writes, "The evolutionary process finds its highest expression in the earth community seen in its comprehensive dimensions, not simply in a human community reigning in triumphal dominion over the other components of the earth community. The same evolutionary process has produced all the living and nonliving components of the planet" (*Teilhard in the Ecological Age*).

While many Americans have been preoccupied with the fanatical attacks by fundamentalist Christians on basic environmental reforms such as lowering the birth rate and protection of endangered species, leaders of Christian denominations in many nations have begun to join with leaders of other religions in bringing forth the relation between religion and ecology. The extensiveness of the discussions and the heartfelt expressions of concern by leaders of many different churches show the power that such a union can have.

For example, the World Wildlife Fund has nourished a continuing series of discussions among church leaders through its Network on Conservation and Religion. In 1991 the World Wildlife Fund participated in a gathering of leaders of eleven major orthodox churches—who for many years were separated by political and historical differences—to discuss their shared commitment to conservation. Out of these discussions came a joint statement in which major orthodox churches agreed:

■ each church will call upon all humanity to adopt a simpler lifestyle based upon the asceticism of the church;

■ each church will dedicate September 1 as a special feast day of the environment to act as a focus for thinking and action;

■ each church will undertake programs of Christian environmental education from Sunday school to schools of theology;

■ each church will evaluate its lands, buildings, and investments to insure they are used in as environmentally friendly a way as possible and to make changes where necessary;

■ each church will gather scientists and environmental advocates in their own countries to help make these changes.

(*The New Road,* Dec. 1991, p. 3).

Ecofeminist writers have questioned some of the basic attitudes of Jewish and Christian religious traditions. Some of these writers point to the value of the cult of the Goddess, the ancient religion of the Middle East, as a counterpoint to the excessive dominating theology of the male-headed theology of western Christianity. Buddhist teachers, including the Dalai Lama, Thich Nhat Hanh, and Joanna Macy have written extensively on the connection between Buddhism and deep ecology. Robert Aiken's provocative collection of essays, *The Mind of Clover: Essays in Zen Buddhist Ethics* (1984), includes in-depth discussion of Buddhist foundations for ecosophy. Numerous Native American speakers and academic philosophers who have examined traditional Native American religions and philosophy have argued that traditional spiritual practices found in many Native American tribes provide a substantial metaphysical basis for ecosophy.

The problem, or so it seems to me, in the context of American and Canadian culture, is partly a political problem and partly a problem of the inertia of organizations. The political problem is based on the extensive use of fundamentalist Christianity by some spokespeople of that view to engage in repressive political action. When politicians such as former Representative William Dannemeyer, a California Republican, speak to Christian church groups and traditional value groups and say that the basic problems in America today are homosexuals and environmentalists, we can conclude only that homosexuals and environmentalists have replaced communists as the "evil empire." The problem of inertia is that organizations tend to do what they have been doing unless prodded into action. When churches see that people are leaving their congregations in droves or when protesters appear at their doors, they tend to begin to listen.

In the congregational model of church found in many Protestant denominations, in the Society of Friends, and in many Buddhist Sanghas, open discussion is encouraged and decisions are made only after near consensus is reached in the congregation. In such settings the process of deep questioning is appropriate. Major religious changes occur after examination of the question, "What does it mean to be human?"

Deep questioning along with deep religious rituals celebrating the successful hunt or the changing of the seasons or the connection between earth and sky are profound ways to "nest" the human in ecological consciousness.

The great Gestalt philosopher Paul Goodman called for a "neolithic consciousness." Ecologist Paul Shepard calls for a "paleolithic consciousness." Theodore Roszak calls it an "ecological unconscious." If churches and religious congregations cannot lead the way to this postmodern exploration of our place in the cosmos, it is unlikely that Christian or Jewish or any other churches can help much in the great social transformations that are necessary to move us beyond the detour of western anthropocentrism and liberal/economic growth policies. If churches do not take a leading role—in recognizing the great "ecological unconscious" from an ecocentric perspective—then they might at least provide a historical model for the kind of social organization that might be appropriate for the Age of Ecology. This model would incorporate the traditional virtues of love and charity in a caring community based on ecocentric principles.

188

CHAPTER 10

ECOCITIES?

Psychologists and writers such as Lewis Mumford, Paul Shepard, and Theodore Roszak see the mega-city as the fullest development of the pathological logic of modern, industrial civilization. Especially in the mega-city, human egoistic domination has shut off communication with what Theodore Roszak calls the "ecological unconscious." The task of the "ecological fieldworker" living in or under the influence of a mega-city is not only to encourage changes in behavior which have been discussed throughout this book—recycling, reduction in extravagant levels of consumption, downscaling, etc.—but to find ways to access the deep "ecological unconscious" as a vital force for self-realization.

Comments concerning lifestyles and behavior for people living in mega-cities, from the perspective of ecocentric philosophy and the practice of deep ecology must, in my opinion, be taken as preliminary. It must be admitted that few major writers or philosophers in the deep ecology movement have discussed the phenomena of mega-cities and the search for "right livelihood" of those who live in and are influenced by mega-cities. By mega-city I mean cities that have grown beyond what demographers called "metropolitan areas," cities which have grown so large in human population and physical domination of the landscape—water systems, power grids, streets and highways, domestic and industrial development—that they have virtually transformed the whole ecosystem. These are cities with human populations from one million to twenty million (the latter was the estimated population of Mexico City in 1990).

While many supporters of the deep, long-range ecology movement live in mega-cities, the major philosophers of deep ecology have focused on wildness, mountains, and the sense of place that comes from long, careful and caring attachment to more "natural" areas. A book on the Norwegian roots of deep ecology is called *Wisdom of the Open Air.* Arne Naess titled his version of ecophilosophy "Ecosophy T" with the "T" standing for "Tvergastein," his mountain place. "Tvergastein" means "crossed stones," referring to angled quartz crystals found in the rockfalls behind his hut. George Sessions in his article "Deep Ecology in California" discusses leading philosophers who spent a great amount of time in wild areas and concludes that the only viable long-range solution to the "environmental crisis" is cessation of both human population growth and the type of economic development which finds it fullest expression in mega-cities.

Gary Snyder, a leading philosopher and supporter of deep ecology, in his much praised book *The Practice of the Wild* (1990), draws inspiration from travels in the wilds of Alaska, from ancient forests of the Pacific Northwest, from indigenous peoples, and from bioregional studies in his home bioregion of the Yuba River watershed on the west side of the Sierra in California.

Dolores LaChapelle, a leading writer on deep ecology, lives in the San Juan Mountains of Colorado.

In my opinion, however, we must address the question of how is it possible to engage the "practice of the wild," or as I have called it in this book "consciousness practice" or the practice of an "ecological fieldworker" while living under the influence of a mega-city?

I refuse to accept that those who live under the influence of mega-cities are condemned, in the words of Chief Seattle, "to the end of living, the beginning of survival."

My preliminary conclusion is that it is possible to engage the "practice of the wild" or "consciousness practice" while living under the influence of a mega-city, but this will be "hard practice." I take that phrase from comments made by my Aikido sensei. For many years, before age and physical ailments caught up with me, I practiced Aikido at a dojo several times a week. Aikido has been called a "martial art," but that term is misleading. Aikido means the practice of learning where our center is, moving from our center, blending, following the flow of energy, and in its philosophy, coming to the realization of "no breaks" between body, mind, and spirit. In other words, harmonious realization.

During my studies in Aikido, the sensei, or teacher, would sometimes distinguish between "soft" practice and "hard" practice. Soft practice is less physically rigorous, focusing on technique and blending exercises. But more than that, in my understanding of the distinction at least, it means learning to yield, gracefully opening to become aware of the flow of energy, or *ki* as it is called in Aikido. Hard practice sessions are both physically demanding, where we learn to take hard falls in rapid succession, and more intense, more focused, and more demanding. Such hard practice sessions were exhilarating and exhausting, with occasional injuries—sprained ankles, broken toes.

Living in or under the influence of a mega-city, whether as a homeless person or living in luxury with all the modern comforts and conveniences, is hard practice from the perspective of deep ecology.

I admit that I do not have extensive experiences from living in a mega-city. I was raised in the bucolic suburbs of Kansas City. I never saw people fighting in the streets, never saw anyone with a weapon on the streets, never saw a homeless person wandering through the streets until after I graduated from college. I attended colleges located in small towns surrounded by farmlands and forests. For the past two decades I have lived in a socially and environmentally progressive town in northwestern California that has been given national recognition for its innovative sewage treatment plant (which is integrated with a wetlands restoration project on the site of a closed landfill dump). Arcata, a city of 15,000 inhabitants, has developed a successful recycling program, and has thus far been successful in efforts to protect the community forest (owned by the city) by implementing ecological forestry practices. It has protected wetlands and farmlands through the city master plan and has vigorously worked to protect air and water quality for its citizens.

In comparison to the situation in many mega-cities, the vital needs of citizens are well provided for, and those vital needs are fulfilled without further destruction of rivers, wetlands, forests, and farmlands in the region wherein the city is located. Indeed some of the ongoing projects of the city are aimed at restoring and healing areas degraded by human activity in the past.

The mega-city, by definition, is such a humanized landscape that even remnants of "wildness" have been exiled to the periphery. Most wild animals—including predators—and many native plants are exterminated or marginalized. Great bureaucracies dominate, control, and domesticate the physical landscape as well as the landscape of mind. The mega-city is qualitatively different from the pueblo or the village.

Some observers see the mega-city as a necropolis, a place of the dead. Some observers envision the future of mega-cities in the scenario of Mexico City in the early 1990s. An estimated twenty million humans are crowded into a valley at seven thousand feet elevation, a valley surrounded by higher mountains. During the winter months typical air-inversion patterns hold in pollution from oil refineries, industrial factories, and auto exhausts. When winds blow they carry dry fecal matter from open dumps. The air in the valley of Mexico, according to many human health experts, during some winter months is unfit for human consumption. Some will see the situation of Mexico City as an extreme case.

In deciding on a lifestyle appropriate for an "ecological fieldworker" in a mega-city, the slogan "Live Simply So That Others Might Simply Live" includes a commitment to the life processes of the ecosystem wherein the city is located, to the lives of species threatened by human encroachment on their habitat—due to the transformation of their habitat into the city's infrastructure and sphere of influence; and, due to the expropriation of their clean air and clean water for the dumping of wastes.

In preparation for writing this book I traveled to the Los Angeles basin. Arriving during the most intense part of an unusually strong series of winter storms, I found the Los Angeles River in flood stage. The radio reported drowning of several people in the upper basin of the Los Angeles River watershed, in the San Fernando Valley. The United States Corps of Engineers many years ago built a flood control dam in the upper watershed to control water under the circumstances of large storms. According to some survivors, the people who escaped from their flooded vehicles did not realize they were on a floodplain that could be expected to flood during major winter storms. "I thought I was in a park," one survivor was quoted on the radio as saying when he was rescued. When the floodplain is dry it is managed as a public park.

For two weeks during these winter storms I stayed on a wooden boat moored in a marina in the Los Angeles harbor at San Pedro near the mouth of the Los Angeles River at Terminal Island. Terminal Island is built on what was once a vast marsh, wetland, sand dune area at the mouth of the Los Angeles River. Especially when arriving at night, driving empty streets under the glare of streetlights, Terminal Island seems a place where machines have taken over from humans. Sounds of mechanical equipment loading and unloading ships, massive hulks of coal ships and container ships loom in the night. Sounds of machines in vast oil refineries and sounds of conveyer belts in faceless warehouses fill the night air.

During the days, I sat with my friends in the cozy cabin of their wooden boat and listened to stories of how they attempt to live simply in the mega-city. From the taped conversations, the following few remarks give a flavor of their "hard practice."

> Even though we live simply in comparison to many, we can cut a lot of fat. I've been experimenting with gardening with plants used by native species, but we are dependent on the web of civilization.

> We live on this boat, twenty-eight feet, and with careful consideration of each other we can live quite well. I consider this boat too big. I don't take it out on frivolous trips. It's our home. We try to eat lower on the food chain most of the time.

> I want to live even simpler. On a stormy day it's hard to imagine a homeless person living a good life, but other than stormy weather, homeless people who are not sick or mentally ill can live a relatively elegant lifestyle. I remember one man in San Francisco who was living with some other people in a basement with cubicles. He had some books, a TV, a rocking chair, and he seemed to be having a fine time.

I think of designing a small homestead, semi-underground, with greenhouses as part of the house, oriented to catch the maximum of sunlight. I'm not against technology. I want designers to apply the principles we already know to simple, elegant, less costly dwelling spaces.

I've been trying to move down the food chain, down the impact chain all the time. It gets better all the time.

I know what a beautiful place the estuary of the L.A. River was. The whole L.A. Harbor development is contrived for profit. We rarely see any wild animals, and when I see a great blue heron landing on a yacht or see a seal swimming in polluted waters in the harbor, I feel sad that we have so damaged their habitat.

We put our garden next to the public lavatory at the marina because we wanted it to be seen by other people coming to the marina. The manager gave us permission and we brought in dirt loaded in sacks. We've harvested lettuce, carrots, broccoli, zucchini, and peas. Yet, the garden is downwind from the small boat repair shop at the marina. Every day they are using toxic paints and all kinds of chemicals on the boats, but for us the garden is an experiment and a demonstration. We eat vegetables from the garden and they probably have some residues of toxins. The whole marina is toxic as far as I am concerned. But we are committed to living here, being an example of simple living. Sometimes it is like working in the emergency ward of a huge hospital. We see dead and dying seals and birds almost every day.

My friends did not use the word "ecocity," but some ecological fieldworkers have used that term to refer to their vision of the city. In some ways I find the term "ecocity" an oxymoron. Every mega-city is a humanized landscape—concrete buildings, asphalt streets, and rivers and streams contained in concrete channels, massive landfills on wetlands, massive alteration of native vegetation to suit the whims and fancies of developers, politicians, planners and landscape designers.

When I read of some so-called ecological restoration projects in a mega-city, I wonder whether these are hopeful experiments or trivial programs developed to give the illusion of wildness. Peregrine falcons are placed in nests on balconies of skyscrapers so the falcons can feed on pigeons that plague the city street-sweeping department with their droppings. Newspapers call this an ecological "success story."

New regulations are implemented to improve air quality in the Los Angeles basin. The removal of products from the market—some paints and starter fluids for outdoor barbecues that are known to cause air pollution—force residents to change a few of their habits. These and other measures result in some improvements in air quality.

How does the ecological fieldworker address the powerful institutions of the city? The banks, business, bureaucracy, government, and institutions of research and higher education are even more threatening to psychological health and well-being than the polluted air is to physical health. When the self becomes a commodity to be traded, sold, manipulated for sale on the marketplace, even the most basic human integrity is lost. The Department of Human Resources Development—a name not unfamiliar in many cities—has the cold ring of the resource development ideology. Intrinsic worth of people is no more honored and respected than the intrinsic worth of wild animals.

The ecological fieldworker contemplates the meaning of ecological restoration. Recovering, and rediscovering the wildness of cities requires penetrating and uncovering the concrete blanket that entombs nature, freeing rivers to spill onto their floodplains and find *their* way to the sea, and clearing the footprints of people from vast areas of urban blight and urban sprawl—undevelopment on a massive scale in concert with downscaling cityscapes and revitalizing urban lifestyles.

The ecological fieldworker in a mega-city asks, "Where in the city do native plants still bloom in the spring? Where along the freeways do some wild or semi-wild animals still burrow and bear their young? Where did native, indigenous peoples in this bioregion gather their wild seed, dig for clams along the bay or estuary, or hunt animals? Where did they hold their rituals and where were their lodges located?"

Previous to this century only a few cities, during limited periods of time, ever had more than a few hundred thousand residents. Rome in the first century, reached a population of one million (and during its period of greatest power imported vast numbers of wild animals, lions, tigers, bears and other great mammals, for the killing sports at the Coliseum). At the beginning of the nineteenth century, London approached a population of one million. In the late twentieth century, cities of three million are common, and more and more cities in third world nations reach into the tens of millions of human residents. There is no historical example of metropolitan regions of the size now exploding—cities of over five million population, upward to twenty million residents as in Mexico City. Never have so many humans lived away from the sources of their food and water, away from wild nature.

Large cities are basically exploitive. There is no known way to sustain the food requirements and water requirements of cities of more than 500,000 residents within a limited bioregion, for example within the watershed of the Los Angeles River. The optimal population of any city based on its biogeographical location, in my opinion, must be addressed before any model of a green city can be envisioned.

City dwellers need to assess the true, ongoing "cost" of the environmental impact of their city. The true environmental costs of cities are staggering—widespread transformation of landscapes for massive oil and gas development, strip-mining operations, and the decimation of natural forests to provide raw resources to cities; destruction of living rivers to fill reservoirs to supply water to cities; huge hydroelectric, fossil-fuel, and nuclear fission plants to provide electricity to cities; industrial farming practices to provide food to cities; toxic waste dumpsites to store hazardous wastes generated in cities; land-fill dumps for trash generated in cities; a pallor of smog that reduces the quality of life and healthfulness of people living in cities—the environmental impacts of cities reach far beyond city limits.

The so-called "cultural benefits" of cities—theater, opera, shopping areas, tourist attractions, museums—are benefits enjoyed by only a small percentage of city dwellers and visitors to cities. The presumed cultural advantages of cities are based on the power of corporations and bureaucracies and of the wealthiest one percent of city residents. Yet the arts and elite cultural traditions of theater and opera are not dependent upon excessive growth and development, and resultant destruction of natural systems. On the contrary, the creative energies in theater, arts and music should flourish in a downscaling society.

When a great storm sweeps through an urban aggregation, such as a hurricane, fire (as in the Oakland hills in October, 1991), or earthquake, the event is, of course, covered in the news as non-normal. Citizens cry that we must "get back to normalcy" as soon as possible. "We must build higher levees along the river. We must contain the river so this tragic loss of human lives and property won't happen again. Our lives, our property must be protected from the ravages of wild nature."

After the immediate, vital needs of citizens are satisfied with emergency aid, provision for adequate food, water, and shelter, citizens have an opportunity to look again at their collective lifestyle. Rebuilding after a hurricane or earthquake or major fire could be an opportunity to apply principles of downscaling, protection of open space, use of native vegetation, and implementation of programs which can bring the wild back into the city.

General principles developed by planners and thinkers can be applied to make the cities more hospitable to humans as well as to the broader community of life. Examples can be found in William McHarg's classic book *Design with Nature,* Christopher Alexander's *A New Theory of Urban Design* and *Timeless Way of Building,* and from critics of cities including Lewis Mumford and Jane Jacobs. Can living rivers and estuaries, native plants and animals, and migratory birds and animals thrive in the presence of large human settlements? General guidelines point us in this direction.

- Minimize alteration of rivers, streams and wetlands and their associated wildlife habitats by designation of flood plains, wetlands, earthquake faults, and fire hazard areas as open space.
- Where possible use solar technology. Apply new design principles for passive solar heating and take advantage of the sunlight for thermal mass heating.
- Redesign our transportation systems to favor mass transport on new subways, monorails, or streetcars.

■ Cluster dwelling units so that each household can have its own plot of ground in which to grow vegetables, and attach greenhouses to dwellings so the residents can grow vegetables during the winter months.

■ Bring people closer to their work place so they don't have to commute so far.

■ Get people out of their vehicles and into other modes of transportation.

■ Integrate the countryside with the city through greenbelts and agriculture preserves which flow through the city.

These, and similar guidelines for urban planning, have been repeated in textbooks written for urban planners for over a generation. In some mega-cities major attempts have been made to implement these and similar guidelines. But the structure of social organization in mega-cities, the politics for growth and economic development, the unwillingness of real estate developers to compromise their profits, the unwillingness of citizens to tax themselves, and the difficulty in motivating various bureaucracies with different priorities—such as planning departments and transportation departments— to coordinate their efforts, have resulted in gridlock for sustainable long-range planning and gridlock on our streets and highways.

While appropriate from a land use perspective, the guidelines for environmentally benign urban planning are not adequately planned or carried out in a pro-growth political climate. Approaching the issues from a lifestyle based on ecocentrism and bioregionalism, imbued with the "practice of the wild" and "consciousness practice," the failures of planning in mega-cities, and adjoining exurbia are obvious.

Even major ecophilosophers provide only long-range goals and vision statements such as this statement, paraphrased from the work of Arne Naess: Large human populations are not necessary for gracious, elegant civilization in the midst of native biodiversity. A city of thirty thousand people can be culturally diverse, lively, interesting, and even exciting in human arts, crafts, music, theater, restaurants, politics, literature, education, and economic activity. Bigger is not necessarily better.

Bringing city dwellers back into awareness of the wild is a daunting task. People are attracted to cities because of jobs, excitement, interest in human diversity and opportunities for interaction with other people. The process has been continuing for centuries and has accelerated during this century. Cities as entities now seem to have a life of their own as destructive organisms. Cities overwhelm us, exhaust us with pollution and traffic and overstimulation, but many people, in their state of delusion, come back for more.

One approach is suggested by Peter Berg, a founder of the Planet Drum Foundation in the San Francisco Bay region and a supporter of the bioregional movement. Berg suggests bringing the bioregional movement into the mega-cities. Berg says:

> Begin with where we're at. We all live in some geographic place. And here's the accompanying mysterious and very critical situation: the places where we live are alive. They are bioregions, unique life-places with their own soils and landforms, watershed and climate, native plants and animals, and many other distinct natural characteristics. Each characteristic affects the others and is affected by them as in any other living system or body. And *biore*gions are all different from each other. . . . People are also an integral part of lifeplaces. What we do affects them and we are in turn affected by them. . . . Cities don't hover on space platforms. They are all within bioregions and can be surprisingly dependent on fairly close sources for food and water, at least. All of them can become more responsible for sustainability by lessening their strain on the bioregions where they are situated ("Growing a Life-Place Politics," 1986).

In articles and books written during the past decade, Berg addresses the question of what's possible for ordinary people. Pursuing sensible goals in the short term can further the overall goal of greening their city.

Focusing on the vision of "green cities" can bring together neighborhoods, people from diverse cultural and religious backgrounds, and can bring together men and women, younger and older people. The slogan used to diffuse multi-ethnic and racial conflict, "Unity in Diversity," has meaning in the deep, long-range ecology movement when it is interpreted to mean working together for the diverse life-forms and on-going life processes of the bioregion within which the city exists.

Focusing on daily habits of mindfulness means remembering and seeking frequently to experience the life processes of the bioregion wherein the city is built. Weekends can be seen as a period not to "escape from the city" into the countryside but to explore the frequently degraded wetlands, rivers, marshes, and other types of landforms upon which the city is built. Participating in the life of the city means participating in tending toxic waste dumps and decommissioned nuclear reactors. It means participating in the process of decomposition as part of the life cycle—decomposing freeways, decomposing conventional attitudes, decomposing the inertia of public agencies and private companies.

Only when residents demand the "freedom of the wild" will the ecocity, which is lurking under the concrete of the humanized landscape, be allowed to emerge. Find the bedrock, the natural contour of the land upon which the city must rest, and build upon that an authentic place in which to dwell.

SOME PRACTICAL (AND SOME IRREVERENT) THOUGHTS FOR LIVING IN A METROPOLIS

■ Practice endless compassion
■ Commit endless random beautiful actions.
■ Meditate on the life of a tree living with its roots under concrete.
■ Discover a path to right livelihood.
■ Remember when the moon is full each month and howl like a wolf.
■ Speak up for coyote and bear.
■ Dream of ravens in the city.
■ Be a raven, a hawk, a fish in the stream, a decomposer.
■ Dwell in wildness and freedom.
■ Remember the season.
■ Celebrate the longest night, the winter solstice.
■ Remember what species of wild animals once lived in the space where you dwell.
■ Oppose arguments by developers, city planners, politicians, business and

civic leaders based only on demands for growth and development.

■ Oppose any development that involves further humanizing and domestication of wetlands, estuaries, native habitat, or habitat of rare, threatened, or endangered species, or channelizing streams, or modifying the landscape with freeways, bulldozing of whole valleys, or dredging harbors for bigger and bigger ships and bigger ports.

■ Visit the dump frequently to witness the amount of trash generated by extravagant consumption and massive population of the mega-city, and participate in restoration projects on the site of dumps that have been closed.

■ Make a pilgrimage to the local nuclear reactor or toxic sites remembering our commitment to future generations of life-forms. Teach children about their nuclear legacy and the causes of their legacy. Help them to be proud to be guardians of nuclear waste sites.

■ Take children to areas where wildness is still felt. Remembering that city parks and playgrounds are humanized landscapes, give children the opportunity to play in relatively unstructured situations in wild regions of mountains, prairies, deserts, seashores, or other types of landscapes within which the city exists. Environmental education programs in public and private schools rarely provide for this type of experience. If children are to discover what Arne Naess calls the "intuition of deep ecology," if they are to make contact with their "ecological unconscious," time to play in relatively wild areas is essential.

■ Teach children their responsibility to far-future generations of the myriad forms of life on this planet.

■ Tear down fences. Oppose fences and walls, oppose massive walls.

■ Make a political statement by riding a bicycle while wearing a mask to reduce exposure to contaminated air, on busy streets.

■ Create art projects in cities that revitalize native diversity. Artists can get away with more than conventional people. Artists can import soil and plant a field of wheat (in cities with appropriate climate such as the American Midwest) on lots in the middle of cities and call it an art project.

■ Create art projects with the rubble from tearing down fences and freeways. Make art out of cast-off tires, pottery, metal and plastic.

■ Walking is a subversive activity in many cities. Demand the right to walk; demand the freedom to walk.

■ Discover the streams, the source of streams in the city, follow the streams, work for free-flowing streams.

■ Oppose golf courses.

■ Oppose any housing developments that use a golf course on the site as a way to attract buyers.

■ Teach children the fundamental laws of ecology.

■ Teach teenagers about the population crisis, about the values of nonparenting and the responsibilities of parenting, about birth control, and about safe sex practices, including the use of condoms.

■ Participate in multicultural dialogue where people discuss the traditions within their own culture for the "practice of the wild."

■ Make every day a day of resistance, a day of affirmation.

■ Defend trees, any trees, but especially older trees, of native species or exotics. It is a community decision to cut a tree or even severely cut the limbs of a tree. Trees have rights to city streets and air space. Trees usually give shelter to plants and animals.

■ Try leaving trees or branches of trees which fall in storms on your lawn. Just as downed trees have a role on the forest floor, so downed trees in the cities have a place for teaching us about recomposing and decomposing in the cycle of life.

■ Keep riding the crest of the emerging green wave, combining the concerns of many for social justice with ecocentric concern for the health of the natural systems.

CHAPTER 11

ECOTOURISM

Dogen, the Buddhist teacher credited with bringing Zen Buddhism to Japan in the twelfth century, advised his students to walk in the mountains. "The mountains are walking," he wrote in his famous "Mountains and Rivers Sutra," and "He who does not know his own walking does not know the blue mountains are walking." John Muir, remembering his mountain walks, "ramblings," he called them, told his readers, "Go to the mountains and get their glad tidings." Dogen was talking about a pathway, an opening to enlightenment. Muir's enlightenment in the Sierra Nevada, his "range of light," was strengthened by an emphatic understanding for the mountains' feeling.

Dogen, John Muir, and Henry David Thoreau were a few travelers among many on journeys to further reaches of transpersonal awareness. They were not looking for just another roadside attraction on their journey. They were engaged in a journey of spiritual growth. Journeying into wild nature on spiritual quests is an ancient practice in many religious and cultural traditions. Tibetans journey to specific holy mountains of Tibet. After ritual preparation, Yuroks in training to "make medicine" journey to the "high country" in the Siskiyou mountains in northwestern California. Australian aboriginals follow "dream lines" that connect the landscape to a cosmological framework. Such types of journeys take careful preparation, skilled guides, and willingness to take physical and psychological risks.

Joan Halifax, an anthropologist and Buddhist teacher, in her book *The Fruitful Darkness: On the Ecology of Initiation—Notes on Crossing the*

Threshold (1993), describes her personal journey, including many travels in Africa, among American Indians, and among indigenous traditional shamans in Asia, to find what she calls "root-truth." She "sought fresh answers in ancient fields." Based on the ancient tradition of initiation, Halifax used her travels to learn truth about the practice of ecology, "an ecology of mind and spirit in relation to the earth." For Halifax, the practice of ecology is "based on the experience of engagement and the mystery of participation."

Contemporary travelers who are engaged in the practice of ecology need new skills and clear intentions, as well as skilled guides, when they enter wild areas or areas of special biological and cultural sensitivity. These contemporary travelers are labeled in this chapter as "ecotourists." Ecotourists are both open to new experience and, paradoxically, carry with them an ideological framework which includes the premise that the traveler should both participate in the ongoing life of the community in which he or she is a visitor and attempt to protect, nurture, help, and defend the ecological integrity of the places visited.

In the following pages I focus on some of the attitudes we carry with us when we begin a vacation or make a short trip into a nature reserve. I offer what I hope are practical suggestions for preparing our attitude and changing our behavior to conform to the needs of the area we are visiting. I am defining nature tourism, or "ecotourism," as it is most frequently called in travel literature, as a visit to an area of biological interest or geological, biological and/or Native cultural interest. Examples of participation in commercial trips featuring themes of ecotourism include boat trips to visit areas frequented by whales, trips designed to help the visitor explore some of the rich biological diversity of the Amazon rainforest, trips to the Galapagos Islands of Ecuador, and visits to the Kodiak area of Alaska to view grizzly bears in their native habitat. For purposes of this chapter I am also including under the term "ecotourism" certain types of adventure—such as organized trips on whitewater sections of rivers, mountain trekking in the Himalayan region, organized diving trips to waters off Belize, and walking trips in mountain regions—travel that focuses on personal growth for the "practice of ecology."

By some estimates of researchers for the travel industry, only about 10 percent of the two trillion dollars a year devoted to tourist travel is spent on ecotourism, but this form of tourism is growing by 20 to 30 percent a year. Even the most dedicated bioregionalist sometimes has the opportunity to travel away from home to enjoy a different area of biological, geological, or ecological interest.

INTENTION OF TRIPS TO NATURE RESERVES AND SPECTACULAR SITES

Ecotourism involves different attitudes than those found in other types of travel. The general theme of tourist travel advertising is basically hedonistic—that is, "enjoy yourself!" This seductive slogan is broadcast in thousands of brochures and advertisements distributed by the tourist industry and by Chambers of Commerce and local governments. Throughout this book I have emphasized the importance of finding multiple sources of joy in our daily experiences; however joyful experiences are not hedonistic. In my definition, hedonism involves unthoughtful indulgence. However, our general desire to find joy should not distract us from our responsibilities as visitors.

For example, millions of people visit national parks and monuments in the United States and Canada each year. The environmental impact of tourist development—including hotels, roads, golf courses, and shopping malls to serve the desires of some tourists and increase profits for concessionaires—on wilderness values in many of these parks, as well as on biodiversity and biological habitats of specific creatures in national parks, has been documented by numerous researchers. The situation in national parks—decline in species diversity, pollution, overcrowded park facilities, lack of restoration programs—has led one sympathetic critic of national parks to call for a "regreening" of national parks (Michael Frome, *Regreening the National Parks,* 1992).

Unless we travel in an " environmental bubble" in poverty-stricken third world nations and poor regions of North America—taking all the conveniences of home with us or staying in hotels built to serve tourists from wealthy nations with conventional conveniences such as hot water and air conditioning—unless we close our eyes to the suffering around us, we must be aware of the wounds to forests, pollution in rivers, and hunger of people in local regions through which we travel.

In my experience, some people who embark on a trip to a nature reserve, wildlife sanctuary, or national park have an intention that is too narrowly focused. They want to see the "most spectacular," whether that be a special rock formation, a famous mountain, or a famous seasonal gathering of wildlife of some species—grizzly bears, for example, gathering to feed on the salmon run in certain rivers in Alaska. An intention that is too narrowly focused may blind visitors to the possibility of learning something new about themselves and something new about the people in different cultures that they encounter on their journey. On virtually all kinds of nature trips, visitors must come in contact with local people, residents of the region. It seems to me that only by engaging in some form of denial can a visitor be unaware of political controversy over local environmental issues. The openness to new experience, for ecotourists, is not without a "filter." The ideological position of an ecotourist is to minimize his or her own impact on the processes of nature and to encourage socially responsible protection of the integrity of nature.

Exploring ways to protect the integrity, beauty, and life of a region visited on a specific trip to a specific location can be seen as part of the discussion within the group. While it is possible to visit some mountains, some deserts, some arctic regions by planning one's own trip, by chartering a boat or plane for a small group of people, or by hiring guides or trackers to find wildlife, tourists more commonly use a tour company.

Let me offer an example of some of the difficulties of intent that I discovered during a nature trip organized by a commercial tour company a few years ago. The trip was advertised by the tour company as a whale-watching trip to winter resting areas for California gray whales in lagoons on the west coast of Baja, California. I flew to San Diego and boarded a one-hundred-foot boat with thirty other intrepid whale watchers—teachers, retired people, a single mother with her teenaged daughter, several businessmen with their wives.

The itinerary included stops on nearly a dozen islands off the coast of Baja, looking at native plants and exploring some of the impact of exotic, introduced plants and animals on island systems. Some of these islands are occupied year-round by local fishermen and their families; others are occupied only during certain months when local fishing cooperatives send small groups of people to fish for specific species. On one island we observed burros grazing hillsides to bare dirt. We were told the burros were brought to the island a decade before to transport material to build a new lighthouse on the island for fishers. When the lighthouse was completed, the burros were left to fend for themselves.

The passengers on this trip had the opportunity to read scientific and naturalistic reports of the areas in an extensive library on board. Each evening the naturalist on board gave an illustrated lecture on the island or natural area we would visit the next day.

When our boat reached Magdalena Bay, we anchored in the zone prescribed by Mexican authorities, outside the area of the lagoon where most of the whales engage in amorous activities and bear their young. Each day while anchored in the lagoon we took small boats across the bay, watching whales playing in the waters. On a few occasions a friendly whale passed under our small boat close enough for us to see the hairs on its back and even to allow some of us to reach our arms into the waters and touch the back of the whale.

I was a young ecophilosopher and environmental activist at the time, and in evening conversations, I kept asking questions about our relationship with whales and about how we could help protect them (at the time there was no worldwide ban on commercial killing of whales). I asked the naturalist on board during conversations after his evening lectures, "Can we write letters to the Mexican government asking the government to take more stringent precautions to protect the whales? About the burros we saw on the island—they are destroying native vegetation. Could we demand that they be transported back to mainland Baja?" After several attempts to ask such questions at dinner time, I was told by other passengers, in polite terms, to shut up. They were on this trip for pleasure, to enjoy their visit with whales, to commune with whales, not to discuss boring political questions or engage in political activism.

At the conclusion of our trip our leader admonished us to "keep in touch with each other" and provided us with the names and addresses of other passengers. I did write each passenger soon after returning home, enclosing a copy of a whale action newsletter from some environmental group and suggesting that we write to a specific politician to get his support for whale protection legislation. I did not receive any responses to my letters.

After that experience I realized that I personally cannot separate my political activism from my recreation. I feel an obligation to do something to help when I visit a natural area. I discovered that my intention for traveling was not only to learn new information, experience different cultures and situations, but also to use my time as a traveler to engage in activism. Having clarified my intention, I have devoted my vacation and recreational travel during the past few years to exploring regions of my own backyard—in the Klamath-Siskiyou Mountains. I have hiked drainages that the U.S. Forest Service planned to clearcut. I have visited sites where massive forest fires burned through tree plantations planted by the Forest Service after ancient forests were clearcut. I have taken trips on the Trinity River by canoe with groups of students seeking body-mind-spirit awareness. We worked with the river as our teacher, carefully listening to birds calling before dawn, diving deep into the pools to watch fish, watching miners dredge in spawning gravels along the river. When I tell my friends, even some environmentalists, that I plan to travel to this watershed or that mountain trail this weekend or for a week long trip, I sometimes receive an incredulous "I've never heard of that place. Why would you want to go there?"

This leads me to discuss another issue concerning our intention when planning trips to natural reserves, wildlife sanctuaries, or wild areas. In some social circles of well-educated, well-traveled people in our culture, it seems that one can score points in conversations on some not-clearly-defined scale of worth with friends or coworkers by visiting a spectacular "named" place, especially a world-class named place.

During the 1960s and 1970s trekking in the Himalayas seemed to be in vogue. In the 1980s the rainforests of the Amazon became more popular with North Americans. In the early 1990s my hip friends are going to Lake Baikal and the farther reaches of Siberia.

Tourists, we are told in news accounts in 1992, are returning to Tibet after the worldwide expression of horror over the Tianamen Square massacre and repression of human rights in China subsided. Western visitors going to Tibet seek not only the spectacular scenery of the mountains and sight of the wildlife but also the beautiful culture of traditional Tibetans. Visitors, however, cannot be blind to the contemporary situation. The Tibetan people have suffered greatly at the hands of Chinese oppression. Tourists in Tibet, and many other regions of the world, may feel compelled to speak out against human rights violations, even—if they happen to be in a public place when the events happen—to film police attacks on protesters, public executions, or damage from government destruction of sacred sites, or damage due to warfare or ethnic violence.

If we do not clarify our intentions as visitors and if we are not psychologically open to the wide range of experiences available during our journey, we may overlook the richness of experience and possibilities for social activism based on our experiences as tourists.

Arne Naess led several expeditions to the Himalayan mountains from his home in Norway and, while looking for a new route up a previously unclimbed mountain, he came to the conclusion that the moral action in that situation would be to leave the mountain unclimbed. He concluded that the intent to conquer mountains can lead to hubris. Going to a mountain and not climbing can encourage modesty. Naess suggests that modesty has little value unless motivated by deep feelings, feelings of how we understand ourselves as part of nature. "The smaller we come to feel ourselves compared to the mountain, the nearer we come to participating in its greatness. I do not know why this is so" ("Modesty and the Conquest of Mountains," in Tobias, *The Mountain Spirit*). *Modesty* is an alien word for some visitors, who take pride in telling other people about their exploits in finding wild grizzlies or kayaking previously unrun whitewater stretches of wild rivers, but Naess suggests that modesty includes maintaining an attitude that emphasizes protecting the integrity of a place we have visited even when talking about and reflecting upon our visit after we return home.

Naess expresses a concern that some nature enthusiasts will increase human impacts on beautiful places by incessantly writing, lecturing, showing pictures about certain places, implying "you *must* visit this area." The implication is that some spectacular places are more important to visit than other places. After he visited the canyonlands of the American Southwest, some people asked Naess to compare them to the fjords of Norway. He admitted that in comparison, the fjords seemed small and cramped. But the comparison had no useful purpose. The fjords of Norway have their own beauty, their own integrity, and their own natural history that visitors can appreciate and learn from. Naess suggests that visitors appreciate the intrinsic value of their experiences in each place and not be caught up in a game of false comparison. This game has many variations: for example, "I've counted X number of species of birds at such-and-such sanctuary," implying that more species are better than the few species that live around one's home.

After experiencing the spectacular, that is the biggest whales, the deepest canyon, the highest mountain, the largest herd of wild rhinos—the tourist is inclined to say, "When will I see again the most spectacular?" The danger is clear, as Naess says, "In the long run such a person mostly will develop an urge and need for the spectacular and a decrease of sensitivity. Using a long range perspective [on our experiences] nothing is gained and something is lost." What can be lost is deep appreciation for the biological diversity, the beauty, indeed the suffering in our own home bioregion—watching the flowering and withering of native plants, caring for the changes in the scenery of our own backyards. Naess concludes that it is wise to consider carefully ways to make our tourist travels relevant to greening our lifestyles and helping to protect the areas that we visit.

GREENING TOURIST TRAVEL

We can incorporate our tourist travels as part of greening our lifestyles. While we do not need to stay in our home bioregions for our whole lives, we should recognize that there are limits on ecotourism that, if transgressed, can reduce planetary and personal quality of life. In an age of easier access to most regions of the earth, the social system as well as ecological processes of vast areas can be damaged by too many tourists traveling through the area within a period of a few years. For example, after the discovery of the tropical rainforests of the Amazon by North American tourists during the 1980s, within a few years the government of Brazil recognized the environmental damage of the tourist boom to certain areas. More port facilities and airports were built. Fossil fuel was imported to run tourist boats, and tour operators dumped empty oil barrels outside of local villages. More wildlife was killed to make artifacts for sale to tourists. Cultural erosion began immediately as tourists began to transfer artifacts they brought with them—such as transistor radios—to indigenous people. In a report published by World Resources Institute, Kreg Lindberg concludes that mass tourism can upset the ecological balance in a region, disrupt the economy of the region, and overwhelm the local culture.

Ecotourism is frequently portrayed as a benign industry, encouraging preservation of wildlife and wild habitat while contributing to the local economy. However, the ecotourist industry—transportation, food supply, accommodations, sales of souvenirs to tourists, wastes created by tourists, introduction of diseases to local human and wildlife populations by tourists—can lead to environmental and social problems in local areas within very short periods of time. Even small groups of tourists regularly visiting the ice-free areas of Antarctica, for example, can contribute to destruction of fragile lifeforms that a visitor might not even notice unless educated by a knowledgeable tour guide. Scientists tell us that only one percent of Antarctica is ice-free, and that one percent supports the greatest variety of organisms on the continent. Facilities for scientists have been constructed on the ice-free area. Construction of tourist facilities in Antarctica in this same area continues the trend toward more road building, runway construction, and creation of dumps by the major signatories to the Antarctic treaty—the USSR, U.S.A., France, Chile, Argentina, New Zealand, and Australia. Reports compiled by Greenpeace indicate that oil drums are rarely taken back to the countries of origin. They are left by the tarmac where their contents are used to fuel the planes used by tourists.

Facilities for traveling scientists and tourists are far from the simple huts and sled dogs that the explorers took with them to Antarctica in the early decades of this century.

How can ecotourists address the problematic moral issues and environmental and social impacts of their own activities as visitors? Recognizing that the interest we have in ecotourism is part of our general concern for environmental quality, protection of endangered habitat, and endangered ecosystems, how can we travel in ways that encourage healing rather disruption of the places we love? How can we avoid, as some commentators have noted, "loving the place to death?" One general principle is to choose activities of intrinsic value rather than activities valued for social prestige. We can avoid traveling to sensitive habitats just to escape from depression, loneliness, and poor human relationships at home. We can place more emphasis on the traveling—enriching our lives along the way—rather than on focusing arrival at some destination.

We can avoid activities that local environmentalists, scientific studies, and government agencies suggest are disruptive to local habitat of wildlife and flora. For example, extensive research has documented the habitat needs of the desert tortoise in certain regions of the American Southwest. It seems irresponsible, therefore, to participate in a mass, cross-country motorcycle race across the California desert or to go offroading in areas of critical habitat in desert regions. Even though many people enjoy the challenge of offroad racing, "the needs of nature come first."

Some visitors have discovered that they find joy in restoring areas that were disrupted by their own trips and by other visitors who followed them. For example, regions of the Himalayan Mountains, favored by climbers and other visitors during the 1960s and 1970s, began showing signs of overuse during the 1980s. In 1992 Sir Edmund Hillary, the first man to reach the summit of Mount Everest, called for a moratorium on climbing the world's highest mountain so that it can recover from tourism. He said that his team, during their 1953 expedition to climb Everest, contributed to the junk heap on the mountain. In their exuberance in climbing a mountain uncontaminated by humans, they unthinkingly began littering the mountain. Peter Stone, a spokesperson for a group of mountaineers attending the

Earth Summit in Rio in June 1992, launched "An Appeal for the Mountains," whose aim is to preserve mountain regions of the earth for small populations of people living in the mountains and for environmentally responsible visitors.

One of the most general guidelines for ecotourism is to develop sensitivity—to the needs of local residents and to the situation of flora, fauna, and whole ecosystems. Stories brought back from tourists in some Himalayan regions indicate, for example, that tourists trekking in the mountains have increased pressure on local wood supplies. Tourists may be required to carry fossil-fuel stoves, and their own fuel supply, in some areas.

A general rule for visitors in designated wilderness areas administered by the U.S. Forest Service is "Pack it in, pack it out." Leave no trash, bury no trash. That rule is useful for ecotourists traveling in many regions of the earth. If you don't take home the personal trash you generated when you fly back from a tourist trip, work with the tour guide to insure that wastes will not create problems for local inhabitants, including nonhuman inhabitants. On trips by canoe or raft on many rivers in the American West, for example, the U.S. Forest Service and Bureau of Land Management require that defecation by humans be carried in containers and transported out of the river canyon at the end of the trip to an authorized organic waste disposal site. Recyclable materials, including bottles and cans, are taken to recycling centers. Part of the cost of the trip is the cost of handling wastes generated on the trip.

There are many guidebooks on how to act like a native in Paris or how to order a meal in Madrid without offending local sensibilities. We need similar guidance on how to relate to local flora and fauna in their native habitats. In the mountain gorilla park in the Central African nation of Rwandi, for example, small groups of tourists under the direction of an experienced guide can take day hikes in the mountain rainforest. If they encounter a group of gorillas, the tourists must stay a designated distance from the gorillas and can observe them only for one hour because humans can transmit respiratory diseases to gorillas and thus endanger their health. When tourists visit the Galapagos Islands reserve, they are required to stay on designated paths, and not attempt to touch any of the native animals which show no fear of humans (sailors in the nineteenth century easily captured giant turtles by turning them on their backs; the turtles were thus kept alive on the ships until the cook butchered them for the crew).

Ecologists use terms like *fragile, threatened,* and *sensitive* to describe regions that are increasingly popular with adventurous ecotourists. These include tundra regions, tropical coral reefs, islands, marine mammal breeding and resting areas, and waterholes in the deserts. In part of North America, some areas that are particularly sensitive to human impact are being zoned as "natural areas" or "botanical reserves," and only authorized scientists or visitors in small groups under the supervision of a qualified naturalist are allowed to visit the area.

Managers of some nature sanctuaries allow limited numbers of visitors who agree to follow guidelines on how to approach, when to approach, and what to wear when approaching wildlife. When contemplating a trip to a park, reserve, or animal breeding area, a visitor can anticipate some of the potential impact of his or her activities. For example, if one is interested in fishing, consider how heavily the area to be visited might be impacted by sports fishing. (Some nature conservancy groups encourage, or even require, catch and release flyfishing with the use of barbless hooks in the areas they manage.)

Hunters can avoid taking trophy specimens—and certainly hunting any threatened or endangered species. While some people object to any hunting on ethical grounds, some ecologists argue for eradication programs of certain introduced or non-native species in fragile and disturbed ecosystems. For example, some government agencies encourage hunting for wild goats and feral pigs on some lands they manage on the Big Island of Hawaii. Animals were introduced by European explorers and they bred prolifically, destroying native wildlife and flora. Killing wild goats, pigs, and burros— or, as an alternative, live-trapping the animals and transporting them out of sensitive areas and fencing them out—is one possibility for returning some of the habitat to native species.

Another general rule to remember in contemplating nature tourism is that visitors should not expect to impose their culture on the native people of the area visited. Unlike religious missionaries or military authorities, ecotourists are in the region to learn about it and to experience natural and cultural diversity. Openness of spirit, openness of mind, willingness to be flexible in daily routines allow a visitor to appreciate the joys of each day.

When a visitor arrives with an open mind, ready to participate as much as possible in local daily routines, ready to be transformed in a spirit of solidarity, and ready to accommodate rather than be accommodated by local residents, an exchange is possible that is beyond an exchange of commodities or exchange of money.

Travels to many areas of interest to ecotourists means travels to areas heavily impacted by industrial civilization or travels through areas of extreme poverty and suffering in third world nations. Buddhist traditions teach us not to avoid suffering but to attempt to understand the causes of the suffering. One implication of this principle is that ecotourists do not avoid visiting damaged ecosystems, areas of massive clearcut forests, toxic waste dumps, nuclear testing sites, and mining districts. Joanna Macy, one of the originators of the Nuclear Guardianship Project, has taken groups of people on pilgrimages to Kiev, Ukraine, to sit with the beings who suffered from the Chernobyl disaster. Just as some people visited the sites of Nazi death camps, which are included on the list of World Heritage Sites, to remember the suffering of the victims of these camps and resolve that this horrible action should not happen again, so some people visit Bhopal, or Three Mile Island, or the Hanford nuclear site, or the Nevada test site, or Alamogordo, or Hiroshima, or Bikini Island to witness the horrors of the atomic age and resolve that this knowledge that humanity now has will not be used to destroy the earth.

An ecotourist who is both socially and environmentally conscious does not overlook injustice, poverty, unequal distributions of power, or irresponsible behavior by government officials who are administering and managing national parks, wilderness areas, nature reserves, or other designated sanctuary areas. They should ask if officials are managing the area for the primary benefit of the flora and fauna, of the ecosystem, or managing it for the aesthetic and personal comfort of visitors. Ecotourists can resolve to be active in political and educational efforts to protect the integrity of the area visited after returning home.

Some people travel specifically to show solidarity with local environmentalists. A former student of mine, a resident of Hawaii, owns a small parcel in the Puna district of the Big Island. He invites groups of students and anyone else who is interested to visit his home and camp on his property. He leads visitors on hikes in the geothermal district. For several years he has been active in exposing the threats of geothermal development on the Big Island. Visitors are encouraged to contact government officials concerning geothermal development when they return home. They are encouraged to take photos, make videos, describe their experiences and, when they return home, to help the effort of protecting endangered rainforests on the Big Island.

Showing solidarity can also mean participating in demonstrations with local environmental groups. One time while visiting Mexico City to attend a conference on a different topic, I learned that a march opposing the opening of the first nuclear power plant in Mexico was being held in the city. On Sunday morning the main streets leading to the Presidential Palace were closed to traffic for several hours, and I and several other American tourists joined tens of thousands of Mexicans—farmers, students, women with children—in the demonstration against the nuclear power reactor. (I was opposed to repeating the mistake made in my home bioregion where we must now be perpetual guardians of the decommissioned, and contaminated, Humboldt Bay Nuclear Reactor site after less than fifteen years of service.) While traveling in a region, visitors can check with local environmental groups on planned actions. A friend recently returned from a southern state where she marched in solidarity with people who were opposing the siting of a toxic waste dump in their neighborhood. Just as visitors to Tibet and other parts of China bring home reports of human rights abuses, so ecotourists, on occasion, have the opportunity to bring back firsthand accounts of abuses to native vegetation, forests, flora, and fauna.

SERVICE TRIPS

Groups of recreationists focused around many different kinds of activities—kayaking, skiing, backpacking, surfing, rockclimbing, sailing, and diving, for example—are increasing the number and variety of service trips designed to engage in work projects in some of their favorite recreation sites. In sporting activities on the land, or in the water, people can see degradation occurring and sometimes suspect that they are suffering possible health hazards from industrial or farming operations near their recreation site.

For example, surfers in California saw, during the 1960s and 1970s, degradation to favorite surfing breaks—from breakwaters constructed by the Corps of Engineers, from dredging operations, and raw sewage from outfall pipes in bays and near surfing reefs, as well as from closure of historic public access to beaches by people building housing projects on beachfront property. A group of surfers in California formed the Surfrider Foundation, a nonprofit organization that engages in educational activities, and discussions with public officials, and serves as an information clearinghouse. Upon hearing the stories of surfers who surfed near the outfall of two pulp mills on the Samoa peninsula near the mouth of Humboldt Bay— stories of dizziness after surfing, eruptions on the skin and other ailments— and after discovering thousands of Clean Water Act violations, the Surfrider Foundation took Simpson Timber Corporation and Louisiana Pacific Corporation, owners of the pulp mills, to court. With the support of the EPA, the surfers won a settlement whereby the corporations agreed to install new equipment designed to reduce the danger of dioxin and to pay the surfers to create a new management plan for the beach area where the outfalls from the pulp mills are located.

The Sierra Club national outings department offers a variety of types of service trips. Trip projects include rebuilding sections of trail in designated wilderness areas, cleaning up campsites in wilderness areas, and other activities designed to restore human-damaged areas.

A group working through Earth Island Institute, located in San Francisco, offers trips to the Lake Baikal region of Siberia designed to assist the Russian national park service in their efforts to develop management plans for two national parks, one on either side of the lake. Among those recruited for these annual trips are social scientists, recreation planners, retired U.S. park administrators, and others who could provide some advice to their Russian counterparts while at the same time learning about and enjoying the Lake Baikal region.

Private conservancy groups sponsor work projects on areas under their management. In my own bioregion, the Friends of Dunes, a membership group that supports a project of the Nature Conservancy called the Lansphere-Christiansen Dunes, a unique coastal dune forest system between Humboldt Bay and the ocean, sponsors an annual trip to the dunes for supporters of the dunes projects. Friends of the Dunes, some of whom live hundreds of miles away, come to take walks with naturalists, watch birds, and help with the annual "lupin bashing": An exotic species of lupin (a shrub) was introduced by timber companies in the last century in an attempt to stabilize the shifting dunes so railroad tracks could be laid over them. As with many exotics, this exotic species of lupin outcompeted native vegetation, including a species of wallflower that is currently listed as threatened and endangered. Each year the Friends of the Dunes engage in manual labor to cut down and tear out lupin and restore the natural conditions that allowed wallflowers and other native plants to flourish on the dune system.

In another example, in southern California waters containing shallow reefs in the Santa Barbara Channel, divers for many years took abalone, a prized shell creature that, when prepared properly, provides a gourmet meal. The state Fish and Game Department noted a rapid decline in the number of mature abalone and put restrictions on the taking of abalone. Fearing that the abalone population would become threatened, scientists began an experimental program to raise abalone seeds—small offspring of abalone. Sport diving clubs were enlisted to help with placing these seed abalone in their natural habitat on the reefs. Sport divers, combining their interest in abalone with a sense of responsibility for the rapid decline in numbers of mature abalone, volunteered to put back abalone and to watch over them by reporting poaching activity.

In the Central American nation of Costa Rica, Americans and Canadians have volunteered to spend their vacations in Monteverde, a tropical forest reserve along the continental divide, working on a variety of projects—scientific studies, development of nature interpretation centers, and restoration of areas now included in the reserve that had been previously logged.

A group organized in Humboldt County, California, traveled to southern Chile to hike through and document on film the ancient temperate forests in that nation. After seeing the invasion of American logging corporations into Chile, this group came home resolved to help protect the forests of Chile and formed a new organization, Ancient Forests International.

Each of these examples shows how people can engage in adventure travel mindfully. These are not "fun trips" with endless parties, luxury hotels, and rich food. These are trips for people who are open to new experience, who want adventure but also recognize that they can help heal the wounds of the earth. They have a commitment to live life richly, rich in experience, compassion, and sharing of knowledge they have acquired in life.

A growing number of people forgo conventional tourist travel all together and devote their vacations, holidays, time away from school or jobs to join with others who are directly addressing gross destruction of nature. During the summer of 1990, hundreds of people—students, retirees, annual vacationers, and some unemployed—came to Humboldt County to participate in Redwood Summer, a series of demonstrations seeking protection for the remaining ancient forests held by private timber corporations and asking for radical reforms in timber harvest practices. A base camp and communication center was set up by local activists, and visitors helped to organize and conduct media campaigns, street theater, demonstrations at the gates of pulp mills, and educational efforts of many kinds. Many of these visitors returned to their homes with renewed commitment to work for reform of forest practices and to speak out for the long-term integrity of forests.

Some local environmental groups in northwestern California have produced information fact sheets to distribute to visitors coming through the redwood region. Environmentally conscious and concerned visitors want to take responsibility, to question the abuses of the forests by the timber corporations. People who love the forests, who are visiting regions experiencing gross deforestation encouraged by government agencies—regions such as British Columbia, Alberta, Maine, Washington, Oregon, California, Montana, Burma, Thailand, Malaysia, Indonesia, Victoria state of Australia, Chile, and Siberia, as well as Brazil—sense they have an obligation to tell those responsible for such deforestation their views on these issues.

Visitors to any areas of deforestation have an obligation, it seems to me, to look behind the "scenic strips" along the roads and to express their grief, concern, even outrage at irresponsible logging practices—nonsustainable harvest rates, clearcuts, destruction of the habitat of threatened and endangered species, and aerial spraying of herbicides. Some environmental groups encourage tourists to boycott certain areas until governments and corporations cease environmentally destructive practices. For example, some environmental groups in British Columbia encouraged tourists to boycott their province and inform the provincial government that they were boycotting the province because of the destructive forestry policy of the provincial government.

One option, which increasing numbers of people are taking, is to join an expedition sponsored by a group such as Greenpeace or The Sea Shepherd Society, or the Costeau Society, to sail to areas that are threatened by inappropriate actions and peacefully witness for the whales and other marine mammals, for the ocean ecosystem threatened by French nuclear testing in the South Pacific, for the life in the oceans threatened by massive drift nets in the North Pacific. Just as visitors go on pilgrimages to sites of nuclear disasters, so they go to sites where massive exploitation of forests, oceans, deserts, and coral reefs is occurring, to witness for the life of these beings.

Some groups specialize in helping volunteers participate in scientific studies, ongoing studies, of ecology, habitat change, wildlife behavior. Ecotourists can become involved in local conservation programs. Some of my former students are working in a valley in Ecuador with an Indian tribe, buying land, mapping reservation boundaries, working in community development.

The ecotourist is a new breed of traveler, both environmentally and socially conscious. As with other lifestyle decisions discussed in this book, decisions concerning whether to travel, when to travel, and the intent of travel open up many questions concerning who we are, our relationship with nature, and how we can engage the process of healing ourselves while helping to heal some of the wounds in the Age of Ecology. We want to experience wild places and wild beings joyfully. We resolve that our presence will not contribute to more degradation of the landscape, more misunderstanding, more suffering.

QUESTIONS TO ASK TOUR COMPANIES

For many people desiring to visit a natural area, wildlife area, or scenic attraction, the first and most important question is which tour company to choose. Seek a responsible tour company, one willing to answer questions about the impacts of tourist travel and willing to discuss all aspects of the trip, including the political actions that might help further protection of native ecosystems. Keep the ecotourist group small.

Questions to ask the tour operator might include the following:

■ Does the operator take local people along on tours, that is, people from that nation or region of that nation?

■ Does the operator hire competent local guides who know the difference between observing wildlife and harassing wildlife?

■ How much of the money spent by tourists on this trip goes directly to the local economy as opposed to leakage—money that goes back to the United States or Canada because the goods bought in the local area were transported to the tourist site—for example film, shampoo, aspirin, even canned foodstuffs that are sold in local stores but made in America?

■ Does the tour operator know local customs, sacred sites, what birds or animals are on the threatened list, and what wood products are from endangered local trees?

■ When a company says that X dollars out of the total fee for the tour will be donated to "protect the rainforest" or "protect the whales," ask specifically if the donation will go to a local grassroots environmental group or to a large, national organization that has a big public relations department but perhaps is not as effective as a local, and frequently underfunded, group.

■ The socially conscious response, "You are helping the local economy," might be explored by asking what segments of the local population are "helped" by my travel? How are women workers treated in the hotels and other public facilities that I use?

■ How are trash and garbage managed on the tour? Small villages near a site of nature observation may have trouble disposing of trash brought by visitors. On some desert islands I have visited, there are only a few places to defecate, and tourists from previous tour boats have discarded trash that does not decompose rapidly.

■ Does the tour operator provide simpler, rather than more luxurious accommodations? Ecotourists who are living a simpler lifestyle at home may feel uncomfortable staying in luxury hotels while on vacation just because the host government wants "tourist development" by multinational hotel chains, auto rental agencies, and national tourist development boards. Tourists who are ecologically conscious will demand facilities that have less impact on—and are more representative of—natural, social, and cultural environments.

12

DILEMMAS OF
SOCIAL ACTIVISM

"Why do you always talk about activism?" an obviously irritated student asked me at the conclusion of a lecture I was giving on the plight of ancient forests. "Can't we just have the facts without you asking that we demonstrate or something? I'm not here to be propagandized by an eco-freak." As I have indicated throughout this book, I consider most of our actions to be political actions. We have choices. We make decisions. We act. From our deep, intuitive identification with suffering, from our broader identification with human and nonhuman beings, we act. Activism takes many forms, many dimensions.

John Muir, considered by many historians to be the founder of the American conservation movement, came back from lobbying politicians for conservation legislation one day in the first decade of this century and wrote with exasperation in his journal, "Politics saps at the heart of righteousness." No doubt many activists in the long struggles for social justice and many environmental activists since Muir's time have felt similar exasperation and even desperation as they toiled on a political campaign to end commercial hunting of whales, protect endangered spotted owls, or require recycling. Many sensitive people experience burnout after toiling in political campaigns and withdraw from political activism when they consider the amount of violence and ignorance in our culture, the drastic and negative impact of industrial civilization on the earth, and the rising species extinction rate due to human impacts. Does the human species have the will and the ability to make wise decisions based on ecocentrism for present and future generations, they ask. Since many humans are motivated primarily by narrow self-interest, greed, and desire for power over other humans, what can one, or a few, or even millions of ecoactivists accomplish?

Other people, however, find renewed strength for themselves, for their personal sense of purpose in life, in their work for social transformation. These activists, many of them in quite humble economic situations in their private lives, give voice to endangered sea turtles, dolphins, ancient forests. Following in the tradition of John Muir, Aldo Leopold, Rachel Carson, David Brower, Chico Mendez, Gandhi, Martin Luther King, Jr., and Bob Brown, they realize that they will make, in Gandhi's phrase, "Himalayan mistakes" in political games. But with clear intent and an open heart, ecoactivists are drawn to the task at hand. What some teachers call *heart politics* involves the activist in open, honest, truthful affirmation. Heart politics is dramatically different from cynical backstabbing, power-grabbing, egotistical game playing that many associate with the mainly masculine game of politics as played in corporations, national and state legislatures, public bureaucratic agencies, and other institutions and organizations of all types. These deeply motivated activists recognize that they are living in a time of war—a great worldwide war against other species, against whole bioregions, against indigenous peoples on every continent.

The environmental movement, by the broadest definition, is the only political movement that provides a loyal opposition to the hegemony of capitalist and socialist economic development in the late twentieth century. So-called conservative and liberal political parties, such as Democrats and Republicans in the United States, have governed as coalition governments by agreeing on major issues including the belief that the nation requires continued, rapid economic growth, massive public works projects, and huge military budgets. Some environmental groups will be infiltrated by secret agents. Some leaders will be corrupted by secret agents. When an environmental group is seen as particularly irritating to state agencies, the group members will be labeled as "terrorists" or "extremists." Environmental activists continue to be arrested and harassed because of their beliefs and actions. The murder of Chico Mendez shows that what many in the United

States call "environmental politics" involves activists in sometimes complex, bitter rivalries between existing political factions who put their narrow interest in their own power first rather than putting the earth first. The plot by the French secret service to bomb the *Rainbow Warrior,* the Greenpeace vessel, in Auckland Harbor is an example of the lengths that some government agencies will go to stop ecoactivists.

Some people may be so wounded by periods of intense activism that they spend the rest of their lives engaged in physical and psychological healing. From a deep-ecology perspective, we are called to ask spiritual, psychological, and philosophical questions concerning our activism. Political action includes many activities besides power politics, political tactics, and political rhetoric.

Suzanne Head is a woman who has engaged in Buddhist practice for many years. She became a leader in the rainforest protection movement and wrote with deep perception on addiction, activism for rainforests, and Buddhist perspective on humans-in-nature. She posed a series of questions concerning political activism to a group of scholars, teachers, and students who attended a conference on Humans in Nature held at Naropa Institute in Boulder, Colorado, in May 1991.

These challenging questions provide a framework within which to discuss political activism in the Age of Ecology. My commentary on each question reflects my current, tentative position. My position concerning some questions has changed over the years as I have reflected on my own political activities and the activities of some of my associates. My position may change in the future. My commentaries are modest. Each reader is encouraged to reflect on these questions based on his or her experience.

■ Is it possible to work for change within the national and international arena and still maintain one's personal integrity and sacred outlook? Is it possible to gain national recognition and influence if one does not play the Washington, D. C., brand of politics? How much influence can one have if one doesn't?

In political circles in Washington, D.C., environmental groups are frequently seen as just another special interest group. Many politicians and government bureaucrats in agencies dealing with nature are still in a state of denial. It is difficult to have influence on a political decision-maker when speaking with moral concern without providing scientific justifications. Since the future processes of nature—greenhouse effect, hole in the ozone, rate of species extinction, interactive effects in complex webs of relationships in forest systems—are uncertain and unpredictable, science cannot provide hard answers concerning the consequences of our actions. Nevertheless, when we speak for Gaia, for dolphins, for any nonhuman creatures on this planet or for the basic processes of ecosystems, of evolution, of life, we are *not* just another special interest group. Put the earth first. That is a basic principle of all who love the planet we dwell upon. We don't compromise on principles.

However, politics, as many have noted, does make for strange bedfellows. Grassroots coalitions focused on specific issues with as broad a range of support as possible can have positive effectiveness in Washington politics. The civil rights movement demonstrated this point. Cooperation with any groups who put the earth first can help further ecosophy. As we search for ecosophical solutions to problems, we can work with many different political parties, ethnic organizations, unions, and consumer groups. There are, of course, honest disagreements concerning what tactics are most appropriate to a particular campaign. Principles, however, are never compromised.

In specific political campaigns, grassroots organizations and national environmental organizations are frequently in disagreement. This can provide healthy tension to the campaign, but it can also lead to a pervasive sense of distrust of national environmental leaders by grassroots activists. Grassroots leaders are frequently motivated by the suffering they have experienced in their own bioregions. Victims of toxic wastes and radioactive wastes, people who have witnessed the clearcutting of ancient forests, citizens who have seen the effects of massive housing subdivision projects on drained wetlands—these are the people who agitate for political solutions. Grassroots leaders see leaders of national reform environmental groups making deals with bureaucrats in federal agencies or with Congressional committees that compromise the principles for which they have fought, deals that create more problems than they solve.

Grassroots groups, sometimes with the cooperation of public interest law firms, have gone to court to obtain decisions on corporate or government actions. Courts are expected to base their decisions on evidence and principles. Seeking court judgments to enforce provisions of the National Environmental Policy Act and the Endangered Species Act provides activists with an arena in which to state principles without compromise. If political regimes corrupt the courts or prohibit certain types of suits, as has happened frequently during the past decade in the United States, then environmentalists take protest to the streets, to the headquarters of timber corporations, to toxic waste sites, and they affirm their principles through civil disobedience.

It is now recognized that the environmental movement has helped to foster democratic decision-making over the past two decades. By insisting on more open discussion of issues, redefining the agenda of politics, refusing to play by the rules of the Washington political game, activists have forced politicians to open the books on dam projects and military projects that drained tax dollars and impaired endangered species.

Let me use an example from my own experience in which I clearly stated my principles and goals and opposed any compromise of those principles. Based on my understanding of the ecology of ancient forests of the Pacific Northwest and my understanding of the extent of clearcutting of ancient forests, as well as my strong emotional identification with the forests, I reached the conclusion (increasingly supported by studies and expert opinion) that our policy should be to end commercial logging of ancient forests on public and private lands. I cannot endorse any legislation that compromises this goal by allowing the timber industry to log a certain percent of the remaining ancient forests.

In *The Lorax,* Dr. Seuss introduces children to the Lorax, a role model for ecoactivists. The Lorax is a being of a forest who warns against cutting the trees in the name of economic growth, development, and affluence. The Lorax speaks out in behalf of the trees and all the beings of the forest that are driven out due to habitat loss and pollution, but he is powerless to stop the devastation. The humans pollute the air and the water and wipe-out the forest, and when they are through they have no more jobs, no more industry. After the forest is gone, the Lorax disappears. A child learns the story and its moral: "Unless someone like you cares a whole awful lot, nothing is going to get better, it's not." The child is given the last seeds and is instructed, "Grow a forest. Protect it from axes that hack. Then the Lorax and all of his friends may come back."

■ How effective can one be if one insists on maintaining purity? How effective can one be if one doesn't?

Effectiveness is a somewhat ambiguous term. To be effective in gaining passage on some legislation may give the impression that ecoactivists are winning the political game, but a compromised piece of legislation may be worse than the status quo. Grassroots activists must always ask, Are we really changing the political game or are we being used by major players in the game?

Effectiveness could be defined as effective in making clear statements based on our principles. Effectiveness means planting seeds of thought that may grow and bear fruit in the far future. Rather than asking, "Am I effective?" I ask, "Am I being true to my principles?"

Purity is also an ambiguous term. If we are clear in our intentions, clear in our goals, clear in our principles, then we have purity. However, we may not fully comprehend the implications of our actions, and we may be deceived by leaders we trusted, even in the environmental movement. Supporters of deep ecology whom I know and admire are modest people. They are not engaged in political action to further their own egos or achieve power for the sake of power. They are not professional politicians nor do they want to be professional politicians or bureaucrats. If purity means to avoid corruption, bribery, and gross manipulation of others to achieve a goal, then I would answer yes—we must maintain our purity in keeping within what Arne Naess calls the "ultimate norms." If purity means always using deep-ecology types of arguments, then I would say no—according to Ralph Waldo Emerson, "A foolish consistency is the hobgoblin of little minds." Arguments should be used that will address the issues and appeal to the intended audience, without pandering or lying.

■ Is it possible to work effectively with power and authority and to maintain integrity in social change work if one has not worked through one's early childhood conditioning and emotional wounds?

Childhood wounds can limit our effectiveness as communicators, but this does not mean we cannot be *activists*. We should recognize what personal healing we need, work on that, and continue healing our relationship with nature. Having emotional wounds should not prevent us from speaking out for non-human beings.

Adults can transcend childhood trauma, can be courageous in the face of a hostile social environment, through entering recovery programs. Various reputable groups and teachers offer "vision quests" for adults, retreats, ongoing support groups where people can work toward acceptance of their own vulnerability, encourage love and companionship between men and women and nonhuman beings, rather than domination. Co-counseling, the twelve-step movement, personal-growth workshops, and many groups focusing on co-dependency are examples of healing in our culture. Supporters of the deep, long-range ecology movement can participate in and encourage others to participate in such healing and bonding activities.

Thich Nhat Hanh, a Vietnamese Buddhist teacher, for example, offers meditation retreats for environmentalists that open the possibilities of sitting and walking meditation to men and women who lead hectic lives as political activists. Retreats offered by Joanna Macy, and others she has trained, help adults move from despair and denial into empowerment.

Transpersonal psychology suggests that adults can be self-realizing beings who explore themselves as leaves on the tree of life. The Council of All Beings developed by Joanna Macy and John Seed provides a ritual for expressing our grief over the loss of many species and a way to empower people to speak for other beings with compassion and power. Some Christian groups have provided opportunities for their congregations to participate in a Council of All Beings.

The deep, long-range ecology movement has a powerful, affirmative message. We do not have to live our lives as victims of military-industrial oppression, victims of toxic wastes, victims of doublespeak by politicians and bureaucrats. Bearing witness to our emotional wounds, our alienation from the rest of nature, we can move into healing relationships with a watershed, with our bioregion, with Gaia.

Supporters of deep ecology do not engage in political activism to advance the ego, to gain power for the sake of power over other persons, but to advance and affirm the myriad of beings, the integrity of our broad and deep self. Our need for ego advancement, our personal likes or dislikes of other people in our activist group, our sexual drives, our emotions, and our motives must be watched, noted, and dealt with compassionately in order to maintain effective activism.

■ Deception plays a central role in the arts of war and politics, both in contemporary political and classical theory. For example, in Sun Tzu's classic book on strategy, *The Art of War,* deception is a basic tactic. Deception in this sense means appearing to do one thing while actually doing something different. If the trickster plays such an important role in political action, how do we avoid self-deception?

Coyote, the trickster in American Indian stories, is a teacher. The trickster calls the attention of the student to the real work by doing some action that seems on the surface to be nonconventional but on a deeper level reveals a profound truth. Deception may also be necessary for mental health of an individual and for the collective health of an entire society. We frequently deceive ourselves with little lies and stories. Some psychologists suggest that deceit is a natural, necessary part of life. We cannot achieve personal well-being and social order without self-deception. Scientists observing pods of dolphins in the Indian Ocean off western Australia conclude that males in one pod will engage in deceit to trick a female into leaving her pod and then capture her for their pod.

The problem is how to deal with our tendency to project what we want the world to be onto the world. If we deceive ourselves into believing our own lies, our own rhetoric, then we cannot be open to "the way things are," to doing what Gary Snyder calls the "real work."

■ How can we go beyond the right wing-left wing dualism—social ecology vs. deep ecology, social justice movement vs. ecocentrism that is currently a conventional mode of discourse in the ecology movement?

An assertion by the German greens is relevant in considering this question. We are neither left or right, we are in the vanguard. The old categories of left and right seem to be losing relevance in the Age of Ecology. Demands for redistribution of wealth and power in society are compelling in terms of historic struggles for human rights and struggles by those seeking more equal sharing of power between men and women, between people in different social classes and different ethnic groups. These demands need to be nestled in an ecocentric perspective with an overall concern for the health of ourselves in nature.

Social movements seeking to redistribute wealth and power have moved into environmental politics with their agendas. The old humanism remains in much leftist, progressive rhetoric. From the extremist statements by Murray Bookchin, through the neo-Marxists, anarchists, and progressive liberals and the women's movement, the demands are framed in terms of what ecocentric philosophers call the "anthropocentric detour." The world is radically out of balance and if demands for social justice can be accommodated into the agenda for politics, as much as possible, some historic wrongs might be addressed. But unless we put the earth first, the world and all its inhabitants will decline.

The real task is to move beyond dualism of all sorts that has characterized so much of leftist politics during the past hundred years. Government regulatory agencies can be creative in implementing social policy from an ecocentric framework, for example, protection of threatened and endangered species for their intrinsic worth under the provisions of the endangered species act. The ecocentric platform discussed in earlier chapters of this book provides a framework for agreement for people coming from different ideological perspectives.

I consider myself a social ecologist. I have studied the social and economic reasons for our current dilemma. I have studied theories of bureaucracy and social class. I find great strength in arguments that identify imperialism and growth of state power as a cause of our problems. I also find great cogency in the arguments by feminists that the patriarchy and anthropocentrism have contributed to the crisis of character and culture that we call the environmental crisis. I feel I am a victim of the patriarchy. I also agree with those who study political economy who argue that the logic of capitalism leads to environmental degradation. I can also agree with those who argue that bureaucracy has social costs and that privatization of some aspects of land can further its long-term environmental quality *if* the stewards of the land respect its integrity. Intellectuals in the deep, long-range ecology movement can debate and discuss these issues honestly. However, when rhetoric replaces discussion and social ecology is defined in a narrow, sectarian way, then divisiveness replaces discussion.

Political revolution and liberal reform have been part of the vocabulary of social change movements in the West for over two centuries. Freedom, individualism, economic development, and progress have also been guiding myths of much modern political theory. All these myths are now questioned. All must be reexamined within an ecocentric perspective.

Supporters of different political ideologies, coming from different religious traditions, both males and females, can agree that we want to enrich the experience of humans on earth by helping humans realize their broad and deep identification with nature.

Believers of any political ideology as well as believers of various religions can affirm the integrity of the principle of preserving native biological diversity, wilderness, forests, and marine ecosystems.

Believers of any political ideology or religion can agree that humans are one modest species among many dwelling on this planet. Humans have no right to cause the extinction of other species nor to alter drastically the habitat of many species in all the ecosystems of the planet.

Believers of any political ideology who support putting the earth first can encourage movements that affirm environmental quality in third world nations, where such movements also tend to strengthen democracy, protect human rights, and encourage social equality among classes, genders, and ethnic groups.

■ Is what we do as important as how we do it?

All actions will initiate reaction. How we engage in political activism is part of our practice. Politicians compete for votes. Activists compete for attention from politicians and from the media. Even if we base our actions on a clear understanding of the situation, we are subject to the whims of the media, to manipulation of our message by those who seek to advance their own narrow self-interest. Our job, as activists, is to present clear messages and constantly to put forth a platform for political change. How we do it is as important as what we do.

All people I have met who embrace the deep, long-range ecology movement have also embraced the norm of nonviolence. The history of environmental movements shows a remarkable adherence to principles of fair play, reliance on appeals to ethics, scientific evidence, and belief in democracy in comparison to many social movements, such as the labor movement, social justice movements, and Marxist-leftist movements. Calls for violent revolution have never been a part of the ecology social movement. Ecology subverts the narrow humanism and materialism of both left and right and rejects both the myth of revolution and the myth of individual ego as supreme in the world.

Nonviolence of course is interpreted differently in different cultural contexts. Nonviolence is not passive. A person acting from the principle of nonviolence can be very assertive, speak out for principles, engage in protest demonstrations, even engage in civil disobedience. To be nonviolent does not mean that one has to be intimidated by threats of violence or threats of legal action by corporations, political regimes or bureaucrats for natural resources agencies, such as the U.S. Forest Service.

Supporters of deep, long-range ecology feel empowered to speak out for right livelihood, for restoration of human-damaged lands. The role of the deep ecology movement is to speak out against narrow humanistic and short-term argumentation and to speak for life-centered, long-term, ecologically sustainable principles. Supporters of deep ecology speak for human-in-nature and politics-in-ecosystem, and humans-in-context-of-ongoing-evolution.

Humans speak in context of their relationships not only to present, but to far-future generations of humans and nonhumans. For example, the Nuclear Guardianship Project places humans in league with beings of future generations. It is a network of citizens working to develop nuclear policies and practices that respect the "poison power" and the responsibility of people in this generation to present and future life.

■ How narrowly do we want to define political action? How broadly do we want to define political activism?

I have a friend who rides his bicycle fifteen miles each way to work each day—rain or shine. He says his bike ride is his Zen practice. He is in pain some days from bike riding. But he continues to ride. He is an example to the rest of us who drive our vehicles each day to work. Is his action political? In a broad sense it is. The deliberate choice of lifestyle is a political action.

What we teach is a political action. When I teach theories of the ecology of ancient forests in my college classes at Humboldt State University, I am engaged in a political act. Ecology, as Paul Shepard noted nearly twenty-five years ago, is a subversive science. It is subversive to the reductionism of conventional science. It is subversive to the dominant social paradigm. In my bioregion of northwestern California, the timber industry uses the ideology of "Natural Resources Conservation and Development," "Managed Forests," "Multiple-use Forests," "Cloned Trees," "Maximum Yield," "Enhancing Nature," "Trees Are for People"—these are the slogans used by those who want business as usual, who want humanistic, capitalist approaches to forest management.

Any statements of solidarity with the integrity of ancient forests are considered political statements. I have received death threats after letters to the editor defending the listing of northern spotted owls as a threatened species. Yes. Freedom of speech is at issue here. Any of our statements, any expression of ideas, even shopping at certain stores is considered a political action.

Political action defined broadly allows people to select the style of activism that suits their own life condition and temperament. If green lifestyles are not stated in political terms, then police, and many school-teachers, will see them as deviant, criminal, or resulting from mental illness. Some groups in my county have organized "Boycott Arcata" campaigns because the city of Arcata has been seen as harboring pro-environmental people. Some businesses located in Arcata have supported the Northcoast

Environmental Center, but other business leaders have said it hurts their business to support the center publicly or advertise in its newsletter, *Econews*.

Whether we like it or not, our green lifestyles, our green opinions, the mode of transportation we choose, our decision to consume less—all these ideas and actions have already been politicized. When I tell some of my acquaintances in Humboldt County that I prefer to wear old but comfortable clothes and shop at small, locally-owned stores rather than at the mall, I am labeled by these people as a "hippie," anti-development, and anti-capitalist. If I put a bumper sticker on my auto proclaiming "Save Ancient Forests," I could be a target for a sniper's bullet. When the president of the United States becomes a promoter of automobile sales, advising us that this is the time to go out and buy a new vehicle because interest rates are low and it is our obligation to help the economy, and we resist his exhortations to "buy more" on the grounds that we are exploring deep green lifestyles, we are taking a political action.

■ How do we integrate our personal and collective shadows so they do not continue to darken the world?

Understanding our own shadows requires courage and skill. We need skillful teachers and therapists to guide us. Teachers and therapists, using skillful means, have a special responsibility in this time of global crisis to help their students and clients integrate themselves so they understand their own suffering in the context of the suffering of the world.

We help ourselves heal when we help the world heal. Political activism should never be a way to impose our dark side on the world. Political action is an extension of the search for what Buddhists call "right livelihood," work that reflects a commitment to the principle "do no harm." We have no desire to project our own neuroses into the world. Compassion and insight are brought forth from our own suffering. When we seek to be healers of the world, we begin by realizing that we are wounded healers. We have been damaged by our experiences of suffering while living on this planet during this era.

We begin our recovery process by accepting that we have been damaged by our socialization to American culture in the late twentieth century. Our collective, cultural shadow includes our fear for "national security," our nationalistic desire to "win," our desire to be number one, our culturally induced desire to find new frontiers to conquer. Strenuous practice may be required to break our psyches of these delusions. We must learn to practice on this planet, not on Mars. We continue to engage in support groups, in critical self-analysis, in seeking to transcend dysfunctional relationships into healthy acceptance.

The courageous stance, it seems to me, is to become a gentle ecowarrior, or in Buddhist terms to become a bodhisattva. Perhaps we can speak for a few ancient forests, a few species that would otherwise have gone extinct without notice. We help as much as we can, for as long as we have energy to bear witness on this earth.

FURTHER READINGS ON THE DEEP, LONG-RANGE ECOLOGY MOVEMENT

Books on the Deep, Long-Range Ecology Movement by Bill Devall

Devall, Bill and Sessions, George. *Deep Ecology: Living as if Nature Mattered.* Salt Lake City, Utah: Gibbs Smith, Publisher, 1985.

Devall, Bill. *Simple in Means, Rich in Ends: Practicing Deep Ecology.* Salt Lake City, Utah: Gibbs Smith, Publisher, 1988.

Published articles on the deep, long-range ecology movement by Bill Devall

"Reform Environmentalism." *Humboldt Journal of Social Relations,* Summer 1979, pp. 129–158.

"The Deep Ecology Movement." *Natural Resources Journal* 20 (April 1980): 299–322.

With Sessions, George. "The Development of Natural Resources and the Integrity of Nature." *Environmental Ethics* 6 (Winter 1984): 293–322.

"Deep Ecology and Its Critics." *The Trumpeter: Journal of Ecosophy* 5 (Spring 1988): 55–59.

"Deep Ecology and Radical Environmentalism." *Society and Natural Resources* 4 (July-September 1992): 247–258.

Major books and articles on the deep, long-range ecology movement

Badiner, Allan Hunt, ed. *Dharma Gaia: A Harvest of Essays in Buddhism and Ecology.* Berkeley: Parallex Press, 1990.

Drengson, Alan R. *Beyond Environmental Crisis: From Technocrat to Planetary Person.* New York: Peter Lang Publishing, 1989.

Drengson, Alan, ed. "The Long-Range Deep Ecology Movement and Arne Naess." *The Trumpeter: Journal of Ecosophy* 9 (Spring 1992).

Fox, Warwick, ed. "From Anthropocentism to Deep Ecology." *Revision: The Journal of Consciousness and Change* 13 (Winter 1991).

Fox, Warwick. *Toward a Transpersonal Ecology: Developing New Foundations for Environmentalism.* Boston: Shambhala, 1990.

LaChapelle, Dolores. *Earth Wisdom.* Silverton, Colo.: Finn Hill Arts, 1978.

LaChapelle, Dolores. *Sacred Land Sacred Sex: Rapture of the Deep.* Silverton, Colo.: Finn Hill Arts, 1988.

Macy, Joanna. *World as Lover, World as Self.* Berkeley: Parallex Press, 1991.

Mander, Jerry. *In the Absence of the Sacred: The Failure of Technology and the Survival of the Indian Nations.* San Francisco: Sierra Club Books, 1991.

Mathews, Freya. *The Ecological Self.* Savage, Maryland: Barnes and Noble Books, 1991.

Naess, Arne, "Deep Ecology and Ultimate Premises," *The Ecologist,* Volume 18, 4/5, 1988, pp. 128–131.

Naess, Arne. *Ecology, Community and Lifestyle.* Cambridge: Cambridge University Press, 1989.

Naess, Arne. "The Shallow and the Deep, Long-Range Ecology Movement." *Inquiry* 16 (1973): 95–100.

Reed, Peter and Rothenberg, David, eds. *Wisdom in the Open Air: The Norwegian Roots of Deep Ecology.* Minneapolis: University of Minnesota Press, 1992.

Rothenberg, David. *Is it Painful to Think? Conversations with Arne Naess.* Minneapolis: University of Minnesota Press, 1992.

Sessions, George. "The Deep Ecology Movement: A Review." *Environmental Review* 8 (1987): 105–125.

Snyder, Gary. *The Practice of the Wild.* San Francisco: North Point Press, 1991.

NOTES AND SUGGESTED READINGS

During the administration of President Jimmy Carter, the annual reports of the Council on Environmental Quality (an advisory council to the president mandated in the National Environmental Quality Act of 1970) were authoritative documents on environmental issues in America. During the administrations of President Reagan and President Bush, from 1981 to 1992, the annual reports of the Council on Environmental Quality were not considered authoritative, and some commentators found some of the contents of the annual reports misleading.

Private organizations began assembling and publishing annual reports which were widely used in classrooms and widely quoted in the press. The annual *State of the World* report published by the Worldwatch Institute in Washington, D.C., is one of the most widely circulated of these reports.

Taking a world systems approach, the work of Donella Meadows and associates presents several scenarios for change in social organization to turn around effectively the deterioration of life processes on earth. Donella H. Headows, Dennis L. Meadows, and Jorgen Randers, *Beyond the Limits: Confronting Global Collapse, Envisioning a Sustainable Future* (Post Mills, Vt: Chelsea Green Publishing Co., 1992).

Vice-president Albert Gore, Jr.'s, book *Earth in the Balance: Ecology and the Human Spirit* (1992) was written when he was a United States Senator. He also was head of the United States congressional delegation to the Rio Summit. Gore's book has been widely praised because it combines understanding of environmental issues, criticizes the shallow political dialogue which occurred during the 1980s, and discusses religious and ethical issues, particularly the need to reconnect science and religion for constructive dialogue. He concludes that the environmental crisis may be seen as a spiritual crisis and that as citizens we have the ethical duty to "be honest with one another and accept responsibility for what we do." (p. 368).

The United Nations Conference on Environment and Development (UNCED) called the Rio Summit, held in Rio de Janerio, Brazil, in June, 1992, brought together delegates from almost all nation states on earth. A parallel conference of nongovernmental organizations, held at the same time in Rio, brought together representatives of thousands of citizen groups to discuss social and environmental issues. There was extensive coverage in the press of the Rio summit focusing on North vs. South, rich vs. poor nations.

One of the most illuminating reports on the philosophical, moral, and ethical issues raised at the Rio Summit appeared in the newsletter of the International Society for Environmental Ethics. The Society was an official observer organization at the UNCED, and two sophisticated philosophers represented the Society, J. Baird Callicott and Holmes Rolston, III. Their report appears in vol. 3, no. 2 (Summer 1992) of the *Newsletter* of the International Society for Environmental Ethics.

A more general discussion of the possible impact of the Rio Summit appeared in a special issue of *Environment* magazine vol. 34 (October 1992) under the title "Earth Summit: Judging its Success."

CHAPTER 1
SISTER/BROTHER, CAN YOU SPARE A HUNDRED BUCKS?

The Decade of Denial—Careening Through the Eighties

The acronym YUPPIE, standing for young, upwardly mobile, middle class professional, was not invented until 1983. Walter Shapiro, writing in *Time,* April 8, 1991, p. 65, says that the word was used in more than 22,000 magazine and newspaper articles between 1983 and 1991. Shapiro argues that the "yuppie mystique" was perpetuated by baby boomers who felt they were entitled to get and spend as much as they could. The "yuppie mystique" came to symbolize the lifestyle of all those who aspired to rapidly increasing incomes, life in the fast lane in large cities, selfish attitudes, hedonism, materialism, and obsessive self-improvement.

There's No Place Like Home—Realities of the Nineties

A number of articles have appeared in newspapers and magazines analyzing data collected by the United States Census Bureau for the 1990 census supplemented with analyses of income distribution information from the Department of Labor and other sources. Following is a small sample of these articles.

One of the longest articles and most comprehensive was written by economist Robert J. Samuelson, "How Our American Dream Unraveled," *Newsweek,* March 2, 1992, pp. 32–39; other articles include the Council on Competitiveness, fourth annual competitiveness index, reported in the *San Francisco Chronicle,* July 10, 1991, "Living Standard Takes First Dip Since 1982," p. 1; Peter T. Kilborn, "The Middle Class Feels Betrayed, But Maybe Not Enough to Rebel," *New York Times,* January 12, 1992, Section 4, p. 1; Ramon G. McLeod, "State Welfare Rolls Growing at Record Rate," *San Francisco Chronicle,* November 19, 1991, p. 1; Louis Uchitelle, "Americans are Just Simulating the Good Life," *San Francisco*

Chronicle, June 18, 1991, Business Section, p.1; *Utne Reader,* July/August, 1991, a collection of articles under the collective title "For Love or Money: Making a Living vs. Making a Life," pp. 65–87; Lee Smith, "How Americans Get By," *Fortune,* October 21, 1991, pp. 53–64; Kenneth Howe, "How Layoffs Affect Workers," *San Francisco Chronicle,* October 28, 1992, Business Section, B1; Jeff Pelline and Kenneth Howe, "Downsizing Corporate America," *San Francisco Chronicle,* October 26, 1992, Business Section, B1; a collection of articles on "What Recovery? The Bite on the Middle Class," *Newsweek,* November 4, 1991; Kenneth R. Hey, "Business as Usual? Forget it," *Inside Guide,* April/May, 1992, pp. 32–37; Sylvia Nasar, "However you Slice the Data, The Richest Did Get Richer," *New York Times,* May 11, 1992, p. C-1; Louis Uchitelle, "Trapped in the Impoverished Middle Class," *New York Times,* November 17, 1991, Section 3, p. 1.

For a general overview of patterns of consumption in rich nations and review of survey data indicating no increase in personal satisfaction and happiness, see Alan Durning, *How Much is Enough? The Consumer Society and the Future of the Earth* (New York: W.W. Norton, 1992).

Chapter 2
Philosophical Roots for Greening Our Lifestyles

General Principles for Deep Green Lifestyles

Arne Naess, "Deep Ecology and Life Style," in Neil Everndon, ed., *The Paradox of Environmentalism* (Toronto: University of Toronto Press, 1984), pp. 57–60.

Language and the Search for Ecosophy

The importance of language in reclaiming our deep roots has been emphasized by most of the leading philosophers in the deep, long-range ecology movement. For example, see the chapter on "Tawny Grammar" in Gary Snyder's *The Practice of the Wild* (1990), and Justin Askins, "The Need for a Deep Ecological Language," in *Wild Earth* (Fall 1991), pp. 74–75.

Facing Ambiguity and Challenge

We may face conflicting claims to priority in many areas of our lifestyle. For example, Michael Soule, a leading scientist in the field of conservation biology first accepted then declined a consulting trip to South Africa, as a protest against apartheid. "Clearly," he writes, "in this case 'humanism' (or is it 'specism'?) triumphed over biological egalitarianism or whatever obligations I have to other species. This realization that I am, after all, a human chauvinist came as a shock." ("A Conservation Biologist's Dilemma: Does Boycotting South Africa Constitute Human Chauvinism?" *Earthwatch,* April 1988, pp. 12–13.

Information on the programs of the Institute for Deep Ecology Education can be obtained from the directors of the Institute, P.O. Box 2290, Boulder, CO 80306.

CHAPTER 3
EXPERIENCING NATURE IN THE AGE OF ECOLOGY

References for Additional Information

Additional Information on the Nuclear Guardianship Project can be obtained from: Nuclear Guardianship Project, 3051 Adeline Street, Berkeley, CA 94703.

Additional information on trainings for consciousness practice can be obtained from: The Institute for Deep Ecology Education, P.O. Box 2290, Boulder, CO 80302.

Additional information on bioregional studies and consciousness practice can be obtained from: Director, Environmental Studies, Naropa Institute, 2130 Arapahoe Avenue, Boulder, CO 80302.

Clearcuts in Ancient Forests

This author has spent considerable time during the past two decades working to radically reform our approach to forests. The tragic destruction of forest ecosystems through clearcutting is presented in an exhibit format book edited by this author which is a project of the Irahiti Foundation for Deep Ecology, *Clearcut: The Travesty of Industrial Forestry* (Earth Island Press, 1993).

Other important books on the ecology of forest ecosystems in the Pacific Northwest and the political battles over the future of these forest ecosystems include Elliott Norse, *Ancient Forests of the Pacific Northwest* (New York: Island Press, 1990); Keith Ervin, *Fragile Magesty: The Battle for North America's Last Great Forest* (Seattle: The Mountaineers, 1989); and, Mitch Lansky, *Beyond the Beauty Strip: Saving What's Left of Our Forests* (Gardiner, Maine: Tilbury House, 1992).

CHAPTER 4
WE'RE ALL NATIVES

Suggested Readings

Andruss, Van, ed. *Home: A Bioregional Reader.* Santa Cruz: New Society Publishers, 1990.

CHAPTER 5
THINKING LIKE A WATERSHED

Ecostery: Another Vision of Dwelling in Place

Information on the Ecostery Foundation of North America can be obtained from Alan Drengson, ed. *The Trumpeter,* P.O. Box 5853 Station B, Victoria, B.C., Canada V8R 6S8.

Thinking Like a Bioregion

Practical considerations in forming a land trust are discussed by Rose Harvey and Evelyn Lee, "Forming a Land Trust," *The Trumpeter,* Winter 1990, pp. 7–12.

See also *Starting a Land Trust* distributed by the Land Trust Alliance, 900 17th St NW, Suite 410, Washington, DC 20006.

Turtle Island Earth Stewards is a non-profit, charitable society incorporated in Canada in 1973 and in the United States in 1984 to assist individuals and community groups to place private lands and forests in trust. They can be contacted by writing the director, Turtle Island Earth Stewards, 101–5810 Battison Street, Vancouver, BC, Canada V5R 5X8.

The Trust for Public Land provides information on forming land trusts. Northeast Regional Office, 666 Broadway, New York, NY 10012–2301. Or Northwest Regional Office, Smith Tower, Suite 1501, 506 Second Ave., Seattle, WA 98104.

Emerging Public Policy and Land-Use Practices for the Next Century

A definitive study of the impact of grazing on the American west is presented by Lynn Jacobs in *Waste of the West* (1992), available from the author at P.O. Box 5784, Tucson, AZ 85703)

On the issue of policies protecting biodiversity from the perspective of conservation biology see Ed Grumbine, *Ghost Bears: The Biodiversity Crisis* (Island Press, 1992).

The views of Frank J. and Deborach E. Popper on the "Buffalo Commons," the future of the Great Plains, is summarized in "The Reinvention of the American Frontier," *Wild Earth,* Spring 1992, pp. 16–18. They consider that the Buffalo Commons "amounts to the nation's most advanced experiment in replacing extraction with preservation."

CHAPTER 6
MAKING A HOME

Downscaling

The article on the new house of rap singer Hammer, discussed in this chapter, appeared in the Eureka *Times-Standard,* February 11, 1992.

For an extensive discussion of homelessness as that term is used in this chapter see Wendell Berry's *The Unsettling of America* (San Francisco: Sierra Club Books, 1977).

Increasing interest in smaller dwelling units led to the reprinting of a book on houses in the 1920s, *Authentic Small Houses of 1920s* (Mineola, N.Y.: Dover Publications, 1987).

Downscaling to the "simple life" is not always easy, as has been emphasized throughout this book. A chronicle of one couple's search for simple living is found in the book by Frank Levering and Wanda Urbanska, *Simple Living: One Couple's Search for a Better Life* (New York: Viking, 1992).

Gardens and Lawns

Efforts to collect native seeds and establish gardens consisting of plants native to specific bioregions has led to renewed interest in ethnobotany of Native Americans. See for example, Gary Nabhan, *Gathering the Desert* (Tucson: University of Arizona Press, 1985).

Given my own difficulties with slugs and snails, I search out articles such as one by Joel Grossman, "Slugging It Out with Snails," *San Francisco Chronicle,* December 4, 1991, Home and Garden Section, p.3.

Gardening can be a form of consciousness practice even when a gardener does not start with that intention. See for example Michael Pollen, *Second Nature: A Gardener's Education* (New York: Atlantic Monthly Press, 1992).

Community Environmental Audits

See Guy Dauncy, "How Green is Your Campus," *The Trumpeter* 8 (Summer 1991): 152.

Selecting a Site and Building a New Dwelling Unit

Noel Bennett, Jim Wakeman, Michael McGuire, *A Place in the Wild: The Dynamics of Structures Integrated into Fragile, Natural Sites,* a report published in 1991 by Shared Horizons, P.O. Box 1175, Corrales, NM, 87048.

Many dwelling structures in America are of wood frame construction. Innovative building materials and methods include rammed earth. P. Beinhauer, Mac Morris, and Janet Venable, "Rammed Earth," *New Settler Interview,* December 1991–January, 1992. P.O. Box 730, Willits, CA 95490.

The work of Christopher Alexander continues to inspire many people who want to build in an organic way. Alexander does not consider space an empty container filled with things but rather as an organic series of interconnected events. These events form intricate and shifting patterns of wholeness. All modes of wholeness share the same structure. Alexander presents a theory of urban design around a "growing whole" involving the qualities of piecemeal, unpredictable, coherent, and full of feeling. Christopher Alexander, *A New Theory of Urban Design* (New York: Oxford University Press, 1987), and *The Timeless Way of Building* (New York: Oxford University Press, 1979).

Suggested Readings

Buzzworm Magazine, eds. *1993 Earth Journal: Environmental Almanac and Resource Directory.* Boulder, Colo.: Buzzworm Books, 1992.

Cohen, Gary, O'Connor, John, eds. *Fighting Toxics: A Manual for Protecting Your Family, Community and Workplace.* Kansas City: Acres U.S.A., 1991.

Dadd, Debra Lynn. *The Nontoxic Home and Office.* Los Angeles: Jeremy P. Tarcher, 1992.

Gershon, David, and Gilman, Robert. *Ecoteam Workbook: A Six Month Program to Restore Your Household to Environmental Balance.* West Hurley, N.Y.: Global Action Plan for the Earth, 1990.

Goldman, Benjamin A. *The Truth About Where You Live: An Atlas for Action on Toxins and Mortality.* New York: Times Books, Random House, 1991.

Harte, John; Holdren, Cheryl; Schneider, Richard; and Shirley, Christine. *Toxics A to Z.* Berkeley: University of California Press, 1992.

Jason, Dan. *Greening the Garden: A Guide to Sustainable Growing.* Santa Cruz: New Society Publishers, 1991.

Naar, John. *Design for a Livable Planet: How You Can Help Clean Up the Environment.* New York: Harper and Row, 1990.

Olkowski, William, et. al. *Common-Sense Pest Control.* Newtown, Ct: The Taunton Press, 1992.

Wells, Phil, and Jetter, Mandy. *The Global Consumer: Best Buys To Help the Third World.* London: Victor Gollancz, 1991.

CHAPTER 7
THE EMPTY NEST IS FULL OF LIFE

Sources for this chapter include Joseph, Roberta. "Deciding Against Motherhood: One Woman's Story,"*Utne Reader,* January 1990, p. 64.

Ehrlich, Anne and Ehrlich, Paul. *The Population Explosion.* New York: Simon and Schuster,1990.

Mills, Stephanie. *Whatever Happened to Ecology.* San Francisco: Sierra Club Books, 1989.

End Piece on Activism

The Carrying Capacity Network, 1325 G Street, NW Suite 1003, Washington, DC 20005, publishes a newsletter under the name "Clearinghouse Bulletin" and a quarterly journal, *Focus.* This journal reprints current and classic environmental essays, furnishes persuasive point-counterpoint discussions by authoritative sources concerning controversial environmental issues, and publishes interviews with different writers on environmental issues.

Suggested Readings

Grant, Lindsey, ed. *Elephants in the Volkswagen: Facing the Tough Questions About Our Overcrowded Country.* New York: W. H. Freeman, 1992.

CHAPTER 8
FOOD AND SUSTAINING ECOSYSTEMS

Suggested Readings

Jacobson, Michael F.; Lefferts, Lisa; Garland, Anne. *Safe Food: Eating Wisely in a Risky World.* Venice, Calif.: Living Planet Press, 1991.

Margen, Sheldon, ed. *The Wellness Encyclopedia of Food and Nutrition.* New York:Health Letter Associates, 1992.

Mokower, Joel. *The Green Consumer Supermarket Guide.* Bergenfield, N.J.: Penguin Books, 1991.

Robbins, John. *Diet For a New America.* Walpole, N.H.: Stillpoint Publishing, 1987.

CHAPTER 9
ORGANIZATIONAL REFORM

Survival and Social Change in Organizations

The network of alternative forestry "practitioners" is one example of communication among people searching for ways that people and forests can coexist in relationships that sustain both. Alternative forestry does not compete with industrial logging corporations. Instead they seek value added options for using wood within the context of local communities. See for example, Michael Goldberg, "New Hope for Forest Communities" *American Forests* (March/April 1992), pp.17–20.

Information on this movement can be obtained from Forest Trust, P.O. Box 519, Santa Fe, NM 87504.

For a discussion of community see Alan Drengson, "Nature, Community and Self," *Communities Magazine,* Summer 1988, pp. 42–49.

Changing Corporate Values

Richard Adams, Jane Carruthers and Sean Hamil, *Changing Corporate Values: A Guide to Social and Environment Policy and Practice in Britain's Top Companies* (London: Logan Page, 1991). This is essentially a reference book on British companies but the format can be applied to reviewing companies in Canada and the United States.

Richard Grossman and Frank Adams, *Taking Care of Business: Citizenship and the Charter of Incorporation,* Cambridge: Charter Ink, 1993. (P.O. Box 806, Cambridge, MA 02140).

Reports on environmental policies and practices of various American corporations are published periodically by the Council on Economic Priorities, 30 Irving Place, New York, NY, 10003.

See Russell Mokhiber, "Corporate Crime and Violence in Review: The 10 Worst Corporations of 1991," *Multinational Monitor,* December 1991, pp. 9–17.

Exposing the pollution practices and public relations doublespeak of corporations helps to inform the public and can lead to public pressure on corporations. Greenpeace and Friends of the Earth, for example, targeted Du Pont as a major producer of CFC which scientists consider a major factor in destroying the earth's protective ozone layer.

Changing Bureaucracies from Within and Without

Jeff DeBonis, a former employee of the United States Forest Service, started the Association of Forest Service Employees for Environmental Ethics (AFSEEE) while working for the Forest Service in Oregon in 1988.

"The idea occurred to us that the *most effective* thing we could do right now would be to organize a committed cadre of dedicated activists working from the *inside* in a *positive* way, toward a new vision of the Forest Service." DeBonis and a small group of friends began publishing *The Inner Voice* to provide expression of facts, thoughts, and feelings contrary to the "agency line"; to provide a support system for those employees who feel isolated because their environmental value system doesn't fit; to lobby at local and national levels for "more environmentally sound resource management within the agency"; to educate other federal employees "on ways we can work for and promote a change in values on our day-to-day jobs"; and, to "spotlight people/projects that are making changes towards this new vision."

By 1992, AFSEEE had built a national network of employees in resource agencies. Association of Forest Service Employees for Environmental Ethics, PO Box 11615, Eugene, OR 97440.

A discussion of John Mumma, regional forester in charge of fifteen national forests in Montana and other states in the northern Rockies, and other whistle blowers in the United States Forest Service, can be found in an article by Paul Schneider, "When a Whistle Blows in the Forest..." *Audubon,* January, 1992.

The STP schools began at the Highlander Center in East Tennessee. The idea for weekend workshops for grassroots environmentalists seeking changes in their own lives and in their communities came from a meeting of environmental activists initiated by the editor of the *Wrenching Debate Gazette,* Richard Grossman. See Paul deLeon, "The STP Schools: Education for Environmental Action," *New Solutions,* Summer 1990, pp. 22–24). Information on the STP schools can be obtained from the Highlander Center, 1959 Highlander Way, New Market, TN 37820.

The importance of deep ecological education has been emphasized by many leading writers in the deep ecology movement. A collection of articles on the environmental crisis, education, and deep ecology is found in *The Trumpeter: Journal of Ecosophy* 8 (Summer 1991).

Reform in the Churches

The topic of ecological spirituality is discussed by Charlene Spretnak, *States of Grace* (San Francisco: Harper Collins, 1991) and by Charles Cummings, *Eco-Spirituality: Toward a Reverent Life* (Mahwah, NY: Paulist Press, 1991).

Continuing dialogue on responsibilities toward the earth from Christian perspectives is encouraged by the North American Conference on Christianity and Ecology which publishes *Firmament: The Journal of Christian Ecology,* 161 E. Front Street, Suite 200, Traverse City, Michigan 49684.

Suggested Readings

Lerner, Michael. *Surplus Powerlessness: The Psychodynamics of Everyday Life,* and *The Psychology of Individual and Social Transformation.* Oakland: The Institute for Labor and Mental Health, 1986.

CHAPTER 10
ECOCITIES?

Notes

Deep anthropology looks at root causes of the contemporary environmental crisis by probing the mindset of civilization in the search for the true world of humans in nature. Some of the most profound philosophical anthropologists have found that true human nature in the paleolithic hunter/gathers. Anthropologist Stanley Diamond influenced Gary Snyder, George Sessions, Paul Shepard, and other influential deep ecology philosophers, especially through his book *In Search of the Primitive: A Critique of Civilization* (Princeton: Transaction Books, 1974).

Domestication of plants and animals, and of the human species, began perhaps 15,000 years ago. Anthropologist Peter J. Wilson, in his book *The Domestication of the Human Species* (New Haven: Yale University Press, 1989) defines domesticated people as those who live in housing groups in hamlets, in villages, in small cities, and who work mostly in their houses, as well as people who live in large cities and work in offices, factories, and other locations separate from their houses.

Wilson argues that nomadic people retain openness and constant attention to nature which allows them to be adaptive to changes in the territory within which they roam. Settled, domesticated people build boundaries, closing themselves off from nature. When humans began erecting artificial barriers such as walls, they allowed pretense and purposeful deception to become important in human social relations.

Peter Berg's writing, and those of his associates, on their views of ways that bioregionalism can help move people toward "green cities" are found in various issues of *Raise the Stakes: The Planet Drum Review* (available from Planet Drum Foundation, P.O. Box 31251, San Francisco, Shasta Bioregion, CA 94131).

See Peter Berg, "Recreating Urbanity," *Raise the Stakes,* Winter 1991, p. 4, and the special issue on "green cities," Summer 1986 in which Peter Berg describes the winter solstice celebration held on December 21, 1985, in San Francisco.

Practical Actions for Living in the Metropolis

It is illustrative to read books on metropolitan regions written during the exuberant 1950s and 1960s. For example a journalist, Christopher Rand, wrote a book *Los Angeles: The Ultimate City* (New York: Oxford University Press, 1967) in which he discusses the sprawl of the Los Angeles metropolitan region, freeways, racial tensions, the dynamic economy. The author is troubled by the danger of unbridled "technological force" being beyond control of democratic processes. The only environmental problem mentioned is smog. He attributes to Aldous Huxley a comment about Los Angeles, that it had the greatest potential of all the places he knew—but whether this was a potential for horrors or fulfillments he simply couldn't tell.

Suggested Readings

Special issue of *The Amicus Journal,* Summer 1992, published by the Natural Resources Defense Council on the topic Metropolis Now: Designing Cities with Ecology.

Register, Richard. EcoCity Berkeley: North Atlantic Books, 1987.

CHAPTER 11
ECOTOURISM

Intention of Trips to Nature Preserves and Spectacular Sites

The difference between journeys and tourism is illustrated in the sensitive narrative of Jim Corbett, *Goatwalking: A Guide to Wildland Living, A Quest for the Peaceable Kingdom* (New York: Viking, 1991). This book is about goats, walking with goats, surviving in the desert, caring about the land and about goats, and about one man's journey of pleasure and discovery and social activism.

Greening Tourist Travel

Articles on the damage caused by rapid growth of tourism in rural, ecologically sensitive areas have appeared in many magazines, journals, and news reports during the past few years. Following is a sample of sources. Ty Harrington, "Tourism

Damages Amazon Region," *The Christian Science Monitor,* 6 June 1989, p. 6; Jim Molnar, "On the Promises and Pitfalls of Ecotourism," *San Francisco Chronicle,* Sunday, 24 November 1991, T-5).

Service Trips

The National Sierra Club approved Guidelines for Ecocultural Tourism on March 2, 1991.

Some magazines have begun to cover issues related to ecotourism on a frequent, even regular basis. For example *Buzzworm* featured a series of articles on ecotourism in Hawaii in their November/December 1992 issue. *Buzzworm* also includes a section on Connections: Volunteer Opportunities and Environmental Jobs, November 1992, pp. 82–85, which includes many opportunities to combine travel with volunteer work on environmental projects. Some are hands-on types of projects; other projects include environmental education and work on research projects.

Suggested Readings

Davis, Mary Dymond. *An Untraditional Travel Guide to the United States.* The Nobel Press, 1991.

Grotta, Daniel, and Grotta, Sally Wiener. *The Green Travel Sourcebook.* New York: John Wiley and Sons, 1992.

Holing, Dwight. *Nature Travel on a Fragile Planet.* Los Angeles: Living Planet Press, 1992.

Johnston, Barbara. "Introduction: Breaking Out of the Tourist Trap." *Cultural Survival Quarterly* 14 (1990): 2–5.

Kaye, Evelyn. *Eco-Vacations: Enjoy Yourself and Save the Earth.* Leonia, N.J.: Blue Penguin Publications, 1991.

Swan, James A. *Sacred Places: How the Living Earth Seeks Our Friendship.* Santa Fe: Bear and Company, 1990.

Whelan, Tensie, ed., *Nature Tourism: Managing for the Environment.* New York: Island Press, 1991.

CHAPTER 12
DILEMMAS OF SOCIAL ACTIVISM

Notes

An earlier version of this chapter appeared in *ReVision,* Winter 1991. I continued my reflections on nonviolence in an article on "Compassionate Activism for Hard Realities: Reflections on Arne Naess' Commitment to Nonviolence" in *The Trumpeter,* Spring 1992.

Various evaluations and criticisms of the performance of mainstream environmental groups in the United States—frequently called the "gang of ten," including the Sierra Club, National Audubon Society, the Wilderness Society, National Wildlife Federation, Environmental Defense Fund, and Natural Resources Defense Council—have appeared in several publications. One of the most thorough critiques was written by Mark Dowie, "American Environmentalism: A Movement Courting Irrelevance," *World Policy Journal,* Winter 1991–92, pp. 67–92.

Reflections on the American environmental movement over the two decades of the 1970s and 1980s written by several social scientists were collected and edited by Riley E. Dunlap and Angela G. Mertig in *American Environmentalism: The U.S. Environmental Movement, 1970–1990* (New York: Taylor and Francis, 1992).

Dave Foreman, one of the co-founders of Earth First! in 1980, who resigned from the Earth First! movement because he did not like the direction it was taking in the late 1980s, has recently described what he calls the New Conservation Movement. The New Conservation Movement, according to Foreman, consists of many grassroots groups advocating biodiversity and big wilderness. Dave Foreman, "The New Conservation Movement," *Wild Earth,* Summer 1991, pp. 6–10. Names, addresses, and descriptions of dozens of groups which Foreman considers part of the New Conservation Movement are included in this issue of *Wild Earth.* For information write Wild Earth, P.O. Box 492, Canton, New York 13617.

Discussions and debates concerning the tactics of radical environmentalism have appeared in many publications over the past several years. It was not my intent in this chapter to review these arguments. Readers can explore these ideas in the pages of the *Earth First! Journal.*

The seminal book which many commentators consider the inspiration of radical environmental tactics is Edward Abbey's novel *The Monkey Wrench Gang* (New York: J.B. Lippincott, 1975).

The seminal book on citizen tactics for dismantling industrial behemoths is Dave Foreman's *Ecodefense,* revisied ed. (Tucson: Ned Ludd Books, 1988).

Dave Foreman tells his story and presents his views on biocentric perspectives on wilderness for its own sake; an analysis of and justification for monkeywrenching; proposals for ecological wilderness preserves; about reforming the mainstream environmental movement; and, about the need for personal action to defend wilderness in *Confessions of an Eco-Warrior* (New York: Harmony/Crown, 1991).

Foreman's dialogue with Murray Bookchin, which was an historic meeting between a critic of deep ecology and a cofounder of the Earth First! movement, is found in a book edited by Steve Chase, *Defending the Earth: A Dialogue Between Murray Bookchin and Dave Foreman* (Boston: South End Press, 1991).

A discussion of some of the disagreements about strategy and tactics in the

Earth First! movement during the late 1980s is found in an article by Bron Taylor, "The Religion and Politics of Earth First!" *The Ecologist* 26 (December 1991): 258–266.

George Sessions' response to the split in Earth First! which led to the resignation of Dave Foreman and the rise of influence of the "social agenda" in Earth First! is found in his article "Radical Environmentalism in the 90s," *Wild Earth,* Fall 1992, pp. 64–70.

Consistent with the approach I have taken throughout this book, I do not wish to tell any reader what specific tactic or type of activism is appropriate for that reader in a specific situation.

As I personally have become more interested in Buddhism and in the campaigns of Gandhi and Dr. Martin Luther King, Jr., I have become more committed to nonviolent, direct social activism. The general norm of nonviolence requires much discussion however. Arne Naess explored the writings and actions of Gandhi and tried to explicate the underlying norms from which he acted. I have found these norms most useful to apply to my own activism. *Gandhi and Group Conflict: An Exploration of Satyagraha Theoretical Background* (Oslo, Norway: University of Oslo, 1974).

Suggested Readings

Hayes, Randall. "Activism: You Make the Difference." in Suzanne Head, ed., *Lessons of the Rainforest.* San Francisco: Sierra Club Books, 1990.

Oelschlaeger, Max, (ed.), *After Earth Day: Continuing the Conservation Effort.* University of North Texas Press, 1992.

REFERENCES

Abbey, Edward. *Desert Solitaire*. Tucson: University of Arizona Press, 1968.

Aitken, Robert. *The Mind of Clover: Essays in Zen Buddhist Ethics*. San Francisco: North Point Press, 1984.

Bateson, Gregory. *Mind and Nature*. New York: Bantam, 1980.

Bennett, Noël; Wakeman, Jim; and McGuire, Michael. *A Place in the Wild: The Dynamics of Structures Integrated in Fragile, Natural Sites*. New Mexico: Shared Horizons, 1991.

Berman, Morris. *Coming to Our Senses: Body and Spirit in the Hidden History of the West*. New York: Bantam, 1989.

Berry, Tom. *The Dream of the Earth*. San Francisco: Sierra Club Books, 1988.

Berry, Tom. *Teilhard in the Ecological Age*. Chambersburg, PA: Anima Books, 1982.

Berry, Wendell. *The Unsettling of America: Culture and Agriculture*. San Francisco: Sierra Club Books, 1977.

Bly, Robert. *Iron John*. New York: Random House, 1992.

Boyd, Doug. *Rolling Thunder*. New York: Random House, 1974.

Brown, Brian. "Native American Religions, the First Amendment, and the Judicial Interpretation of Public Land." *Environmental History Review* 15 (Winter 1991): 19–44.

Byers, Bruce. "Deep Ecology and Its Critics: A Buddhist Perspective." *The Trumpeter* 9 (Winter 1992): 33–34.

Callahan, Debra. *The Wise Use Movement*. Charlotteville, Va.: W. Alton Jones Foundation, 1992.

Carson, Rachel. *Silent Spring*. Boston: Houghton Mifflin, 1964.

Commoner, Barry. *The Closing Circle: Nature, Man and Technology*. New York: Knopf, 1971.

Cronon, William. *Nature's Metropolis: Chicago and the Great West, 1848–1893*. New York: W.W. Norton and Company, 1991.

Crosby, Alfred. *Ecological Imperialism: The Biological Expansion of Europe, 900–1900*. Cambridge: Cambridge University Press, 1986.

Daly, Herman E., and Cobb, Jr., John B., *For the Common Good: Redirecting the Economy Toward Community, the Environment, and a Sustainable Future.* Boston: Beacon Press, 1989.

Dasmann, Raymond. *The Destruction of California.* New York: Macmillan, 1966.

Dauncey, Guy. "How Green Is Your Campus?" *The Trumpeter* 8 (Winter 1991).

Drengson, Alan. *Beyond Environmental Crisis: From Technocrat to Planetary Person.* New York: Peter Lang, 1989.

Drengson, Alan. "The Ecostery Foundation of North America (TEFNA): Statement of Philosophy." *The Trumpeter* 7 (Winter 1990): 12–16.

Ehrlich, Paul. *The End of Affluence.* New York: Ballantine, 1974.

Ehrlich, Paul. *The Machinery of Nature.* New York: Simon and Schuster, 1986.

Ehrlich, Paul, and Ehrlich, Anne. *The Population Explosion.* New York: Simon and Schuster, 1990.

Eiseley, Loren. *The Invisible Pyramid.* New York: Scribner, 1970.

Eldredge, H. Wentworth, ed. *Taming Megalopis: How To Manage an Urbanized World,* vols. 1, 2. Garden City: Doubleday, 1967.

Evernden, Neil. *The Natural Alien: Humankind and Environment.* Toronto: University of Toronto Press, 1985.

Evernden, Neil, ed. *The Paradox of Environmentalism.* Toronto: University of Toronto Press, 1984.

Foreman, Dave. *Confessions of an Eco-Warrior.* New York: Harmony Books/Crown, 1991.

Fox, Warwick. *Toward a Transpersonal Ecology: Developing New Foundations for Environmentalism.* Boston: Shambhala, 1990.

Frankl, Victor. *The Unheard Cry for Meaning.* New York: Simon and Schuster, 1978.

Frome, Michael. *Regreening the National Parks.* Tucson: University of Arizona Press, 1992.

Gershon, David, and Gilman, Robert. *Ecoteam Workbook.* Global Action Plan for the Earth, 1990.

Golden, Sephanie. *The Women Outside: Meanings and Myths of Homelessness.* Berkeley: University of California Press, 1992.

Goodman, Paul, and Goodman, Percival. *Communities: Means of Livelihood and Ways of Life.* New York: Vintage, 1960.

Gore, Al. *Earth in the Balance: Ecology and the Human Spirit.* Boston: Houghton Mifflin Company, 1992.

Halifax, Joan. *The Fruitful Darkness: On the Ecology of Initiation—Notes on Crossing the Threshold.* San Francisco: Freeman, 1993.

Harrington, Michael. *The Other America: Poverty in the United States.* New York: Macmillan, 1969.

Harte, John, Cheryl Holdren, Richard Schneider and Christine Shirley. *Toxics from A to Z.* Berkeley: University of California Press, 1991.

Head, Suzanne, and Heinzman, Robert, eds. *Lessons of the Rainforest.* San Francisco: Sierra Club Books, 1990.

Hunter, Linda. *The Healthy Home: Attic to Basement Guide to Toxic Free Living.* New York: Pocket Books, 1989.

Jacobs, Jan. *The Death and Life of Great American Cities.* New York: Random House, 1961.

Kroeber, Theodore. *The Inland Whale.* Berkeley: University of California Press, 1963.

Leopold, Aldo. *A Sand County Almanac.* New York: Oxford University Press, 1949.

Lerner, Michael. *Surplus Powerlessness; The Psychodynamics of Everyday Life,* and *The Psychology of Individual and Social Transformation.* Oakland, Calif.: The Institute for Labor and Mental Health, 1986.

Linder, Steffan B. *The Harried Leisure Class.* New York: Columbia University Press, 1969.

McHarg, Ian. *Design With Nature.* Garden City: Natural History Press, 1969.

McKibben, Bill. *The End of Nature.* New York: Random House, 1989.

Macy, Joanna. *Despair and Personal Power in the Nuclear Age.* Philadelphia: New Society Publishers, 1983.

Macy, Joanna. *World as Lover, World as Self.* Berkeley: Parallex Press, 1990.

Manes, Christopher. "Ecology and the Language of Humanism." *Wild Earth,* Spring 1991, p. 61.

Manes, Christopher. *Green Rage: Radical Environmentalism and the Unmaking of Civilization.* Boston: Little Brown, 1990

Maser, Chris. *Global Imperative: Harmonizing Culture and Nature.* Walpole, N.H.: Stillpoint Press, 1992.

Mills, Stephanie. *Whatever Happened to Ecology?* San Francisco: Sierra Club Books, 1989.

Mumford, Lewis. *The Myth of the Machine,* vol. 1: *Technics and Human Development.* New York: Harcourt Brace Jovanovich, 1967.

Mumford, Lewis. *The Myth of the Machine,* vol. 2: *The Pentagon of Power.* New York: Harcourt Brace Jovanovich, 1970.

Naess, Arne. "Deep Ecology and Life Style," in Neil Everndon, ed., *The Paradox of Environmentalism.* Toronto: University of Toronto Press, 1984.

Naess, Arne. "Modesty and the Conquest of Mountains," in Michael Tobias, ed., *The Mountain Spirit.* New York: Overlook Press, 1979.

Norton, Jack. *Genocide in Northwestern California.* San Francisco: Indian Historical Press, 1979.

Regan, Tom. *All That Dwell Therein: Animal Rights and Environmental Ethics.* Berkeley: University of California Press, 1982.

Reisner, Marc. *Cadillac Desert: The American West and Its Disappearing Water.* New York: Penguin, 1986.

Rifkin, Jeremy. *Beyond Beef: The Rise and Fall of the Cattle Culture.* New York: Dutton, 1992.

Rifkin, Jeremy. *Time Wars: The Primary Conflict in Human History.* New York: Henry Holt and Company, 1987.

Roberts, Elizabeth. *Earth Prayers.* New York: Harpers, 1991.

Roszak, Theodore. *The Voice of the Earth.* New York: Simon and Schuster, 1992.

Sale, Kirkpatrick. *Dwellers in the Land: The Bioregional Vision.* Santa Cruz: New Society Publishers, 1991.

Samuelson, Robert. "How Our American Dream Unraveled." *Newsweek,* 2 March 1992, pp. 32–39.

Sax, Joseph L. *Mountains Without Handrails: Reflections on the National Parks.* Ann Arbor: The University of Michigan Press, 1980.

Schumacher, E.F. *Small Is Beautiful; Economics as if People Mattered.* New York: Harper, 1973.

Scitovsky, Tibor. *The Joyless Economy: An Inquiry into Human Satisfaction and Consumer Dissatisfaction.* New York: Oxford University Press, 1976.

Seed, John, Joanna Macy, Pat Fleming, Arne Naess. *Thinking Like a Mountain: Toward a Council of All Beings.* Philadelphia: New Society Publishers, 1988.

Seuss, Dr. *The Lorax.* New York: Random House, 1971.

Shames, Lawrence. *The Hunger for More: Searching for Values in an Age of Greed.* New York: Times Books, 1986.

Shepard, Paul. "A Post-Historic Primitivism," in Max Oelschlaeger, ed., *The Wilderness Condition: Essays on Environment and Civilization.* San Francisco: Sierra Club Books, 1992.

Shepard, Paul. *The Sacred Paw; The Bear in Nature, Myth, and Literature.* New York: Viking, 1985.

Shepard, Paul, and McKinley, Daniel, eds. *The Subversive Science: Essays Toward an Ecology of Man.* Boston: Houghton Mifflin, 1969.

Simon, Julian. *The Ultimate Resource.* Princeton: Princeton University Press, 1981.

Snyder, Gary. *The Practice of Wild.* San Francisco: North Point Press, 1990.

Snyder, Gary. *No Poems.* New York: Pantheon Books, 1992.

Sun Tzu. *The Art of War.* New York: Oxford University Press, 1963.

Taylor, Paul. *Respect for Nature: A Theory of Environmental Ethics.* Princeton: Princeton University Press, 1985.

Tobias, Michael, ed. *Deep Ecology.* San Diego: Avant Books, 1985.

Tobias, Michael, and Drasdo, Harold, eds. *The Mountain Spirit.* Woodstock, New York: The Overlook Press, 1979.

Trump, Donald. *The Art of the Deal.* New York: Random House, 1987.

Udall, Stuart. *The Quiet Crisis.* New York: Holt, Rinehart and Winston, 1963.

Vogt, William. *The Road to Survival.* New York: William Sloane Associates, 1948.

Vogt, William. *People: Challenge to Survival.* New York: William Sloane Associates, 1960.

Wachtel, Paul. *The Poverty of Affluence: A Psychological Portrait of the American Way of Life.* Philadelphia: New Society Publishers, 1989.

Wallace, David Rains. *The Klamath Knot: Explorations of Myth and Evolution.* San Francisco: Sierra Club Books, 1983.

Watts, Alan. *The Book: On the Taboo Against Knowing Who You Are.* New York: Random House, 1966.

Watts, Alan. *Nature, Man, and Woman.* New York: Pantheon Books, 1958.

Whyte, Lynn, Jr. "The Historic Roots of our Ecological Crisis." *Science* 155 (1967) 1203–1207.

Wilson, Alexander. *The Culture of Nature: North American Landscape from Disney to the Exxon Valdez.* Cambridge: Blackwell, 1992.

Worster, Donald. *Nature's Economy: The Roots of Ecology.* San Francisco: Sierra Club Books, 1977.